ELECTRICITY

Energy in Action

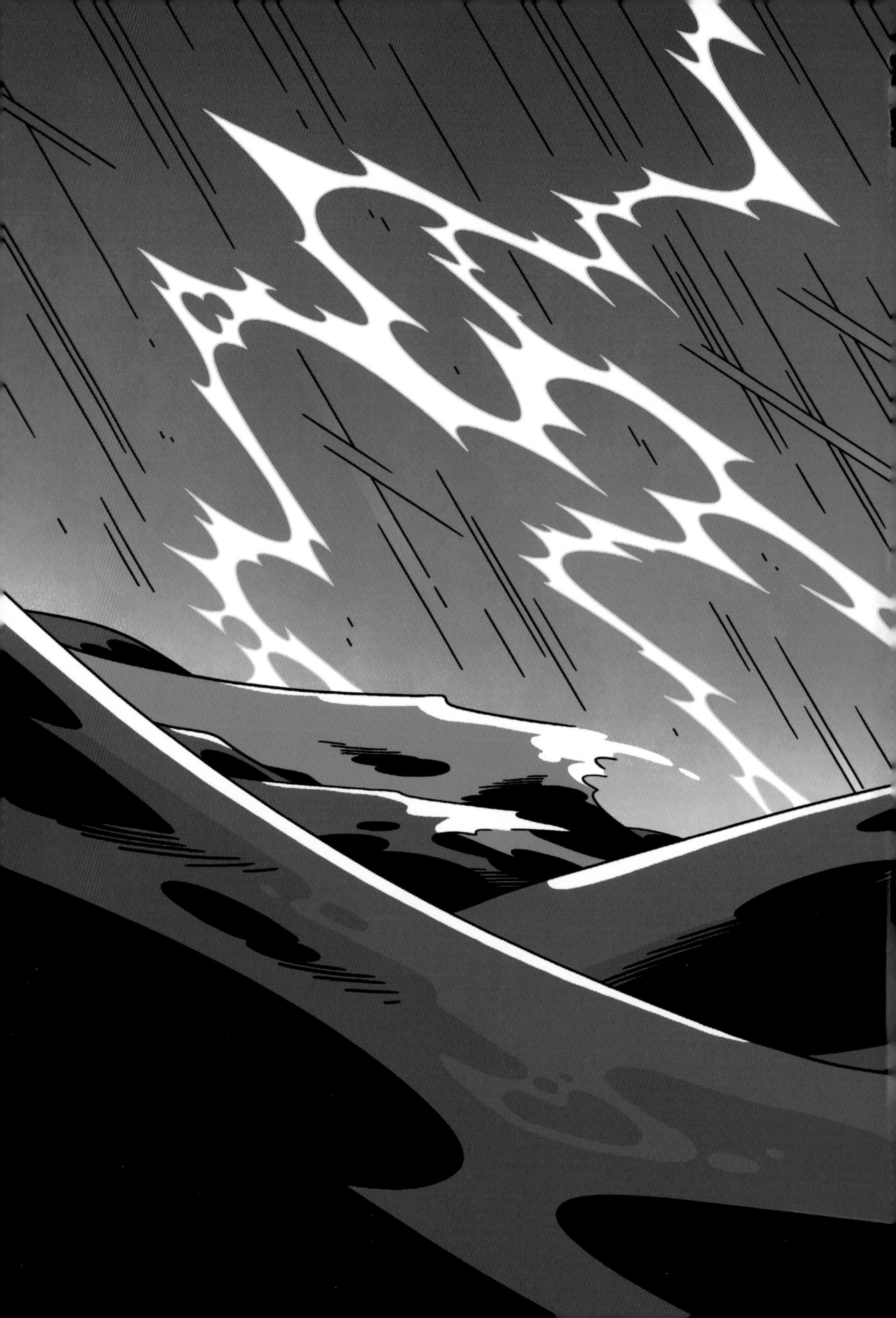

ELECTRICITY

Energy in Action

Andy Hirsch

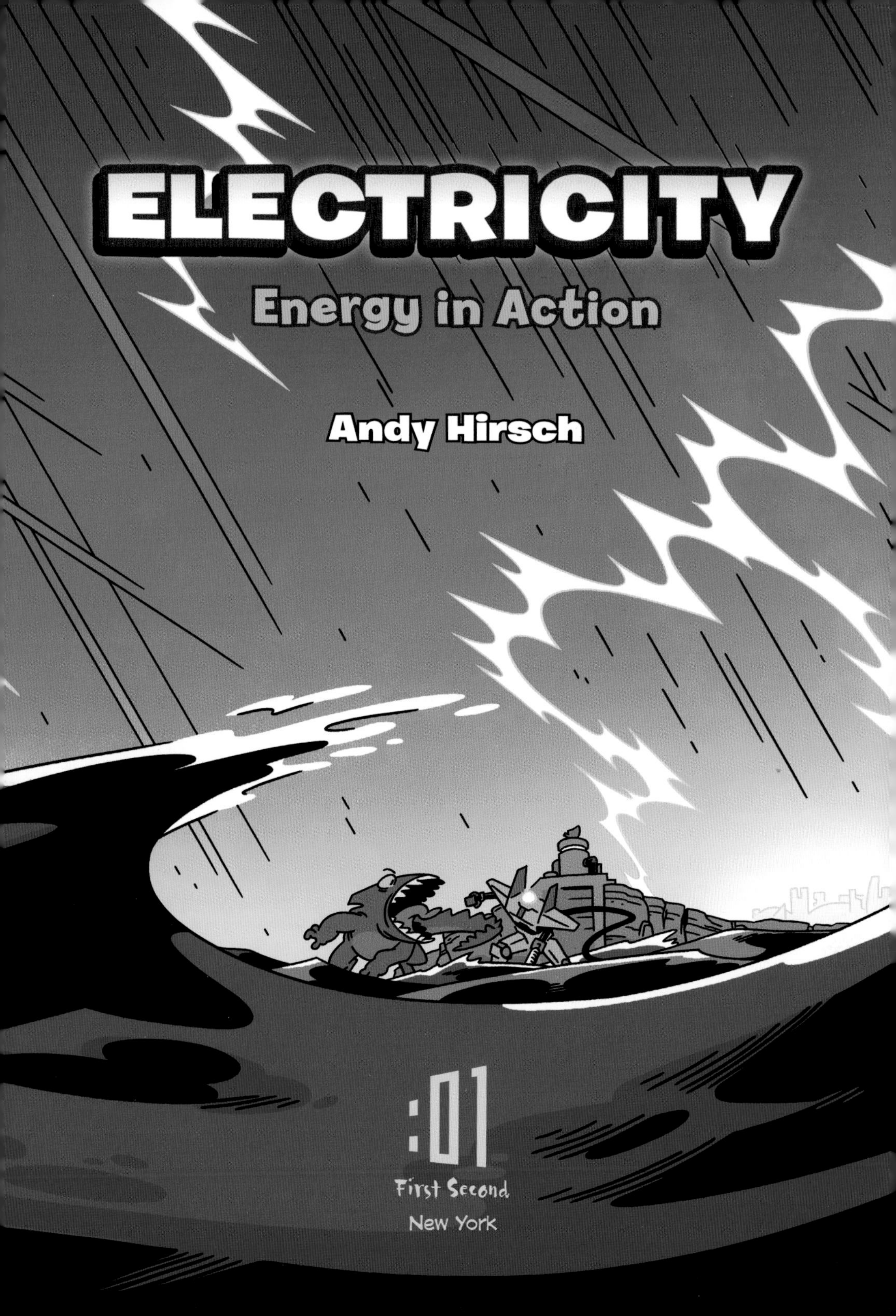

:01 First Second
New York

First Second

Published by First Second
First Second is an imprint of Roaring Brook Press,
a division of Holtzbrinck Publishing Holdings Limited Partnership
120 Broadway, New York, NY 10271
firstsecondbooks.com
mackids.com

Library of Congress Cataloging-in-Publication Data is available.

Our books may be purchased in bulk for promotional, educational, or business use. Please contact your local bookseller or the Macmillan
Corporate and Premium Sales Department at (800) 221-7945 ext. 5442 or by email at MacmillanSpecialMarkets@macmillan.com.

First edition, 2023
Edited by Dave Roman and Tim Stout
Cover design and interior book design by Molly Johanson
Production editing by Avia Perez
Electricity consultants: Eduardo Cotilla-Sanchez and Rob Maher

Drawn in Clip Studio Paint. Colored in Adobe Photoshop CC. Lettered with the Comicrazy font from Comicraft.

Printed in China by Toppan Leefung Printing Ltd., Dongguan City, Guangdong Province

ISBN 978-1-250-26585-2 (paperback)
10 9 8 7 6 5 4 3 2

ISBN 978-1-250-26584-5 (hardcover)
10 9 8 7 6 5 4 3 2 1

Don't miss your next favorite book from First Second!
For the latest updates go to firstsecondnewsletter.com and sign up for our enewsletter.

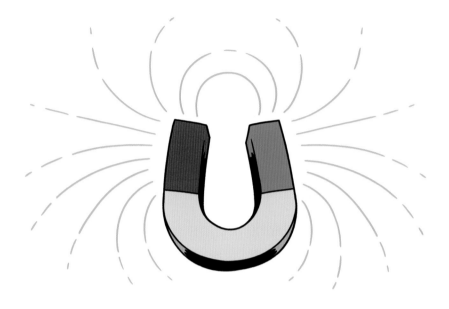

Magnets fascinated me, starting when I was a kid. Do you have any magnets in your home? My folks used a magnet to hold my school artwork on the front of our refrigerator, and I marveled that the magnet knew how to stick but never became tired, didn't require batteries, and just held on securely like magic. Yet a small grip with even my little fingers could remove it when Mom and Dad swapped out the featured artwork.

I became equally fascinated later by a magnetic compass that I was given to carry when we went out hiking or camping. How did that magnetic needle somehow keep track of which way was north? Day or night, rain or shine, hot or cold, it would swing around so that the *N* pointed to the north!

I remember when my older brother showed me that you could trick the direction needle by holding a toy magnet near the compass: one end of the needle would follow the magnet! And if you switched which end of the toy magnet was near the compass, the other end of the compass needle would swing toward it. It really seemed like magic.

But the coolest application of magnetism I remember from when I was a kid was the gigantic electromagnet on a crane, used at the scrap metal yard. Unlike the kitchen refrigerator magnet and the compass pointer that are always on, the giant electromagnet could be turned on and off at the flip of the operator's switch! The crane could lift a big pile of metal with the electromagnet, swing it around to the desired location, and then—*clank cronk cong*—it all fell into a neat pile when the electromagnet was abruptly switched off. The electromagnet could be controlled by a switch!

Since you are reading this book, I bet you are like me: You love to observe a physical property, like magnetism, and study how it behaves in different forms.

Now, you might be thinking, "Hey, this book is supposed to be about *electricity*. Why are we talking about *magnets*?" That's a good question. And there is a clue to the answer in what I just mentioned about the big electromagnet at the scrap metal yard...

An amazing fact is that an electric current flowing in a wire creates a magnetic field around that wire, and if we gather many, many loops of wire in a coil, the total magnetic field created by the electric current in all those wires working together can be strong enough to lift an entire junk car! The giant electromagnet creates magnetism because of the strong electric current flowing in many coils of wire hidden inside its lifting plate. When the operator turns off the electric current, the magnetic field disappears, too.

Not only does the flow of electric current create magnetism, but a moving magnetic field will cause a current to flow through a wire that is positioned in that changing magnetic field. This remarkable link between electricity and magnetism is what makes electric motors spin and what allows spinning electrical generators to power our electrical grid. Isn't it fun to be curious about the physics around us?

Now that I am a grown-up, my job is to be an electrical engineer. Engineers like me are educated in math, physics, chemistry, and other scientific fields, then we learn how to apply that knowledge of math and science to solve problems that help people live better and more joyful lives. My own work in electrical engineering is in audio engineering, which is the design of microphones, recording systems, and loudspeakers.

In fact, loudspeakers use the electromagnetic principle to make sound. The audio signal is sent through a coil of wire hidden behind the speaker, and that electricity makes a magnetic field that alternately attracts and repels a fixed magnet also located behind the speaker cone, causing the cone to vibrate and emit the sound we hear. Yes, electricity and magnetism have a beautiful partnership!

I really hope you enjoy this fun book about electricity as much as I did when I read it. Keep a lookout for mention of the partnership between electricity and magnetism! Who knows, maybe you will design the world of the future as an electrical engineer like I do! But whatever you choose to do as you learn more about math and science, I know your future will be bright—and not only because of electricity. ☺

—Robert C. (Rob) Maher, PhD, PE
Professor of Electrical and Computer Engineering
Montana State University, Bozeman, Montana, USA

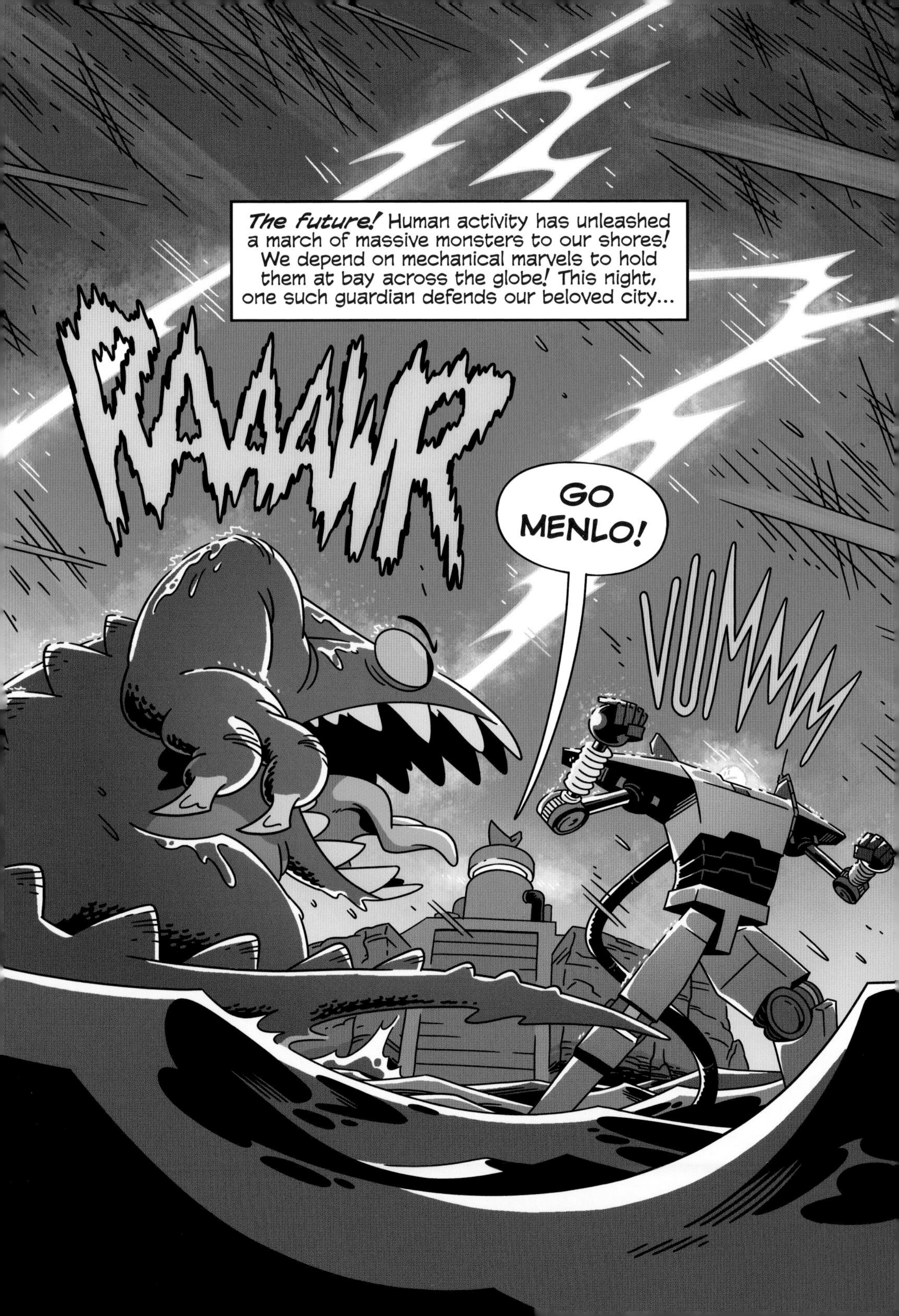
The future! Human activity has unleashed a march of massive monsters to our shores! We depend on mechanical marvels to hold them at bay across the globe! This night, one such guardian defends our beloved city...
RAAWR
GO MENLO!
VUMMM

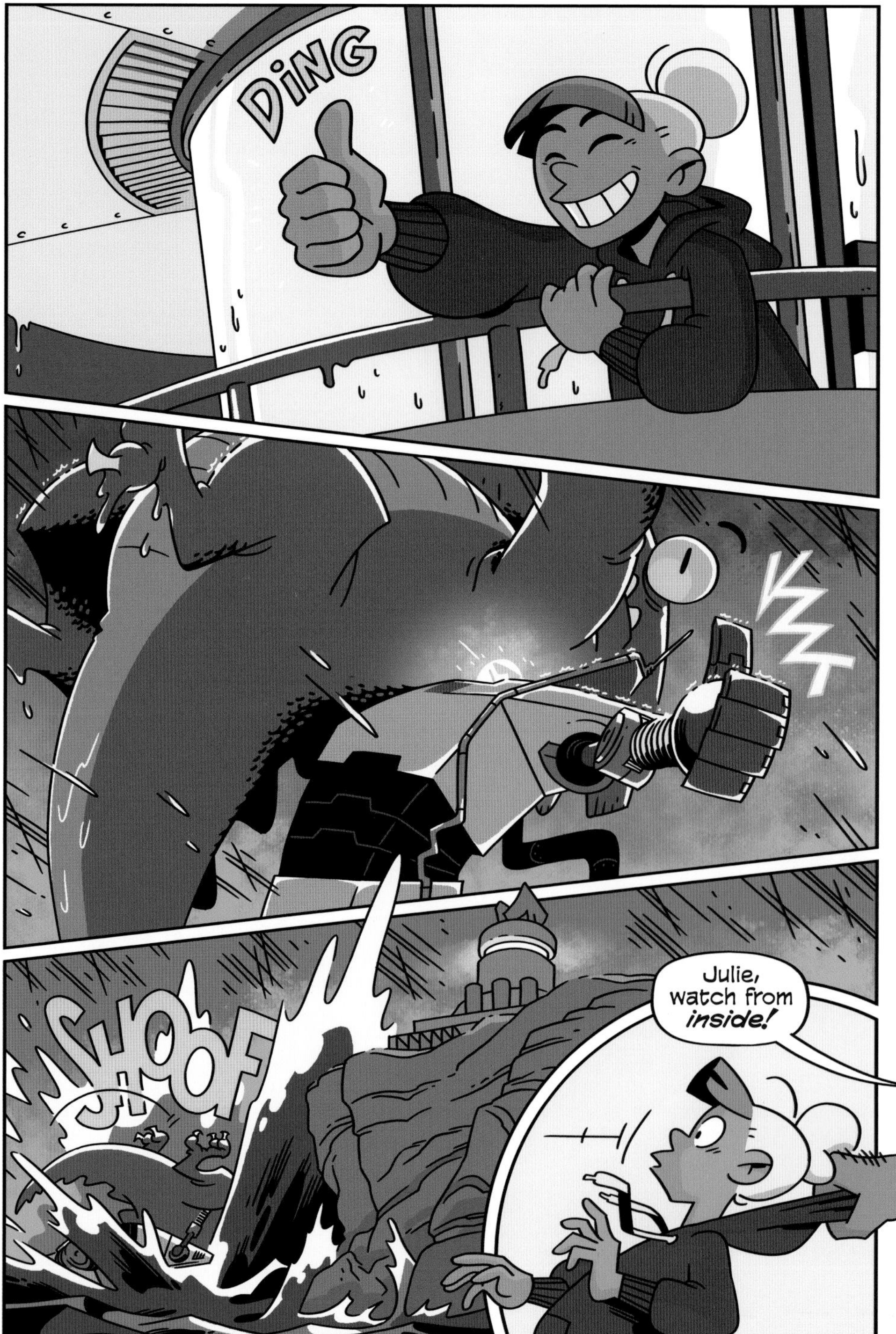
DiNG
KZZT
SHOOF
Julie, watch from *inside!*

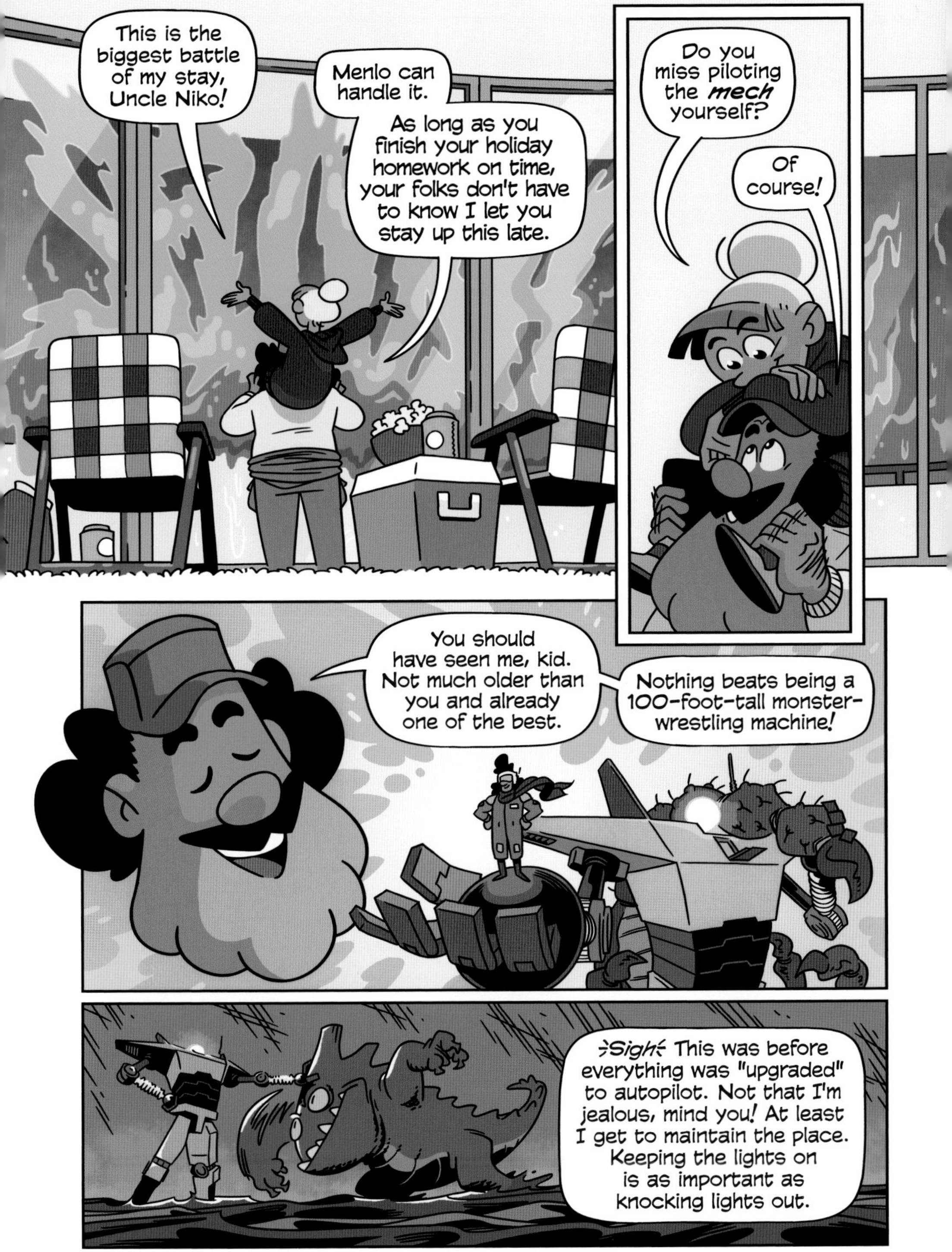
This is the biggest battle of my stay, Uncle Niko!
Menlo can handle it.
As long as you finish your holiday homework on time, your folks don't have to know I let you stay up this late.
Do you miss piloting the *mech* yourself?
Of course!
You should have seen me, kid. Not much older than you and already one of the best.
Nothing beats being a 100-foot-tall monster-wrestling machine!
Sigh This was before everything was "upgraded" to autopilot. Not that I'm jealous, mind you! At least I get to maintain the place. Keeping the lights on is as important as knocking lights out.

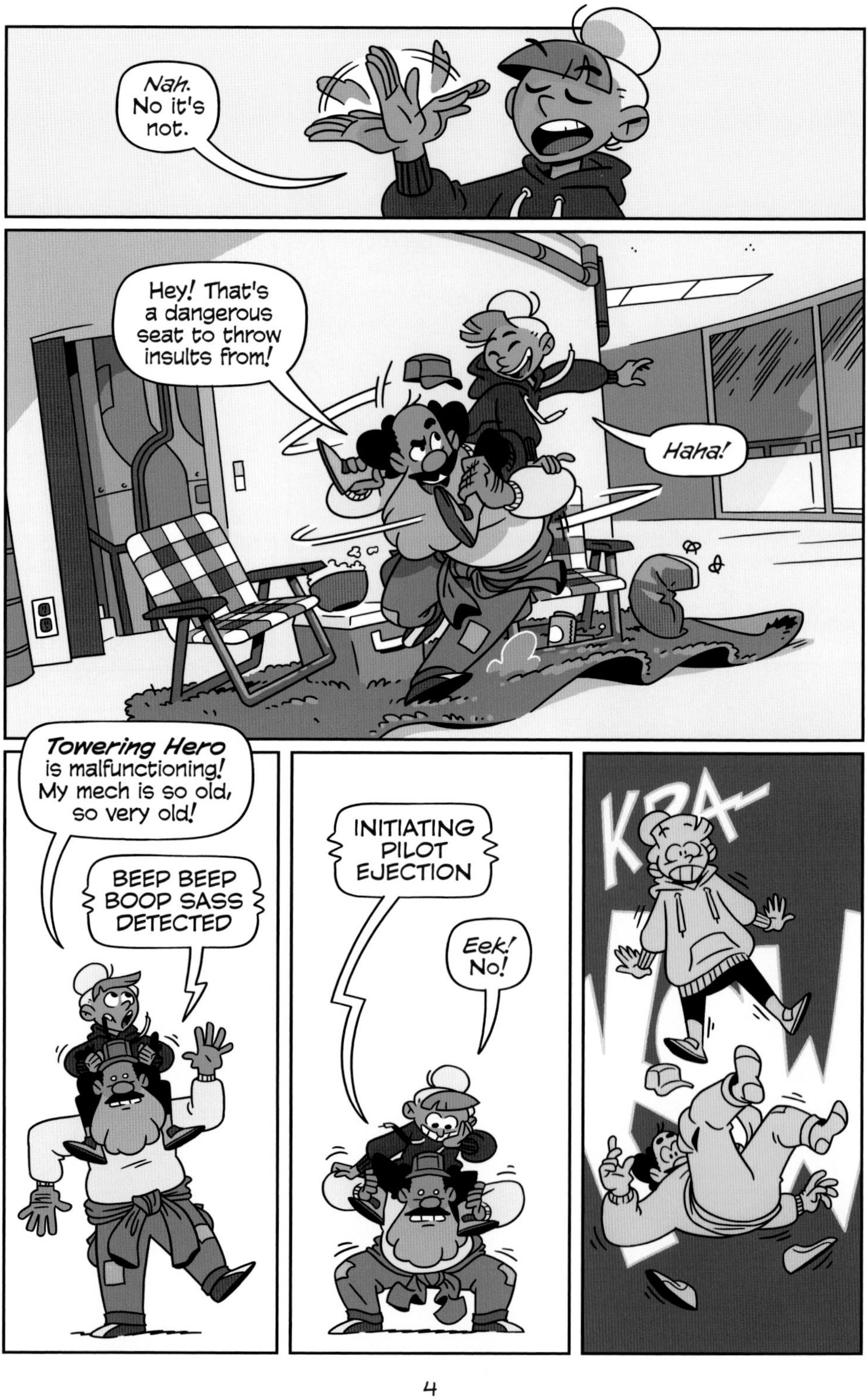
Nah. No it's not.
Hey! That's a dangerous seat to throw insults from!
Haha!
Towering Hero is malfunctioning! My mech is so old, so very old!
BEEP BEEP BOOP SASS DETECTED
INITIATING PILOT EJECTION
Eek! No!
KRA-

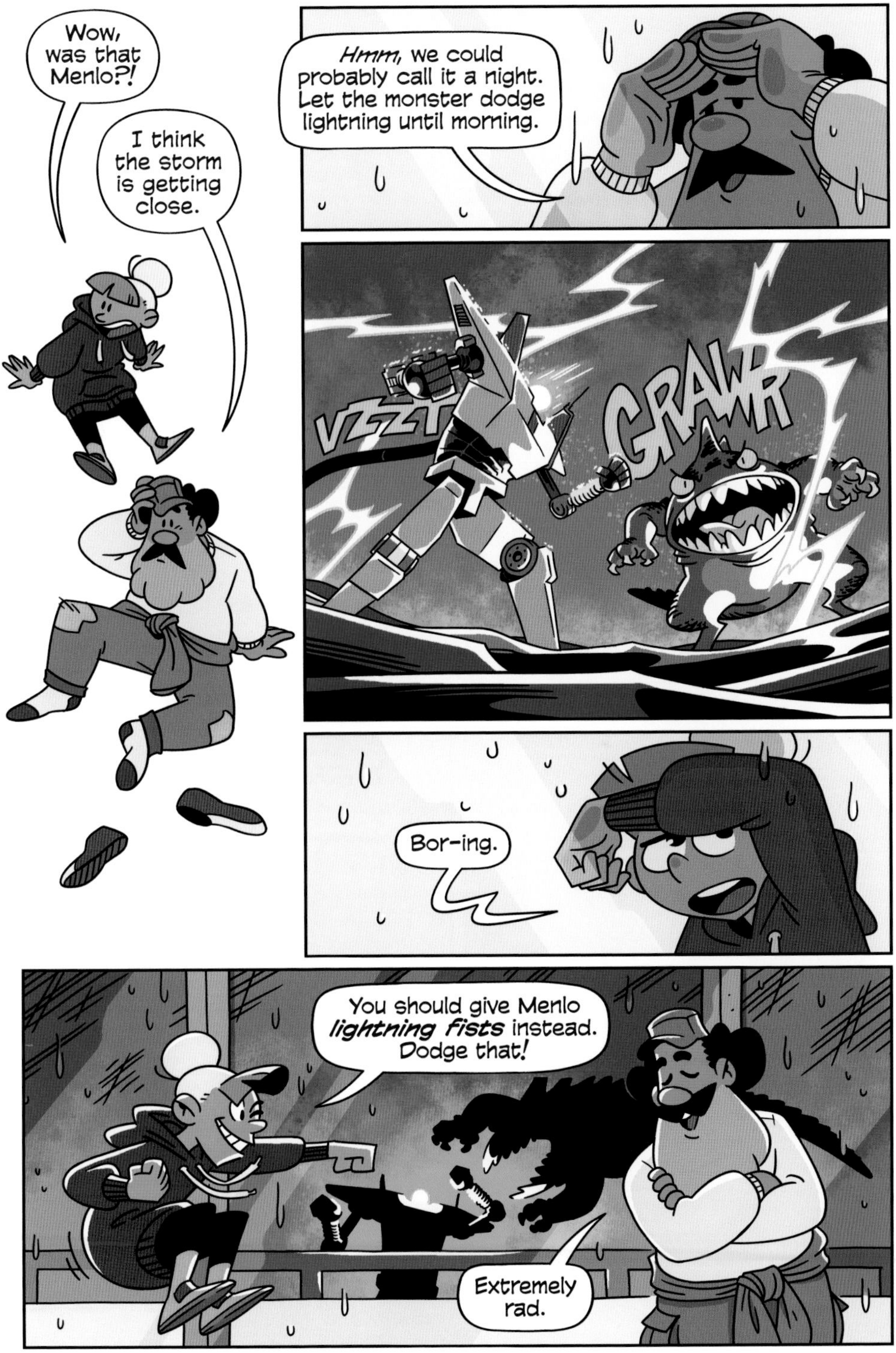
Wow, was that Menlo?!
I think the storm is getting close.
Hmm, we could probably call it a night. Let the monster dodge lightning until morning.
VZZT
GRAWR
Bor-ing.
You should give Menlo ***lightning fists*** instead. Dodge that!
Extremely rad.

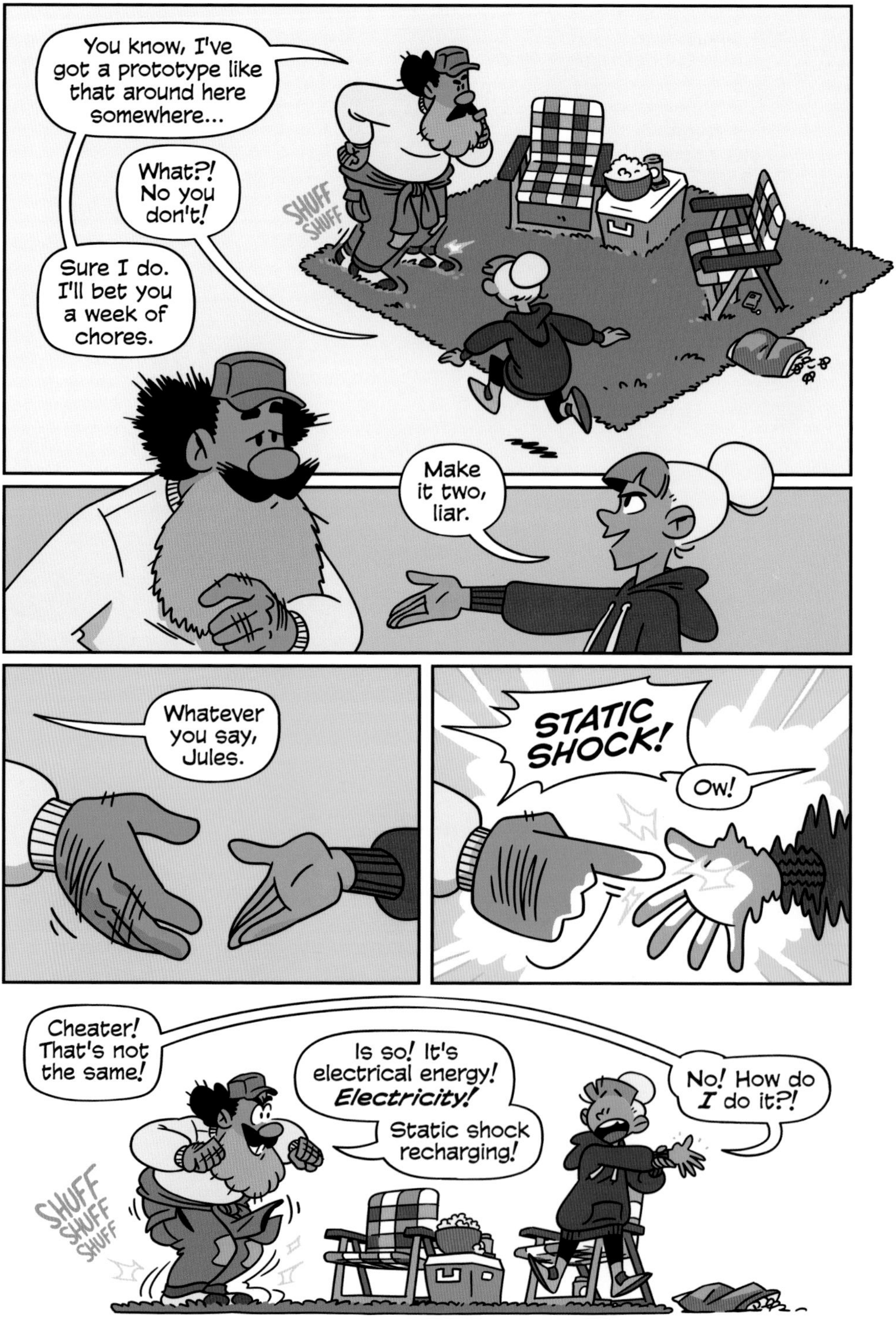
You know, I've got a prototype like that around here somewhere...
What?! No you don't!
SHUFF SHUFF
Sure I do. I'll bet you a week of chores.
Make it two, liar.
Whatever you say, Jules.
STATIC SHOCK!
Ow!
Cheater! That's not the same!
Is so! It's electrical energy! *Electricity!*
Static shock recharging!
No! How do *I* do it?!
SHUFF SHUFF SHUFF

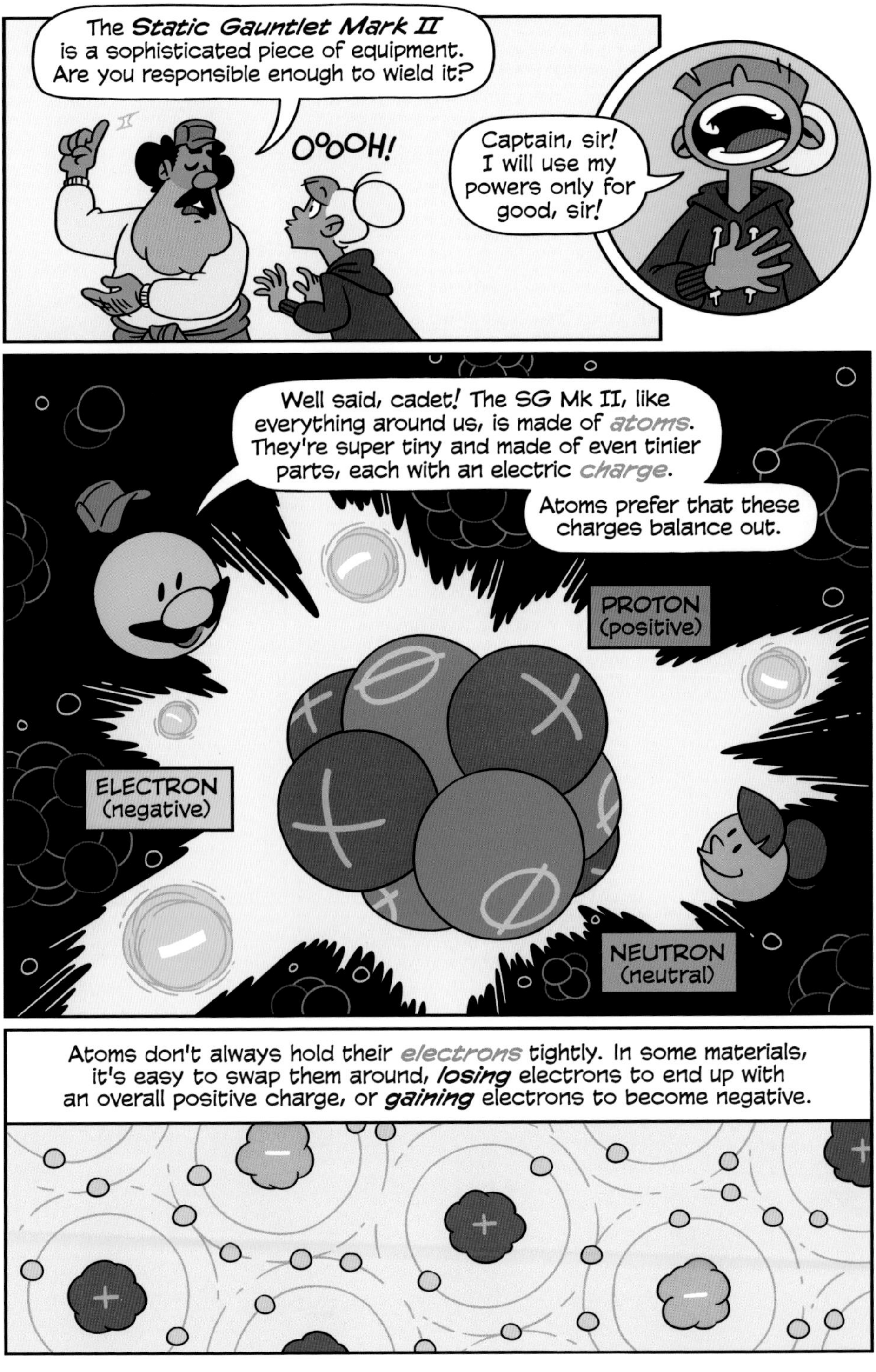
The Static Gauntlet Mark II is a sophisticated piece of equipment. Are you responsible enough to wield it?
II
OOOOH!
Captain, sir! I will use my powers only for good, sir!
Well said, cadet! The SG Mk II, like everything around us, is made of atoms. They're super tiny and made of even tinier parts, each with an electric charge.
Atoms prefer that these charges balance out.
PROTON (positive)
ELECTRON (negative)
NEUTRON (neutral)
Atoms don't always hold their electrons tightly. In some materials, it's easy to swap them around, losing electrons to end up with an overall positive charge, or gaining electrons to become negative.

Here's the key: The invisible *electric field* around a charge makes *like charges repel* each other and *opposite charges attract* each other.

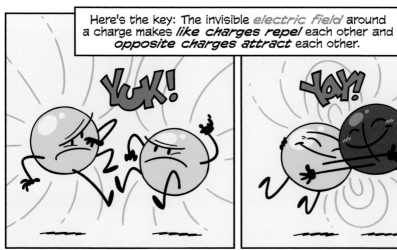

Not only that, but fields become stronger the closer together they are.

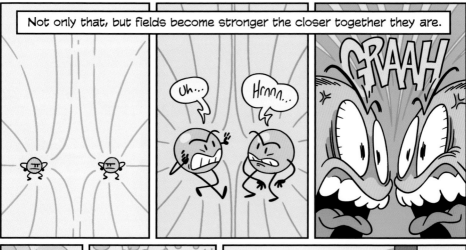

Uh...

Hrnnn...

GRAAH!

These forces create the chemical bonds that create the molecules that create the matter that creates *all of this!*

It's all because like repels like and opposites attract!

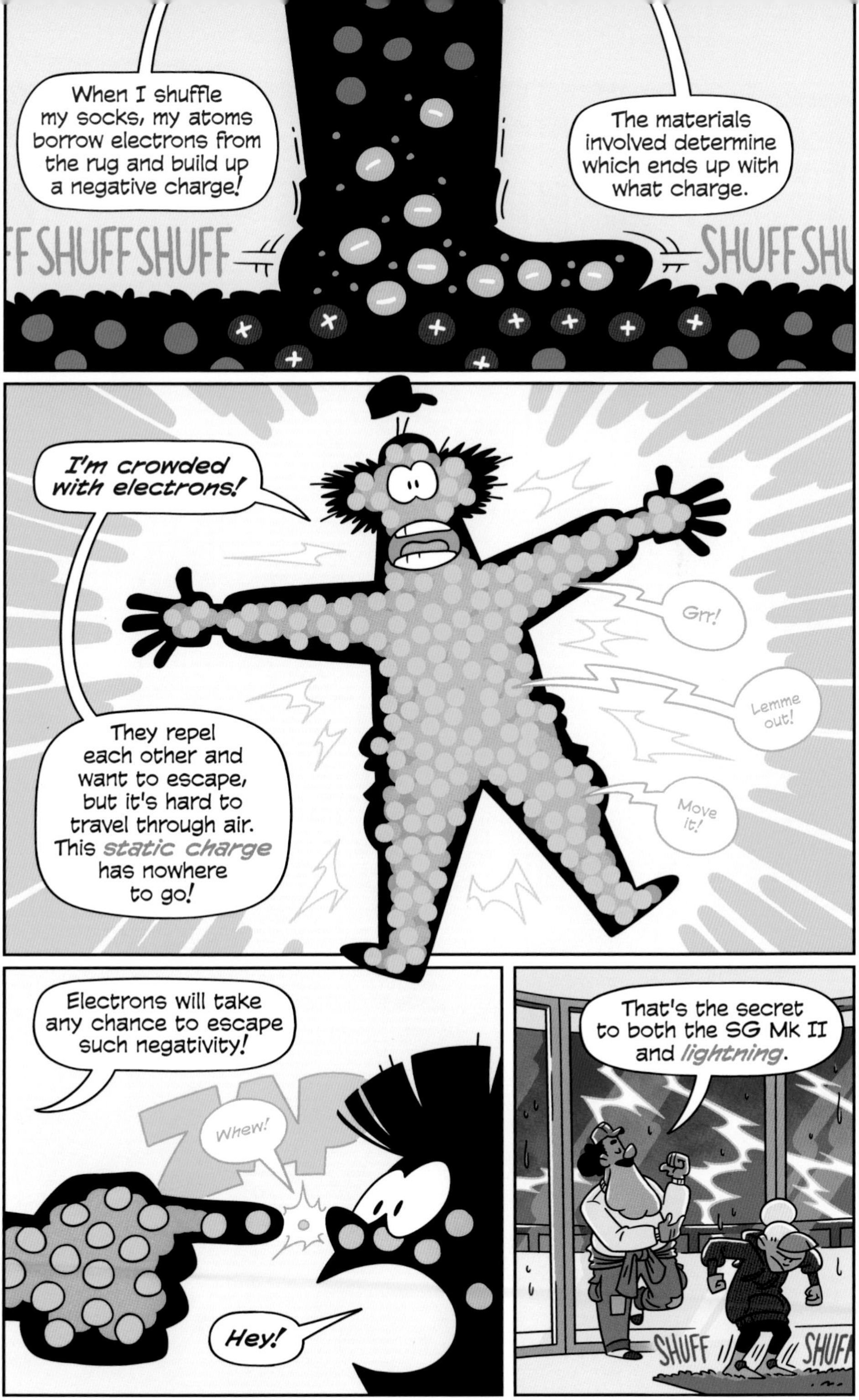
When I shuffle my socks, my atoms borrow electrons from the rug and build up a negative charge!
The materials involved determine which ends up with what charge.
FF SHUFF SHUFF
SHUFF SHU
I'm crowded with electrons!
Grr!
Lemme out!
Move it!
They repel each other and want to escape, but it's hard to travel through air. This static charge has nowhere to go!
Electrons will take any chance to escape such negativity!
Whew!
Hey!
That's the secret to both the SG Mk II and lightning.
SHUFF
SHUFF

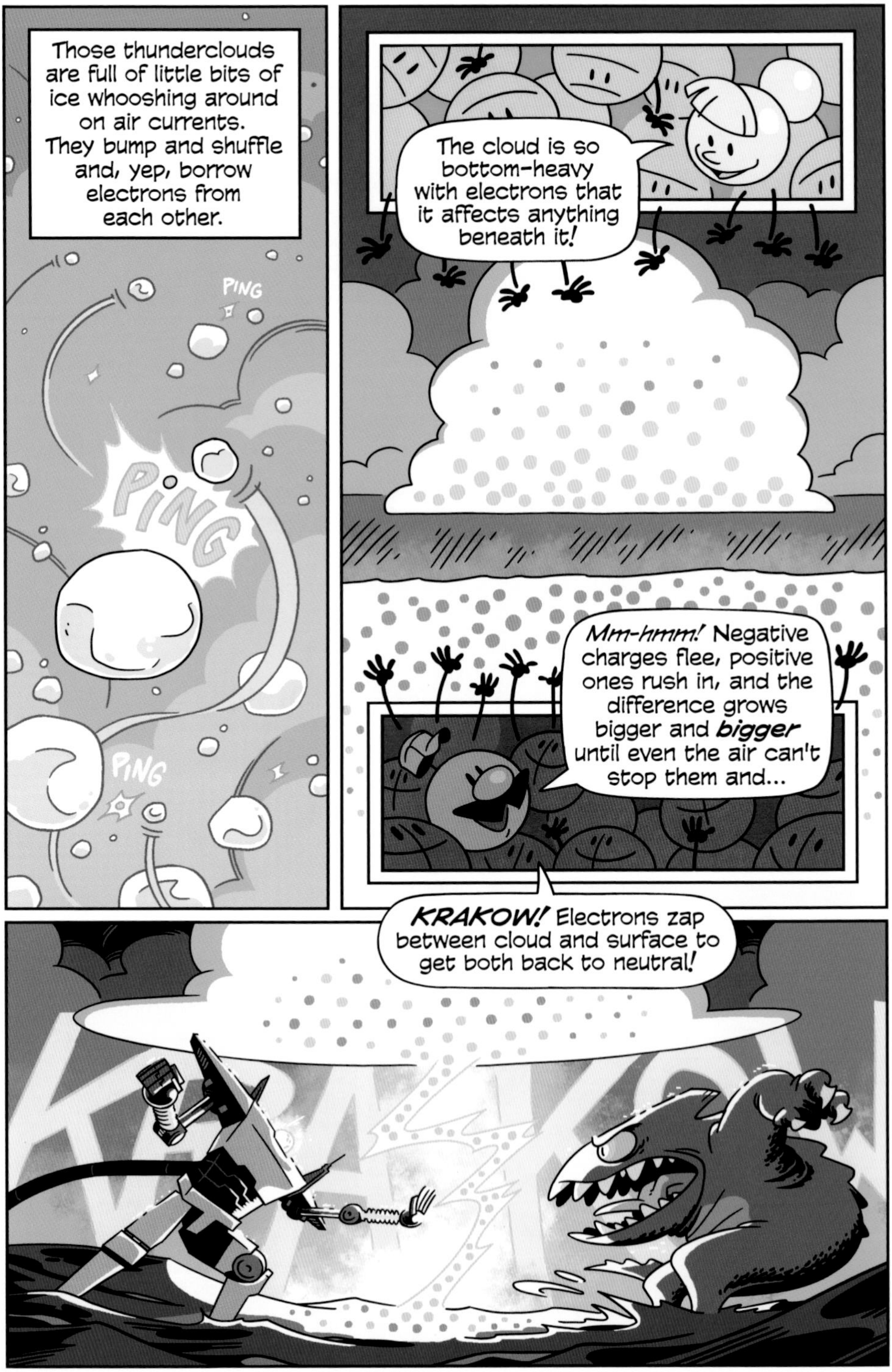
Those thunderclouds are full of little bits of ice whooshing around on air currents. They bump and shuffle and, yep, borrow electrons from each other.
PING
PING
PING
The cloud is so bottom-heavy with electrons that it affects anything beneath it!
Mm-hmm! Negative charges flee, positive ones rush in, and the difference grows bigger and bigger until even the air can't stop them and...
KRAKOW! Electrons zap between cloud and surface to get both back to neutral!

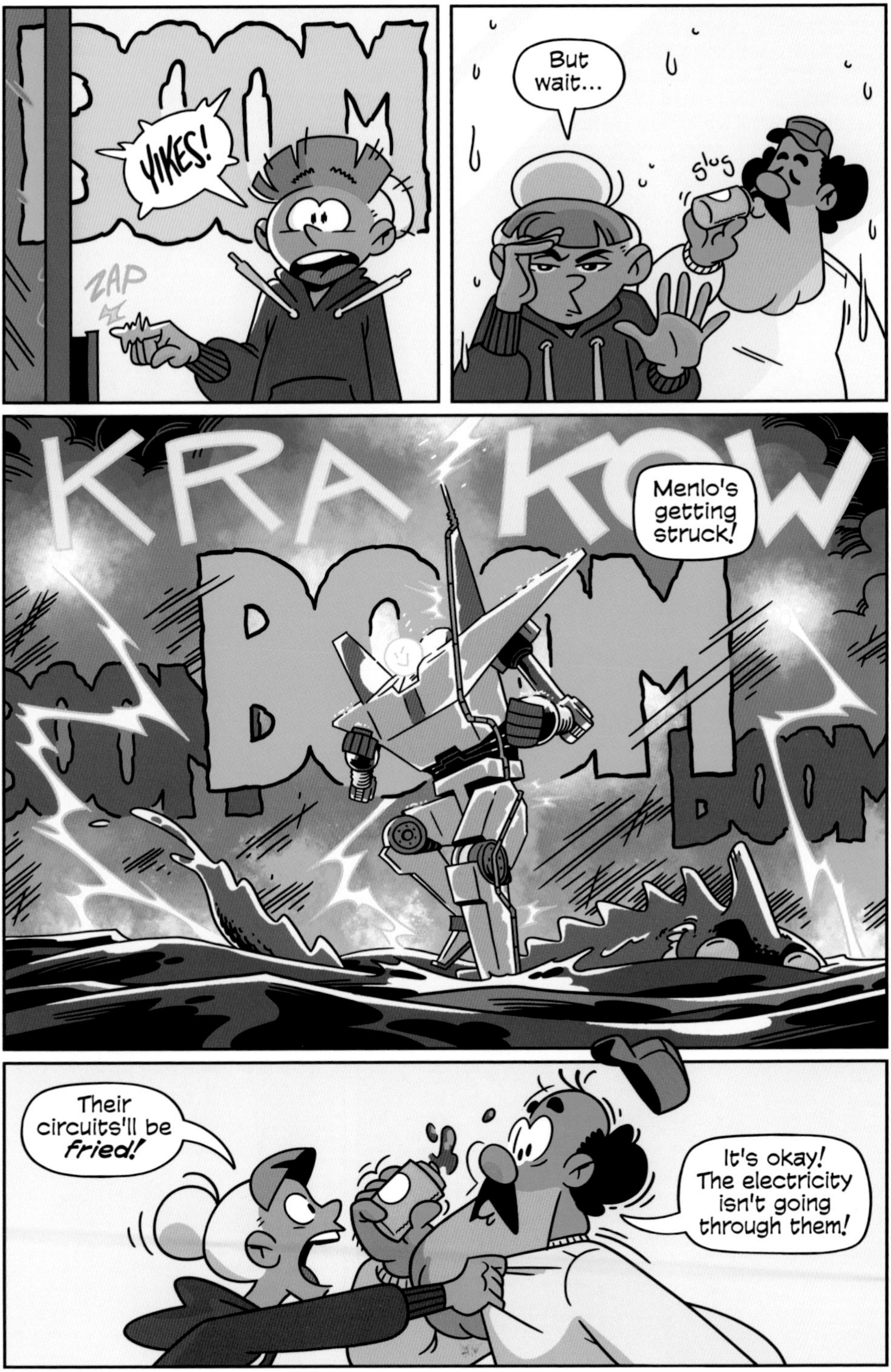
BOOM
YIKES!
ZAP
But wait...
slug
KRA KOW
Menlo's getting struck!
BOOM
Their circuits'll be *fried!*
It's okay! The electricity isn't going through them!

Electricity always wants to take the easiest path, and Menlo's *grounding wire* gives it one. It's easier for electricity to travel through *that* than the mech, so that's what it does.

What if that easy path wasn't there?

Well, it'd find another, less safe one.

RAWR HA HAR

SWK

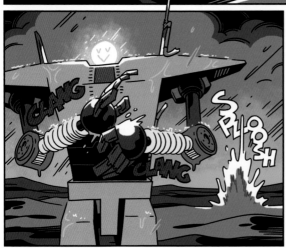

CLANG

CLANG

SPLOOSH

Could *monster claws* break the easy path?

Huh. You know, that's never come up.

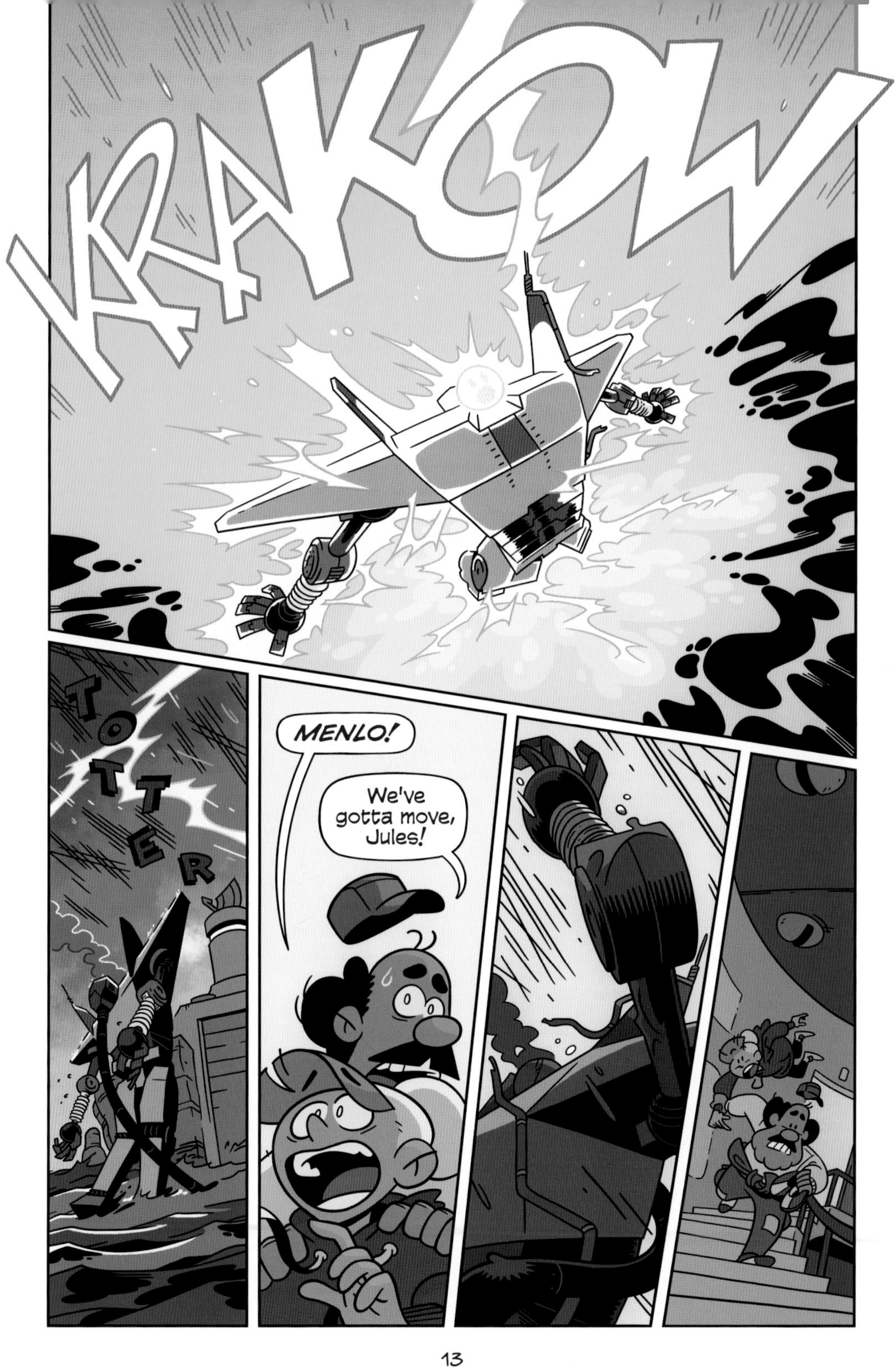
KRAKOW
TOTTER
MENLO!
We've gotta move, Jules!

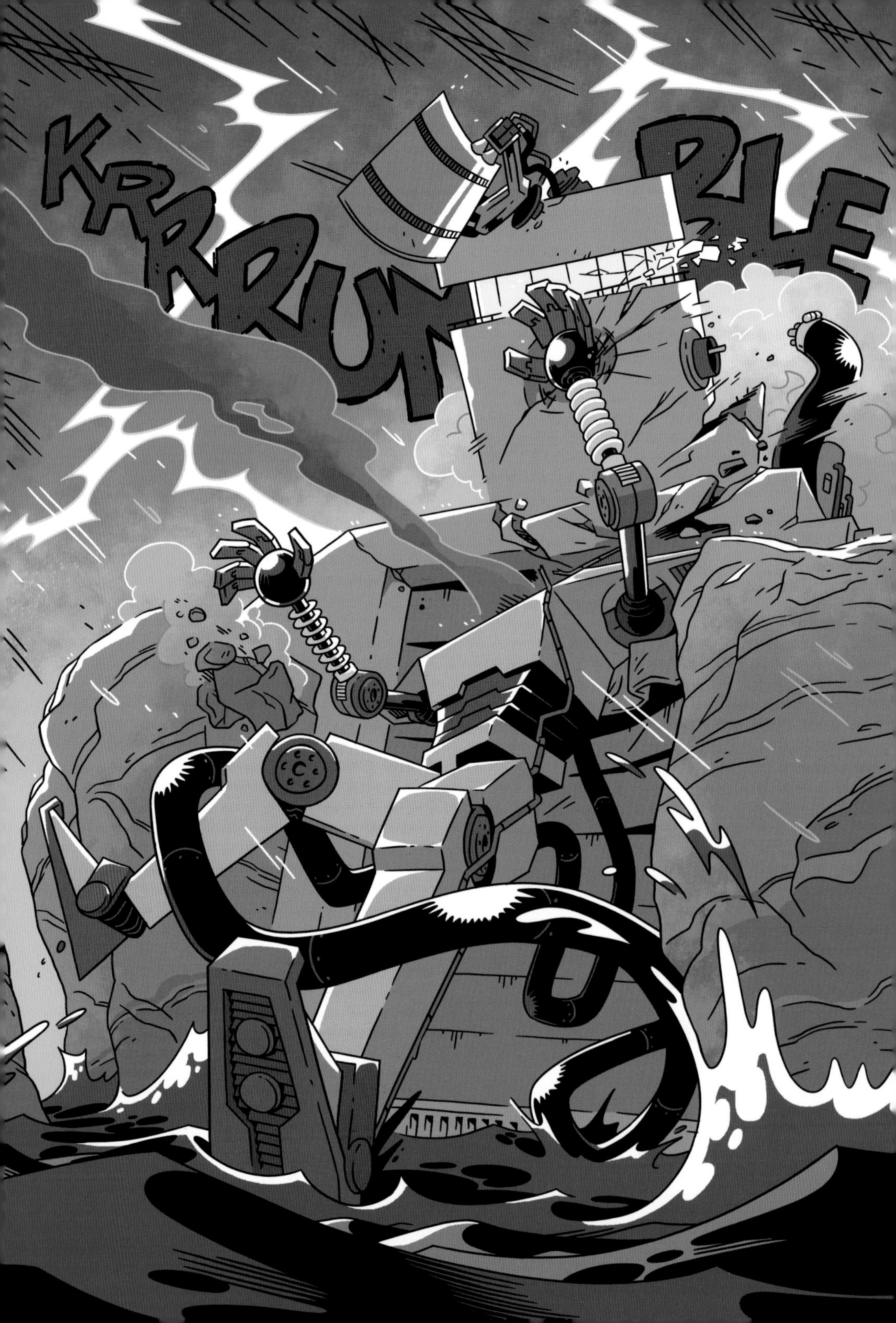
KRRRUMBLE

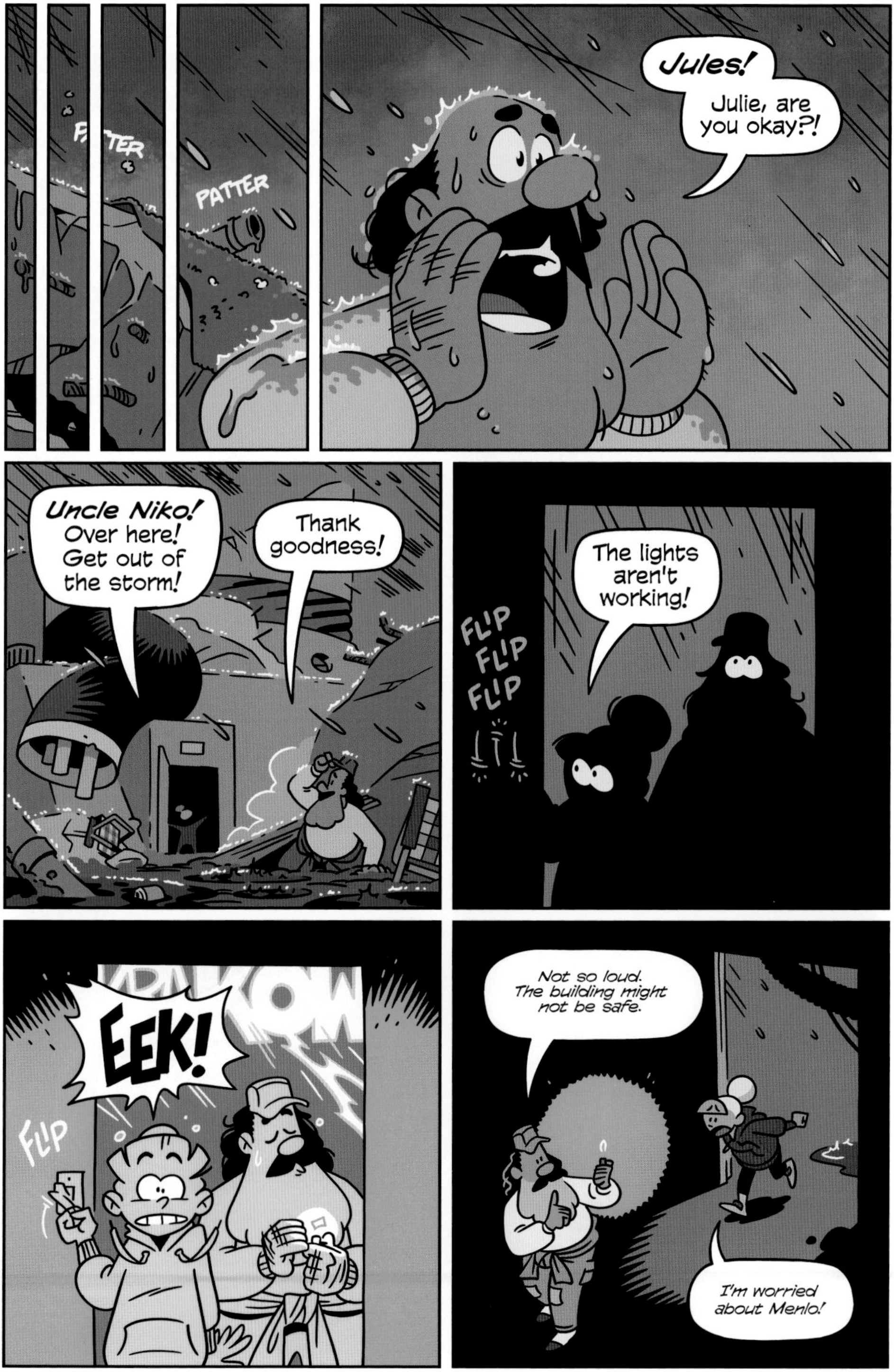
PATTER
PATTER
Jules!
Julie, are you okay?!
Uncle Niko! Over here! Get out of the storm!
Thank goodness!
FLIP
FLIP
FLIP
The lights aren't working!
EEK!
FLIP
Not so loud. The building might not be safe.
I'm worried about Menlo!

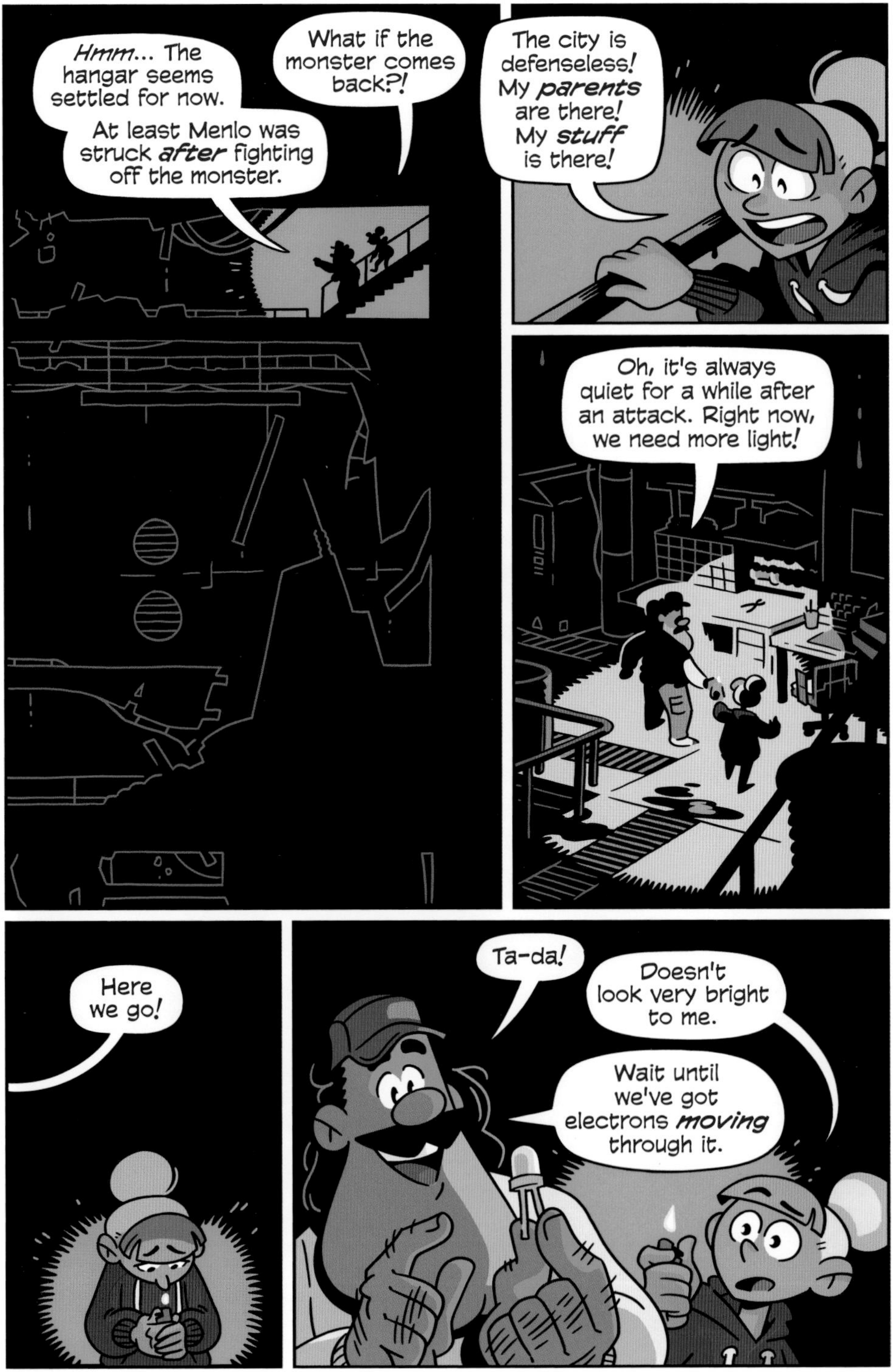
Hmm... The hangar seems settled for now.
At least Menlo was struck ***after*** fighting off the monster.
What if the monster comes back?!
The city is defenseless! My ***parents*** are there! My ***stuff*** is there!
Oh, it's always quiet for a while after an attack. Right now, we need more light!
Here we go!
Ta-da!
Doesn't look very bright to me.
Wait until we've got electrons ***moving*** through it.

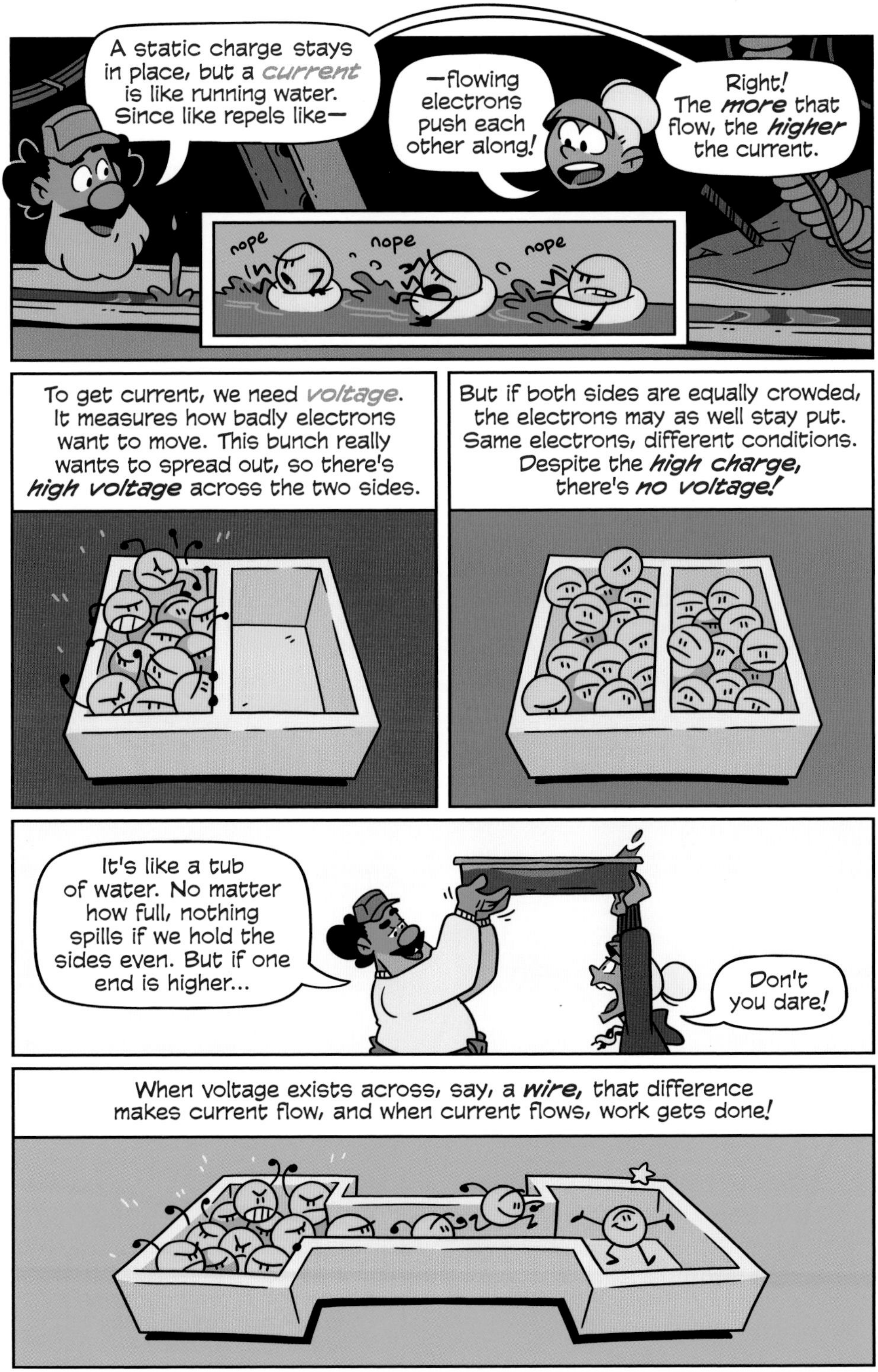
A static charge stays in place, but a *current* is like running water. Since like repels like—
—flowing electrons push each other along!
Right! The ***more*** that flow, the ***higher*** the current.
nope
nope
nope
To get current, we need *voltage*. It measures how badly electrons want to move. This bunch really wants to spread out, so there's ***high voltage*** across the two sides.
But if both sides are equally crowded, the electrons may as well stay put. Same electrons, different conditions. Despite the ***high charge,*** there's ***no voltage!***
It's like a tub of water. No matter how full, nothing spills if we hold the sides even. But if one end is higher...
Don't you dare!
When voltage exists across, say, a ***wire,*** that difference makes current flow, and when current flows, work gets done!

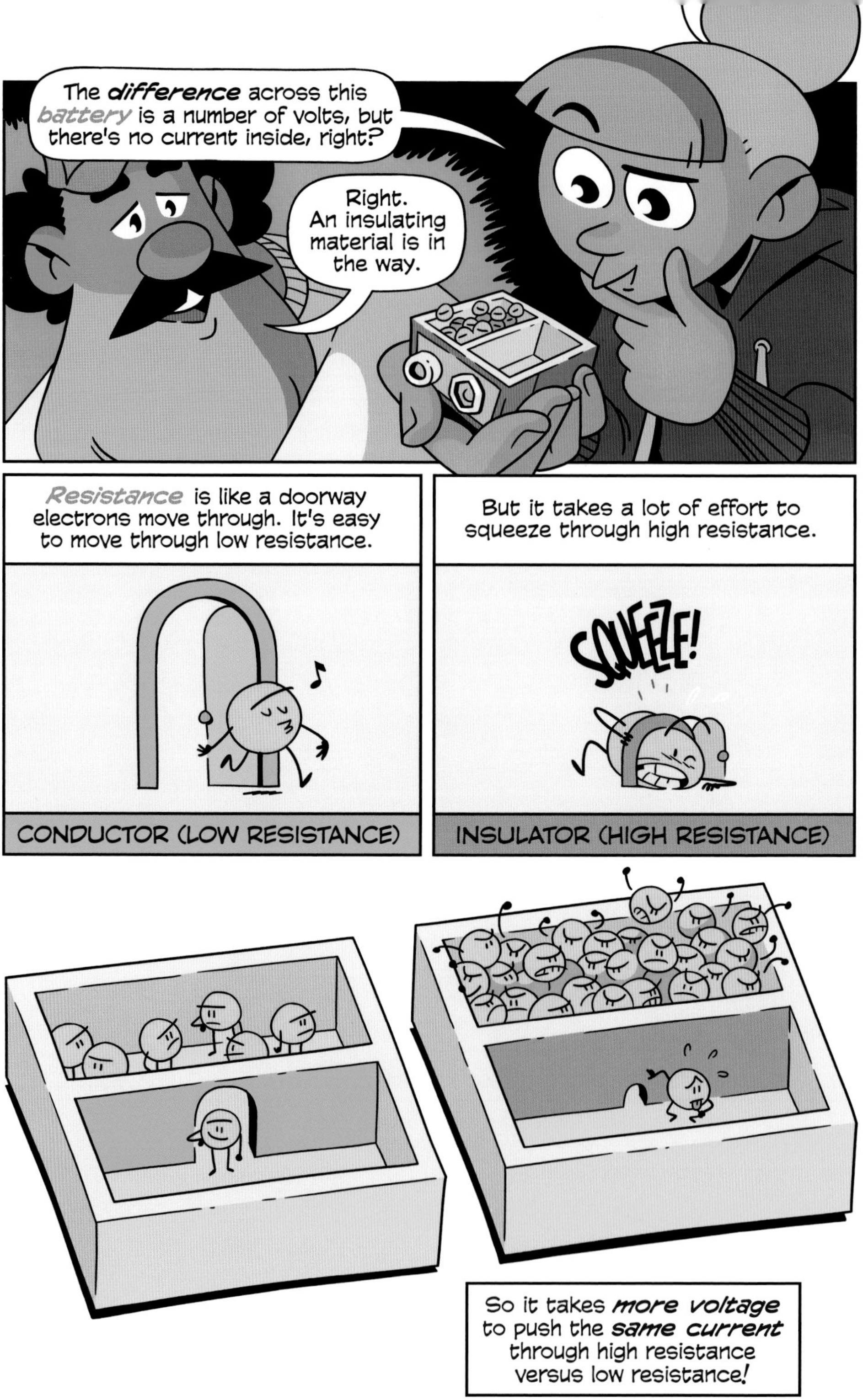
The *difference* across this battery is a number of volts, but there's no current inside, right?
Right. An insulating material is in the way.
Resistance is like a doorway electrons move through. It's easy to move through low resistance.
But it takes a lot of effort to squeeze through high resistance.
CONDUCTOR (LOW RESISTANCE)
SQUEEZE!
INSULATOR (HIGH RESISTANCE)
So it takes ***more voltage*** to push the ***same current*** through high resistance versus low resistance!

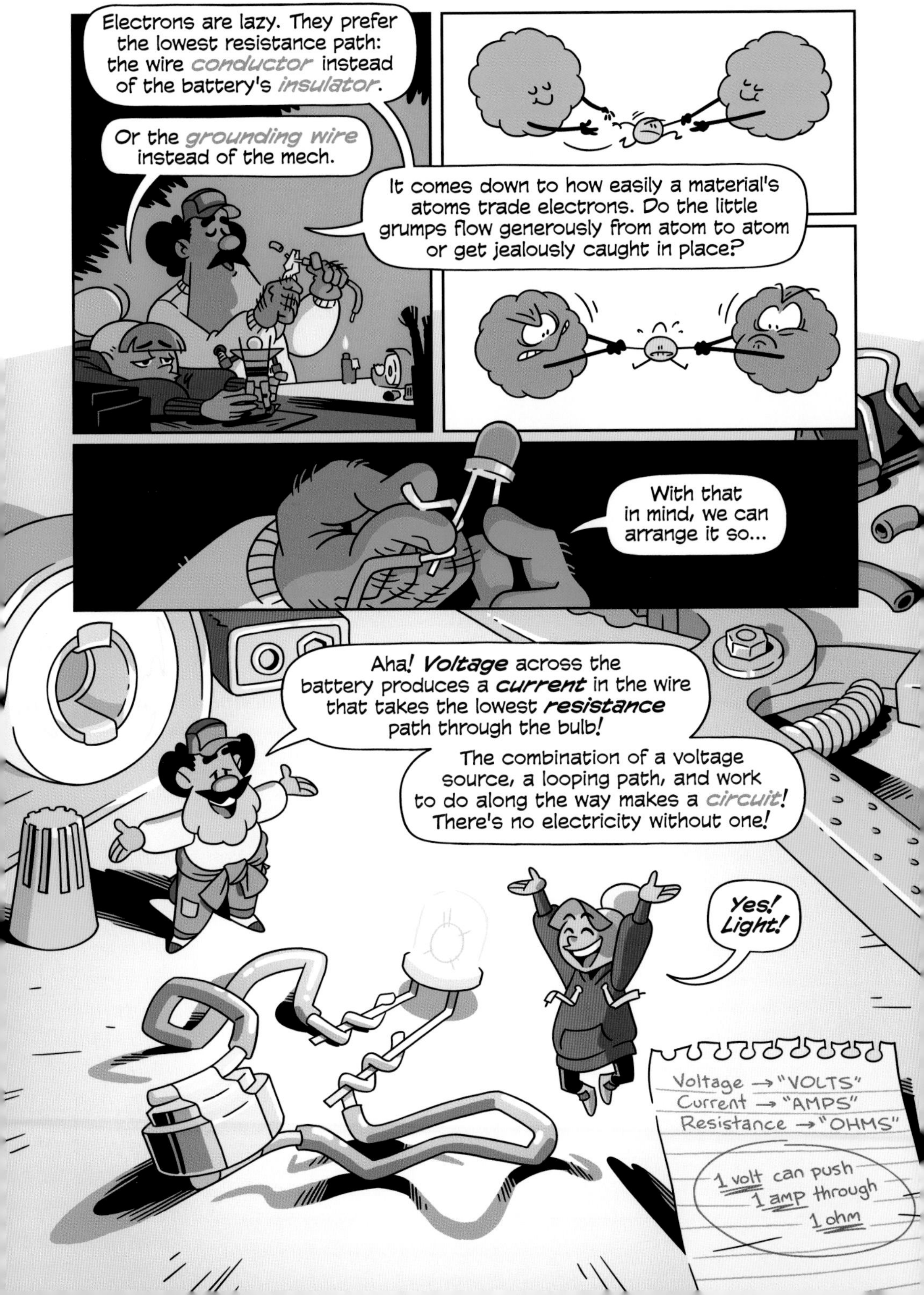

Electrons are lazy. They prefer the lowest resistance path: the wire *conductor* instead of the battery's *insulator*.
Or the *grounding wire* instead of the mech.
It comes down to how easily a material's atoms trade electrons. Do the little grumps flow generously from atom to atom or get jealously caught in place?
With that in mind, we can arrange it so...
Aha! ***Voltage*** across the battery produces a ***current*** in the wire that takes the lowest ***resistance*** path through the bulb!
The combination of a voltage source, a looping path, and work to do along the way makes a *circuit*! There's no electricity without one!
Yes! Light!
Voltage → "VOLTS"
Current → "AMPS"
Resistance → "OHMS"
1 volt can push 1 amp through 1 ohm

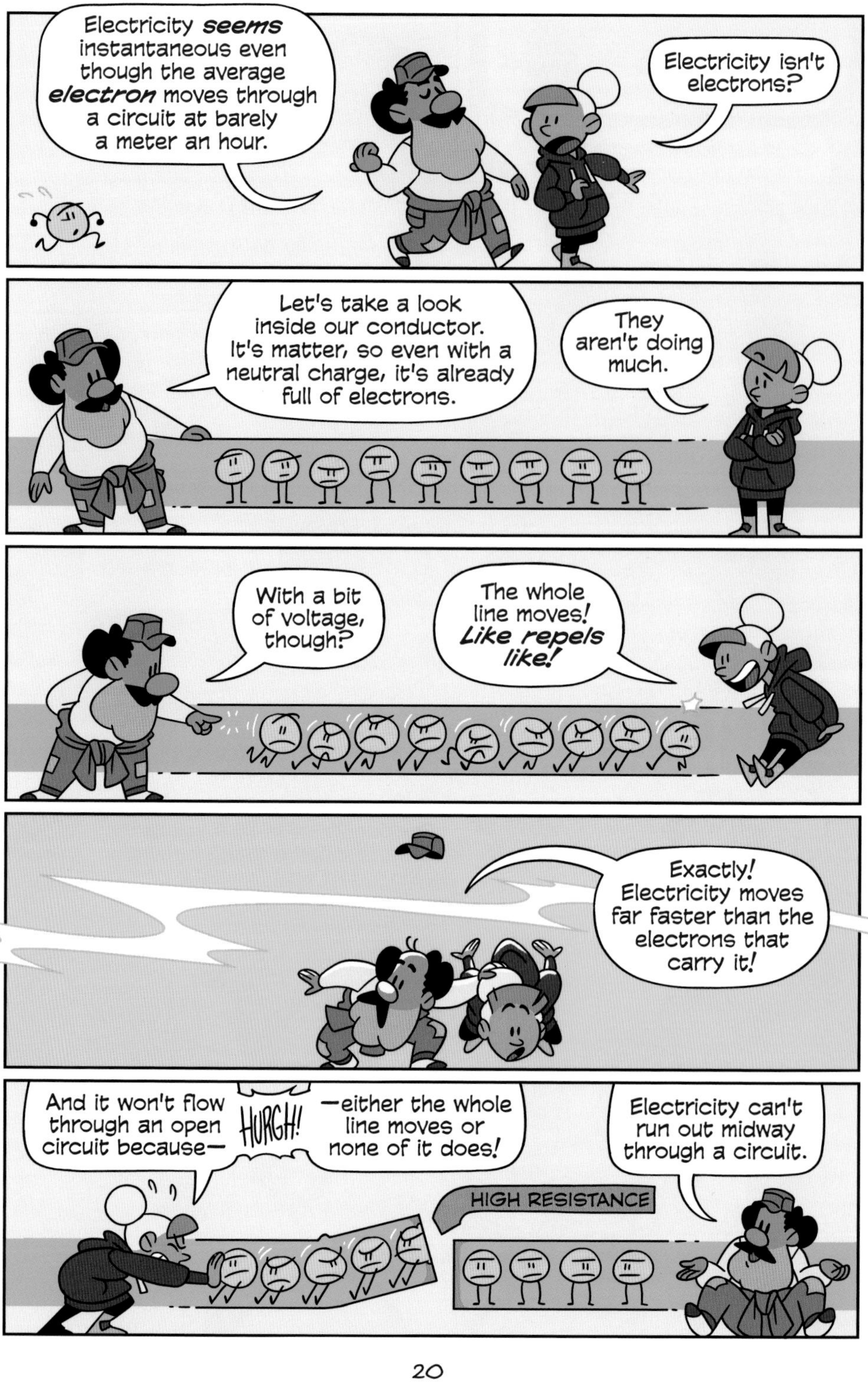
Electricity **seems** instantaneous even though the average **electron** moves through a circuit at barely a meter an hour.
Electricity isn't electrons?
Let's take a look inside our conductor. It's matter, so even with a neutral charge, it's already full of electrons.
They aren't doing much.
With a bit of voltage, though?
The whole line moves! ***Like repels like!***
Exactly! Electricity moves far faster than the electrons that carry it!
And it won't flow through an open circuit because—
HURGH!
—either the whole line moves or none of it does!
HIGH RESISTANCE
Electricity can't run out midway through a circuit.

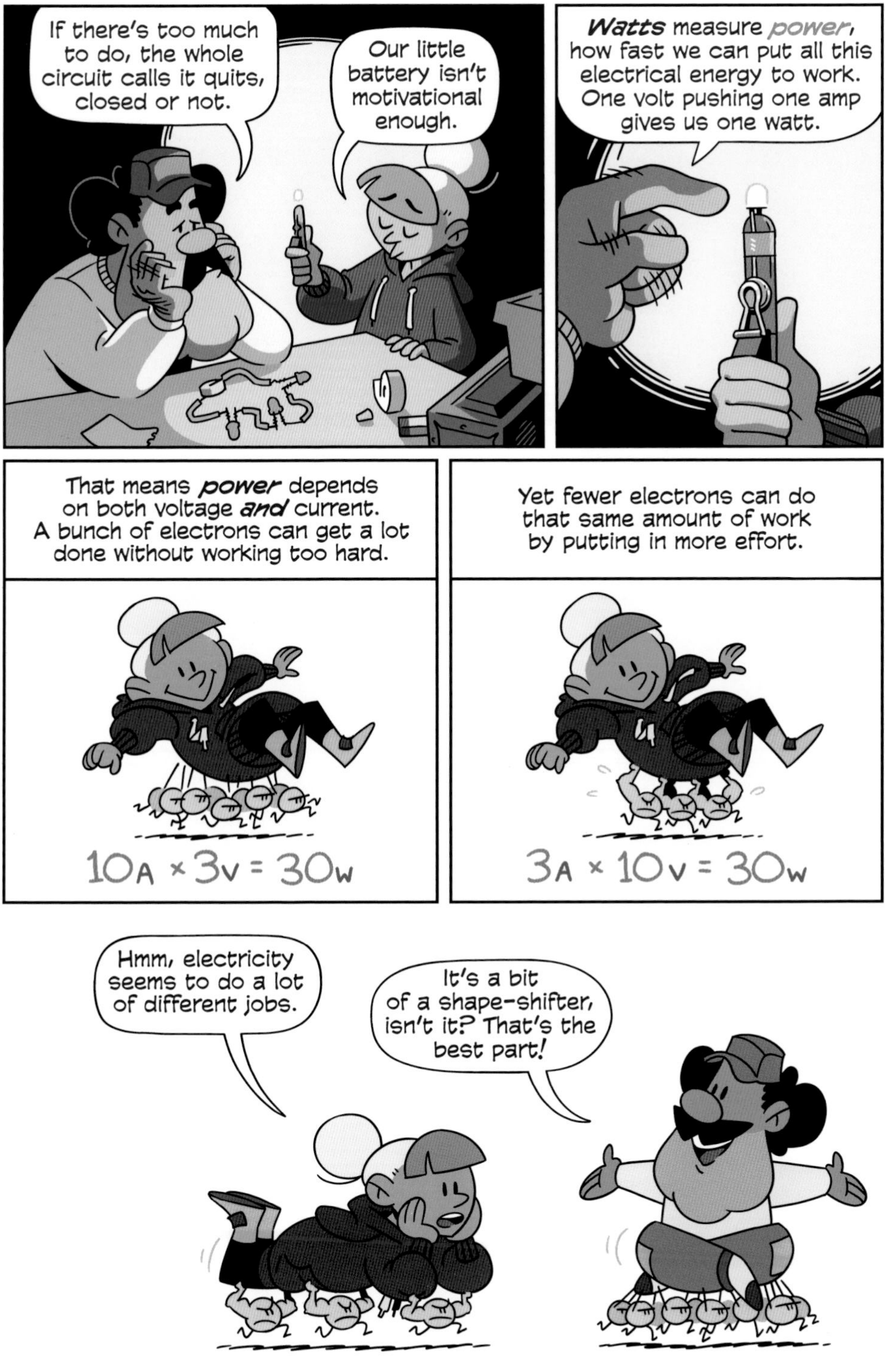

If there's too much to do, the whole circuit calls it quits, closed or not.
Our little battery isn't motivational enough.
Watts measure *power*, how fast we can put all this electrical energy to work. One volt pushing one amp gives us one watt.
That means *power* depends on both voltage *and* current. A bunch of electrons can get a lot done without working too hard.
10A × 3V = 30W
Yet fewer electrons can do that same amount of work by putting in more effort.
3A × 10V = 30W
Hmm, electricity seems to do a lot of different jobs.
It's a bit of a shape-shifter, isn't it? That's the best part!

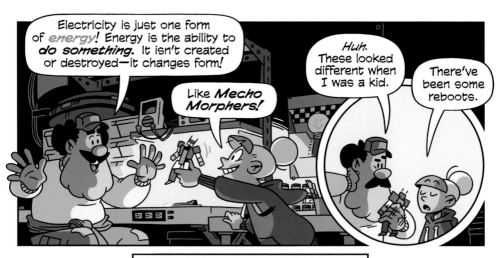

Electricity is just one form of *energy*! Energy is the ability to ***do something.*** It isn't created or destroyed—it changes form!
Like ***Mecho Morphers!***
Huh. These looked different when I was a kid.
There've been some reboots.
All energy forms are one of two types.
POTENTIAL ENERGY is still and can do something later.
KINETIC ENERGY is in motion, doing something now.
NUCLEAR
Stored within atoms
RADIANT
Electromagnetic waves like light
CHEMICAL
Stored as bonds between atoms
THERMAL
Heat from vibrating molecules
ELASTIC
Stored by stretching or compressing
SOUND
Compression waves through matter
GRAVITATIONAL
Stored at height
MECHANICAL
Any sort of moving object
And, of course...
ELECTRICAL
Charges moving in one direction

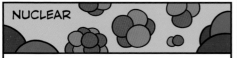

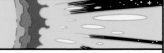

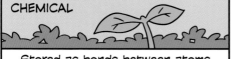

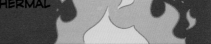

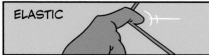

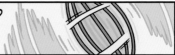

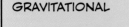

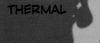

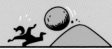

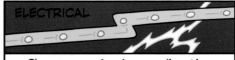

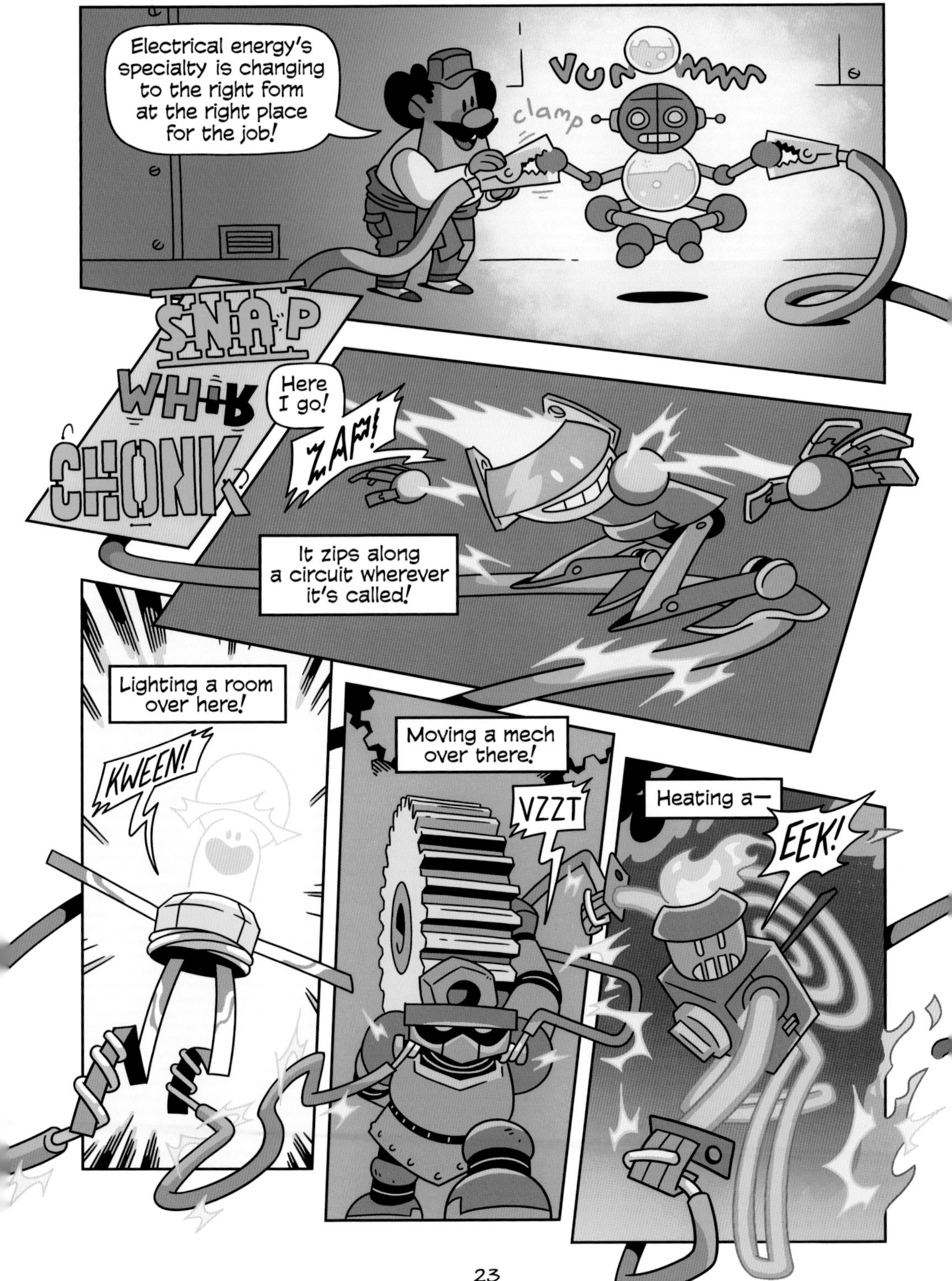

Electrical energy's specialty is changing to the right form at the right place for the job!
VUMMM
clamp
SNAP
WHIP
CHONK
Here I go!
ZAP!
It zips along a circuit wherever it's called!
Lighting a room over here!
KWEEN!
Moving a mech over there!
VZZT
Heating a—
EEK!

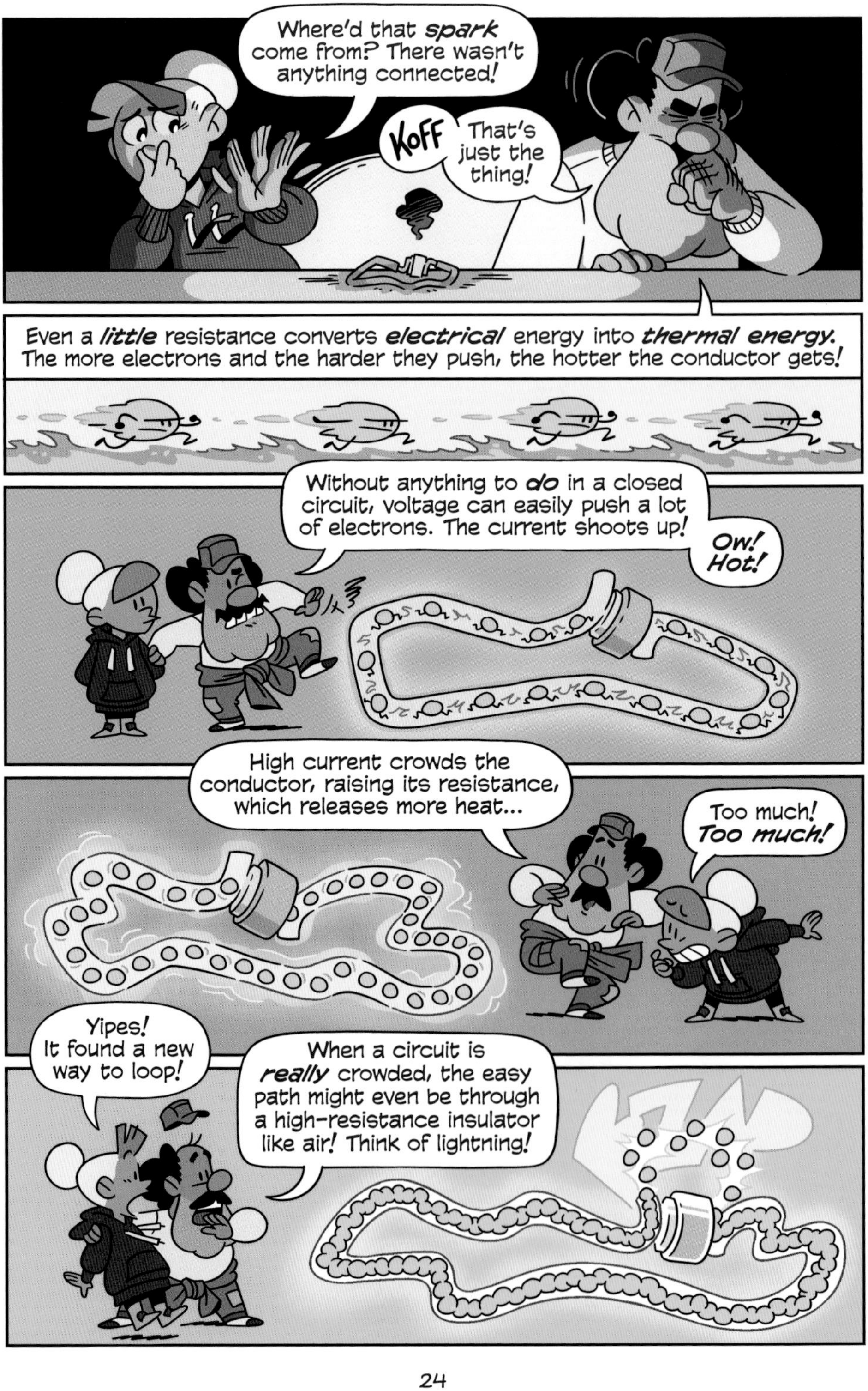
Where'd that *spark* come from? There wasn't anything connected!
KOFF
That's just the thing!
Even a *little* resistance converts *electrical* energy into *thermal energy.* The more electrons and the harder they push, the hotter the conductor gets!
Without anything to *do* in a closed circuit, voltage can easily push a lot of electrons. The current shoots up!
Ow! Hot!
High current crowds the conductor, raising its resistance, which releases more heat...
Too much! *Too much!*
Yipes! It found a new way to loop!
When a circuit is *really* crowded, the easy path might even be through a high-resistance insulator like air! Think of lightning!

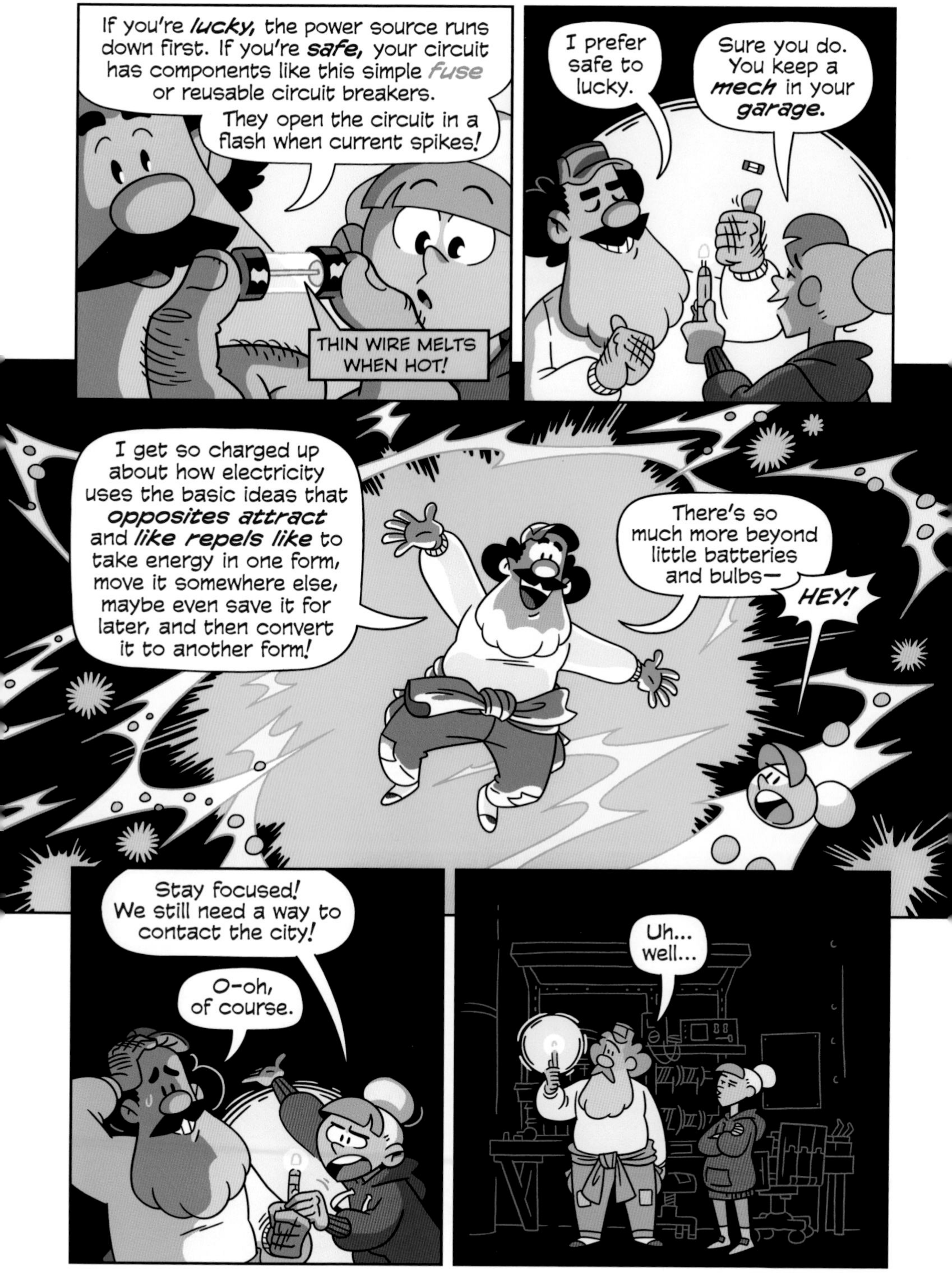

If you're *lucky,* the power source runs down first. If you're ***safe,*** your circuit has components like this simple *fuse* or reusable circuit breakers.
They open the circuit in a flash when current spikes!
THIN WIRE MELTS WHEN HOT!
I prefer safe to lucky.
Sure you do. You keep a ***mech*** in your ***garage.***
I get so charged up about how electricity uses the basic ideas that ***opposites attract*** and ***like repels like*** to take energy in one form, move it somewhere else, maybe even save it for later, and then convert it to another form!
There's so much more beyond little batteries and bulbs—
HEY!
Stay focused! We still need a way to contact the city!
O-oh, of course.
Uh... well...

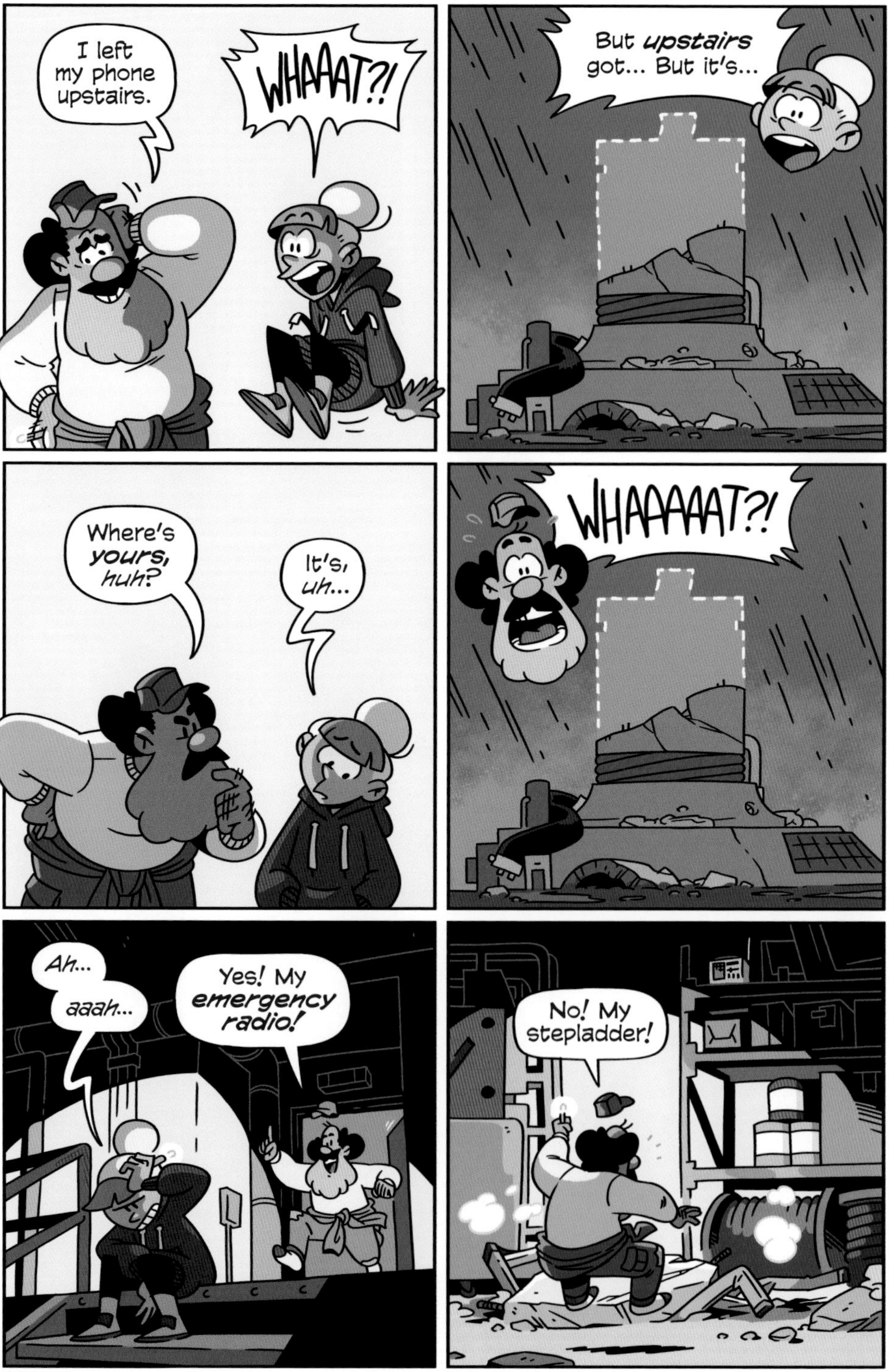
I left my phone upstairs.
WHAAAT?!
But upstairs got... But it's...
Where's yours, huh?
It's, uh...
WHAAAAAT?!
Ah...
aaah...
Yes! My emergency radio!
No! My stepladder!

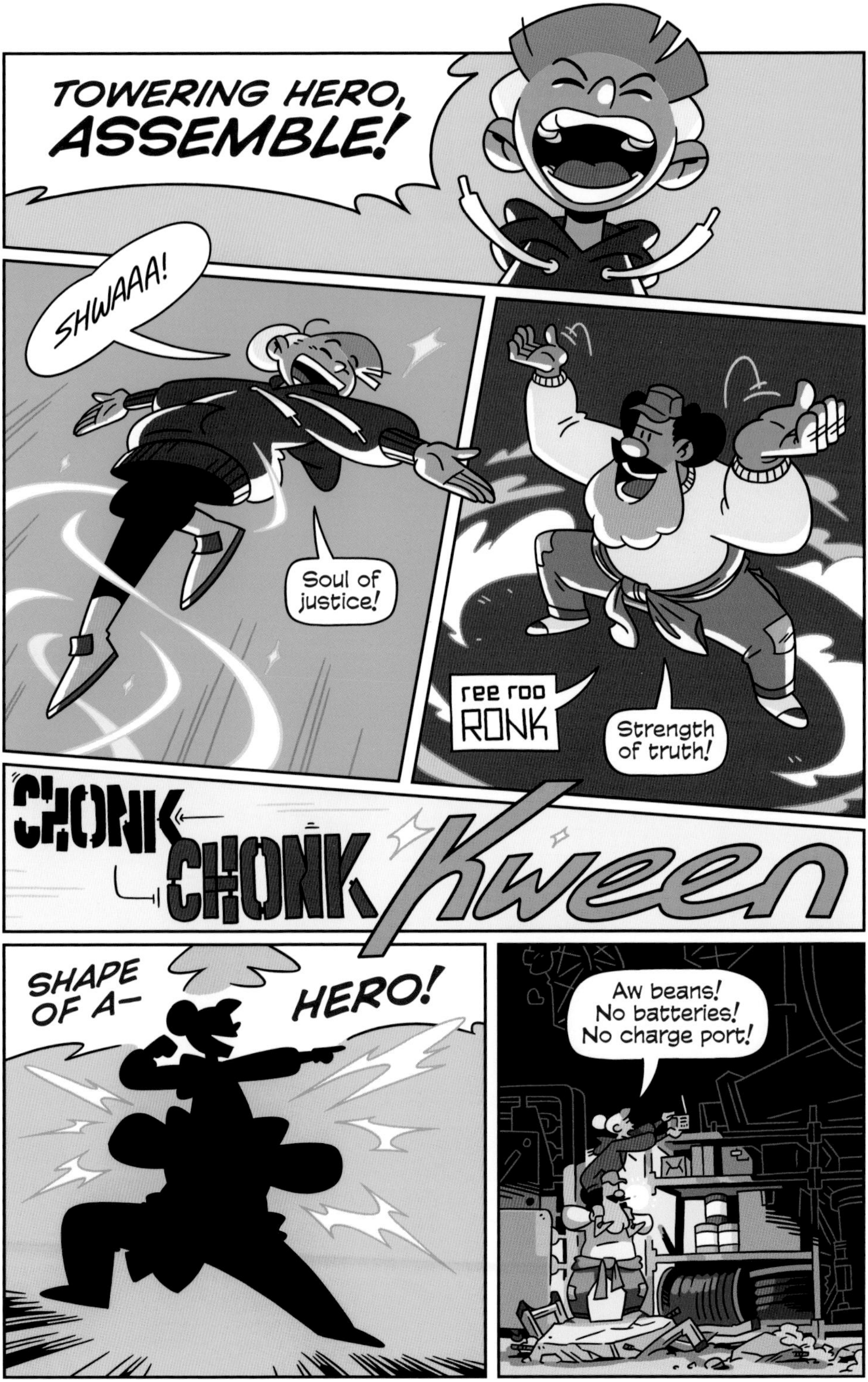

TOWERING HERO, ASSEMBLE!
SHWAAA!
Soul of justice!
ree roo RONK
Strength of truth!
CHONK
CHONK
Kween
SHAPE OF A—
HERO!
Aw beans! No batteries! No charge port!

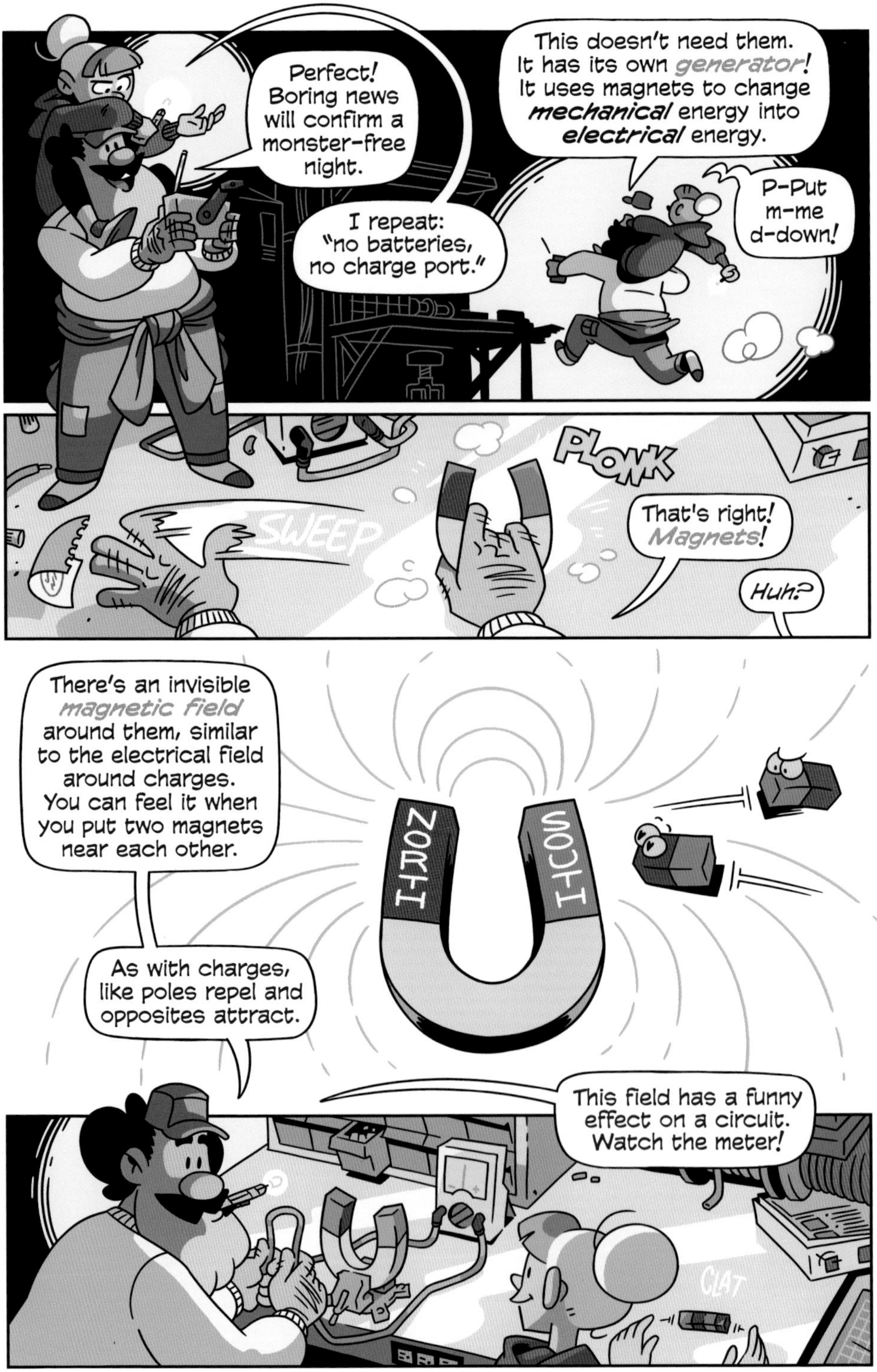
Perfect! Boring news will confirm a monster-free night.
I repeat: "no batteries, no charge port."
This doesn't need them. It has its own generator! It uses magnets to change mechanical energy into electrical energy.
P-Put m-me d-down!
PLONK
SWEEP
That's right! Magnets!
Huh?
There's an invisible magnetic field around them, similar to the electrical field around charges. You can feel it when you put two magnets near each other.
NORTH
SOUTH
As with charges, like poles repel and opposites attract.
This field has a funny effect on a circuit. Watch the meter!
CLAT

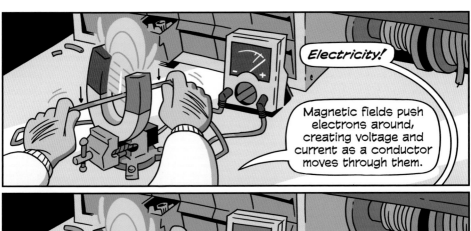

Electricity!

Magnetic fields push electrons around, creating voltage and current as a conductor moves through them.

But look! The current's direction depends on *which way* this wire is moving.

When we turn this loop of the conductor, called a *winding*, one side moves *up* through the field and the other *down*.

Its shape lets current go both ways!

Right! But as it keeps turning...

VWOOP

Up is down and down is up. Mayhem!

The trick is to "reset" up and down with a *commutator*.
Back to square one here.
N
S
Now a no-current hiccup.
N
S
Oh! The winding flips over, but the current doesn't!
Good start, right?
N
S
If you watch our meter, though, the voltage wobbles a ***lot.*** It hits zero twice each turn, right where the magnetic field and the winding's movement point the same way.
We won't get steady power from that.
Let's multiply it all!
VOLTAGE
TURN

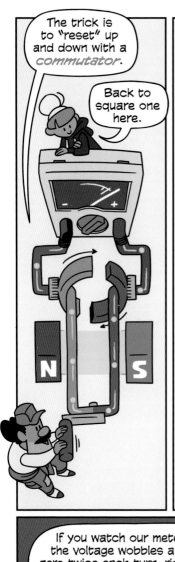

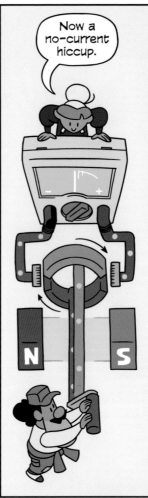

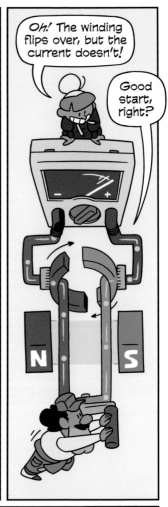

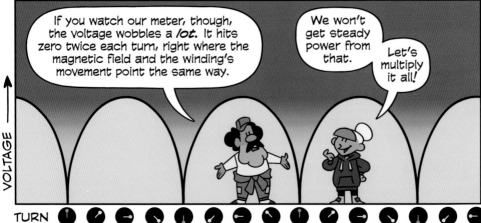

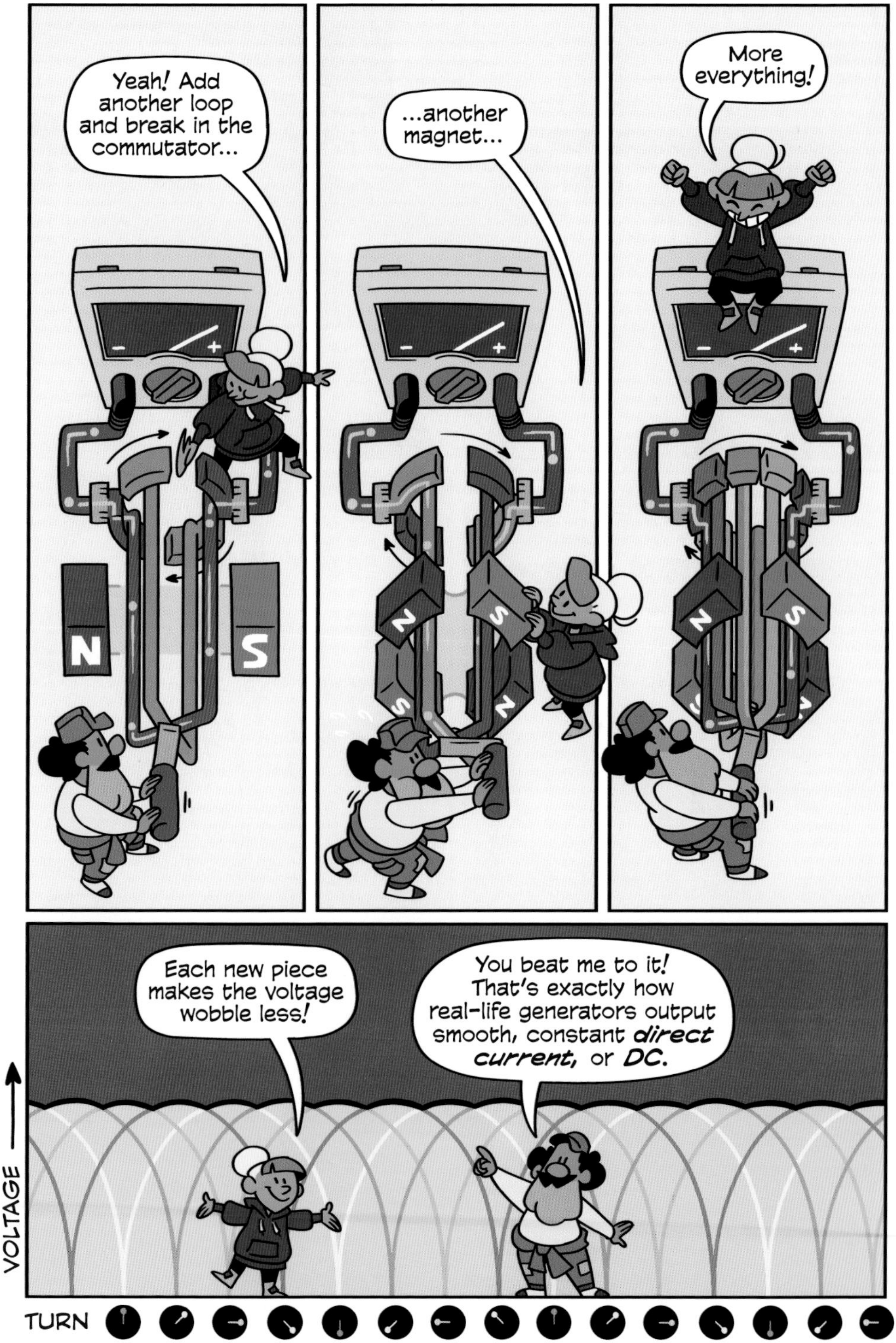

Yeah! Add another loop and break in the commutator...
-
+
N
S
...another magnet...
-
+
N
S
S
N
More everything!
-
+
N
S
Each new piece makes the voltage wobble less!
You beat me to it! That's exactly how real-life generators output smooth, constant *direct current,* or *DC.*
VOLTAGE
TURN

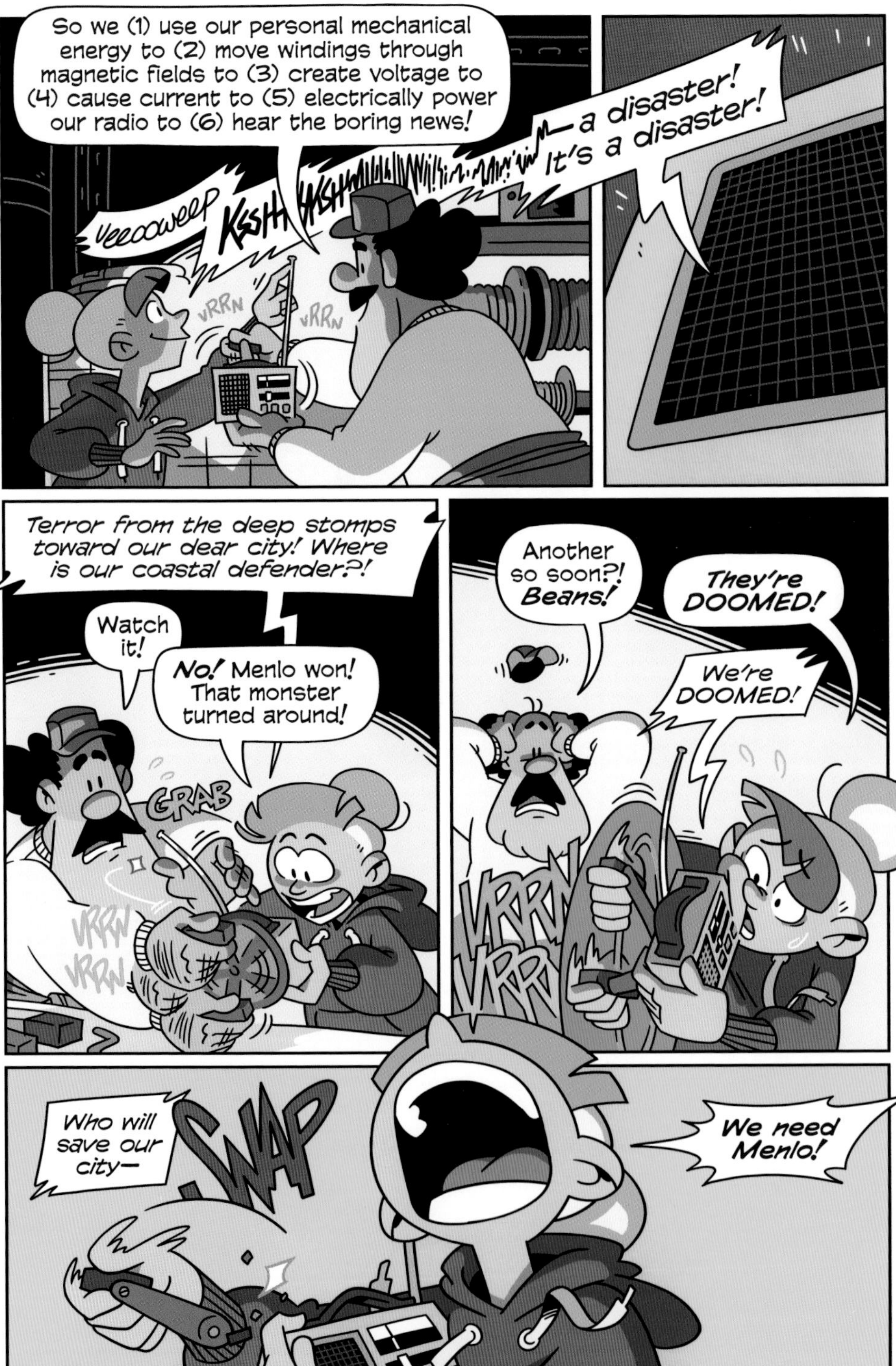
So we (1) use our personal mechanical energy to (2) move windings through magnetic fields to (3) create voltage to (4) cause current to (5) electrically power our radio to (6) hear the boring news!
VEEOOWEEP
KSHH KSHH
—a disaster! It's a disaster!
VRRN
VRRN
Terror from the deep stomps toward our dear city! Where is our coastal defender?!
Watch it!
No! Menlo won! That monster turned around!
GRAB
VRRN
VRRN
Another so soon?! Beans!
They're DOOMED!
We're DOOMED!
VRRN
VRRN
Who will save our city—
SNAP
We need Menlo!

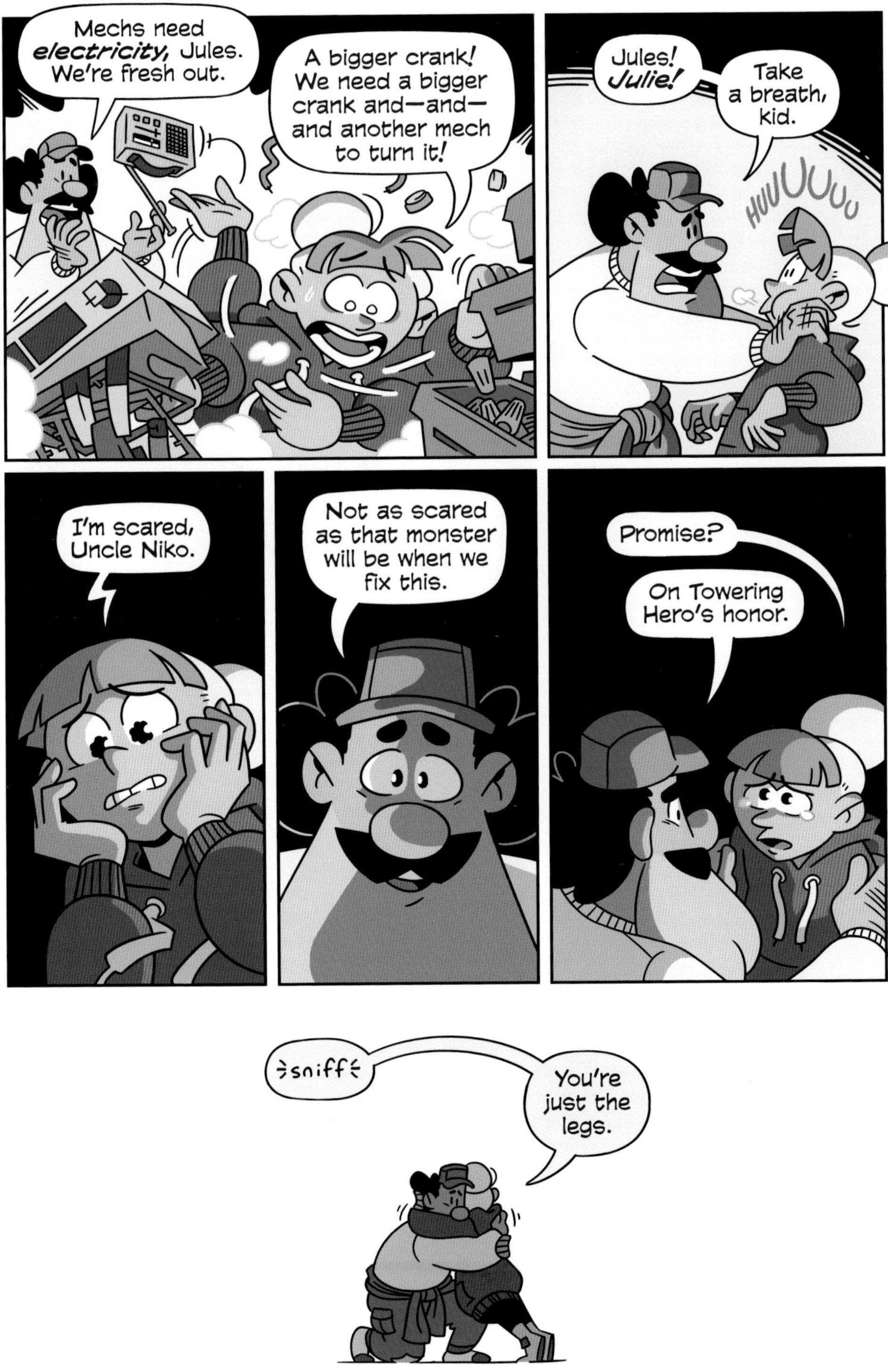
Mechs need *electricity,* Jules. We're fresh out.
A bigger crank! We need a bigger crank and—and—and another mech to turn it!
Jules! *Julie!*
Take a breath, kid.
HUUUUUu
I'm scared, Uncle Niko.
Not as scared as that monster will be when we fix this.
Promise?
On Towering Hero's honor.
sniff
You're just the legs.

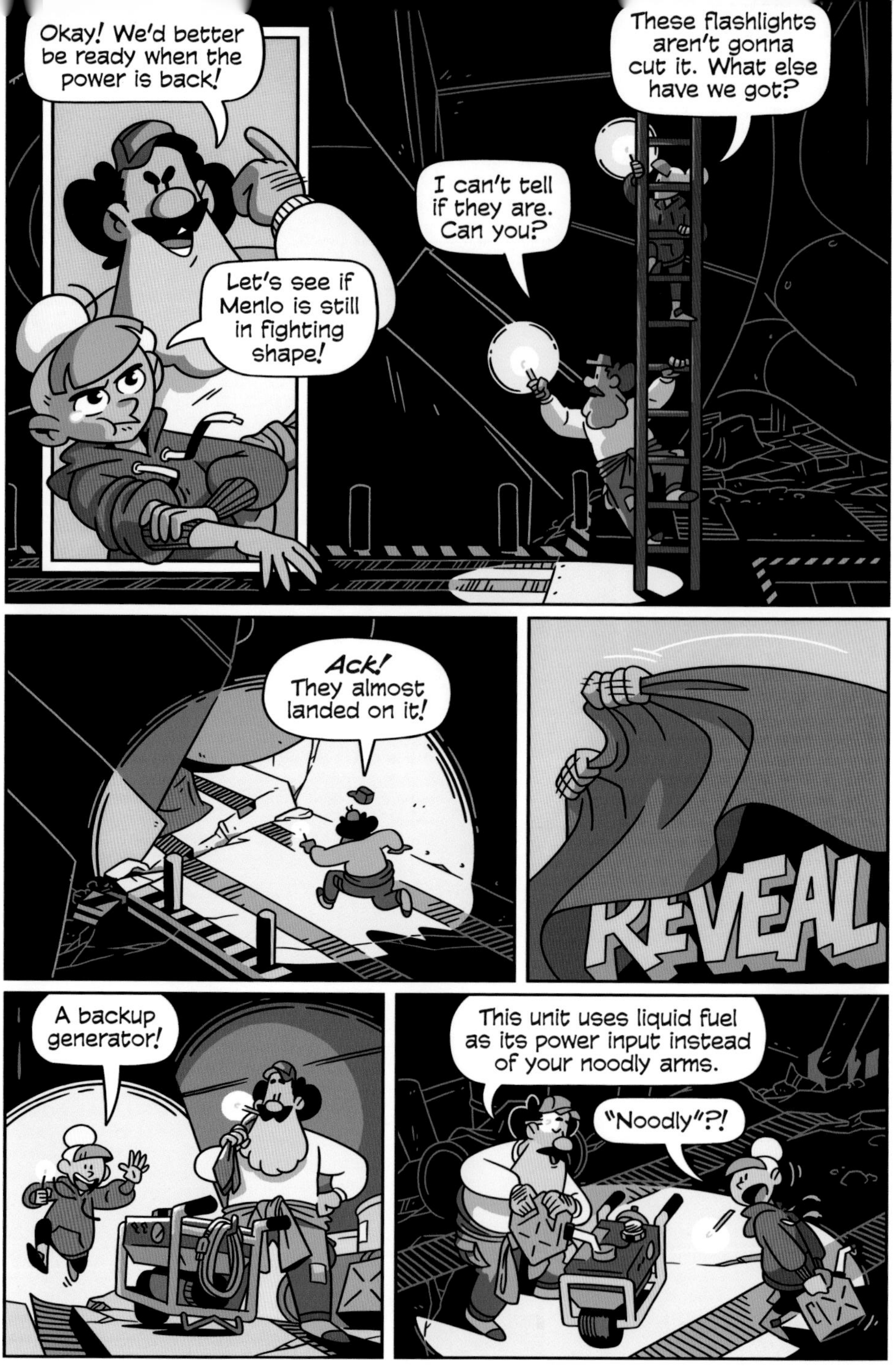

Okay! We'd better be ready when the power is back!
Let's see if Menlo is still in fighting shape!
These flashlights aren't gonna cut it. What else have we got?
I can't tell if they are. Can you?
Ack! They almost landed on it!
REVEAL
A backup generator!
This unit uses liquid fuel as its power input instead of your noodly arms.
"Noodly"?!

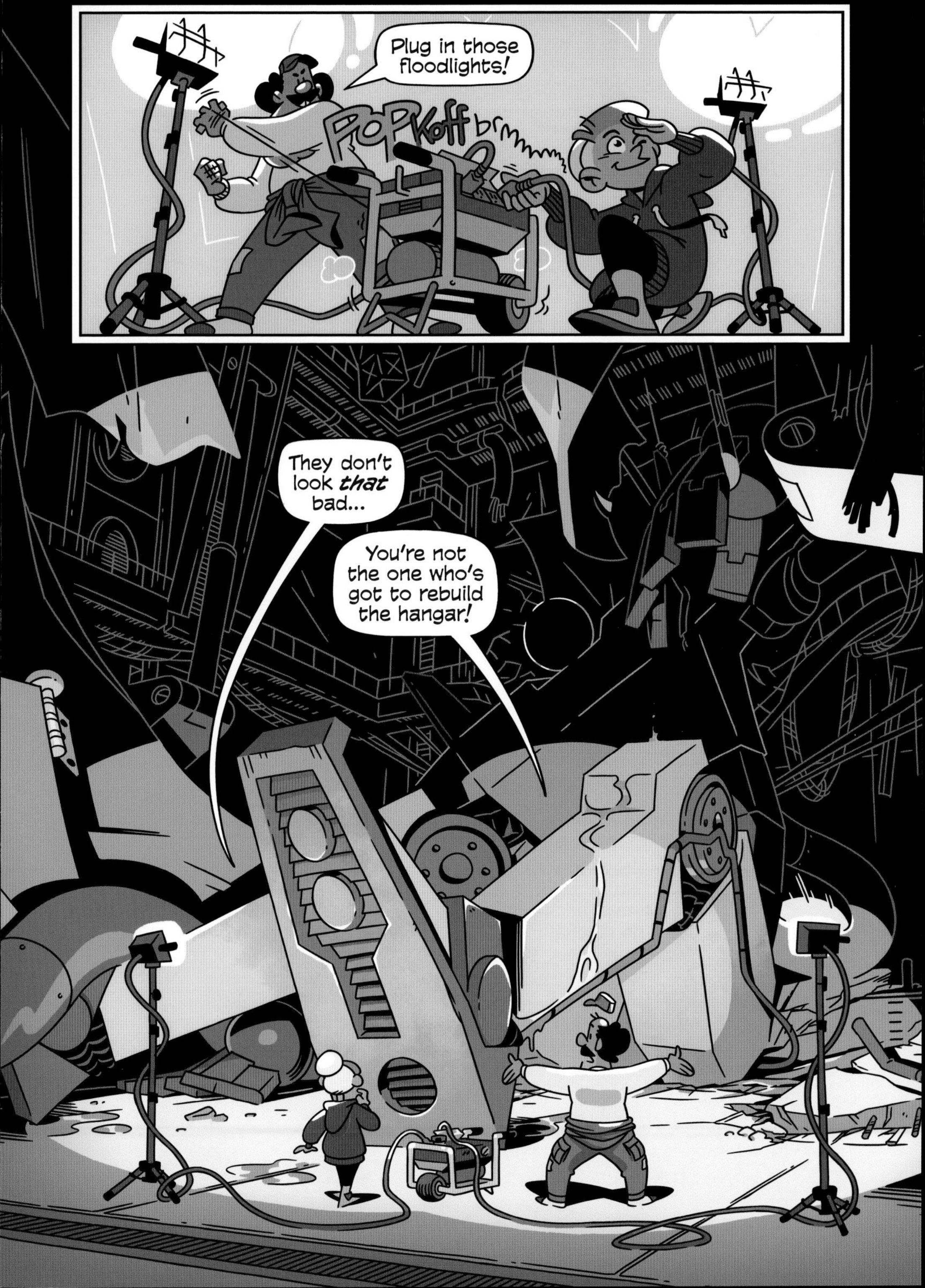
Plug in those floodlights!
POP Koff brmmmm
They don't look *that* bad...
You're not the one who's got to rebuild the hangar!

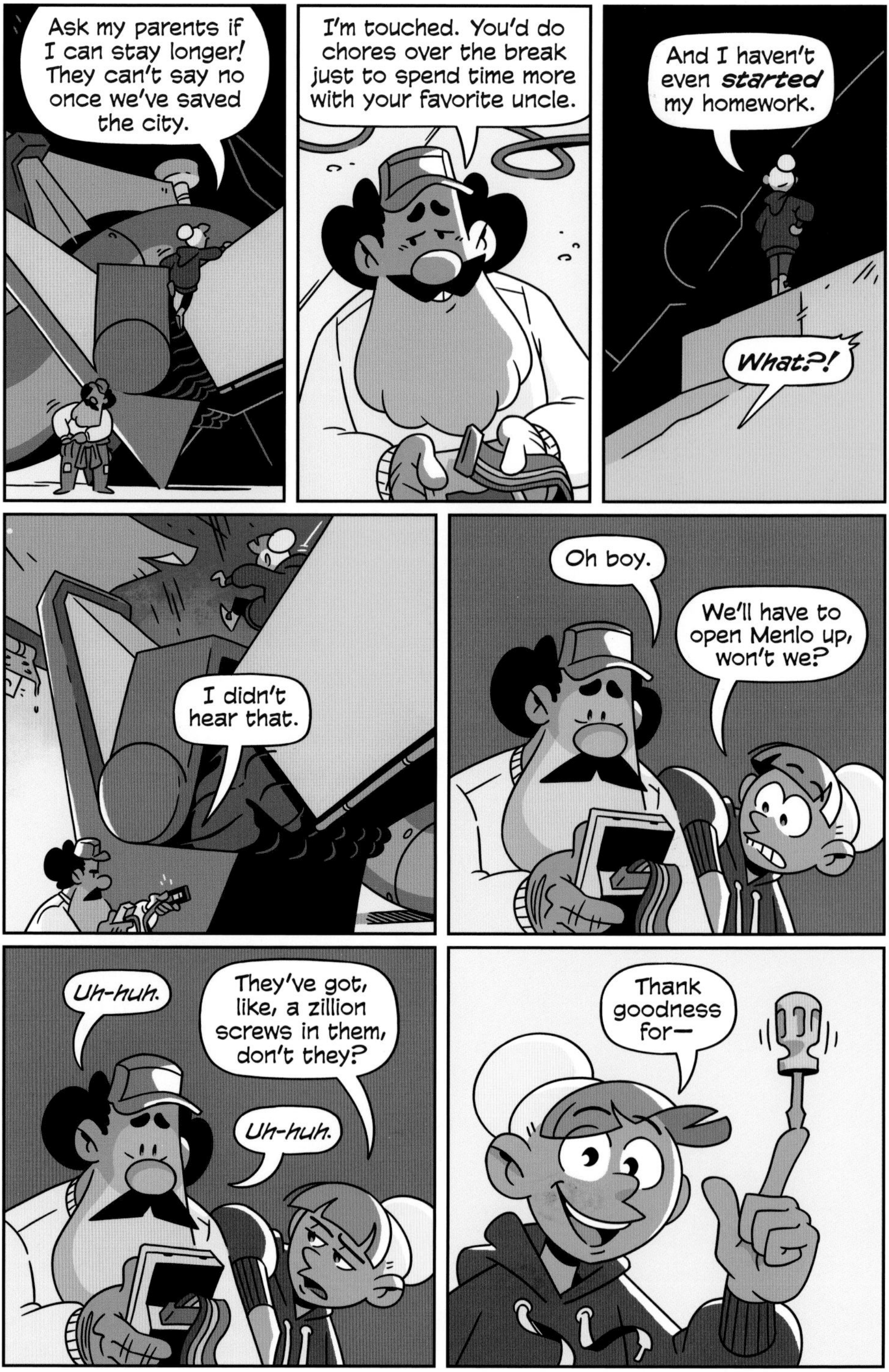
Ask my parents if I can stay longer! They can't say no once we've saved the city.
I'm touched. You'd do chores over the break just to spend time more with your favorite uncle.
And I haven't even *started* my homework.
What?!
I didn't hear that.
Oh boy.
We'll have to open Menlo up, won't we?
Uh-huh.
They've got, like, a zillion screws in them, don't they?
Uh-huh.
Thank goodness for—

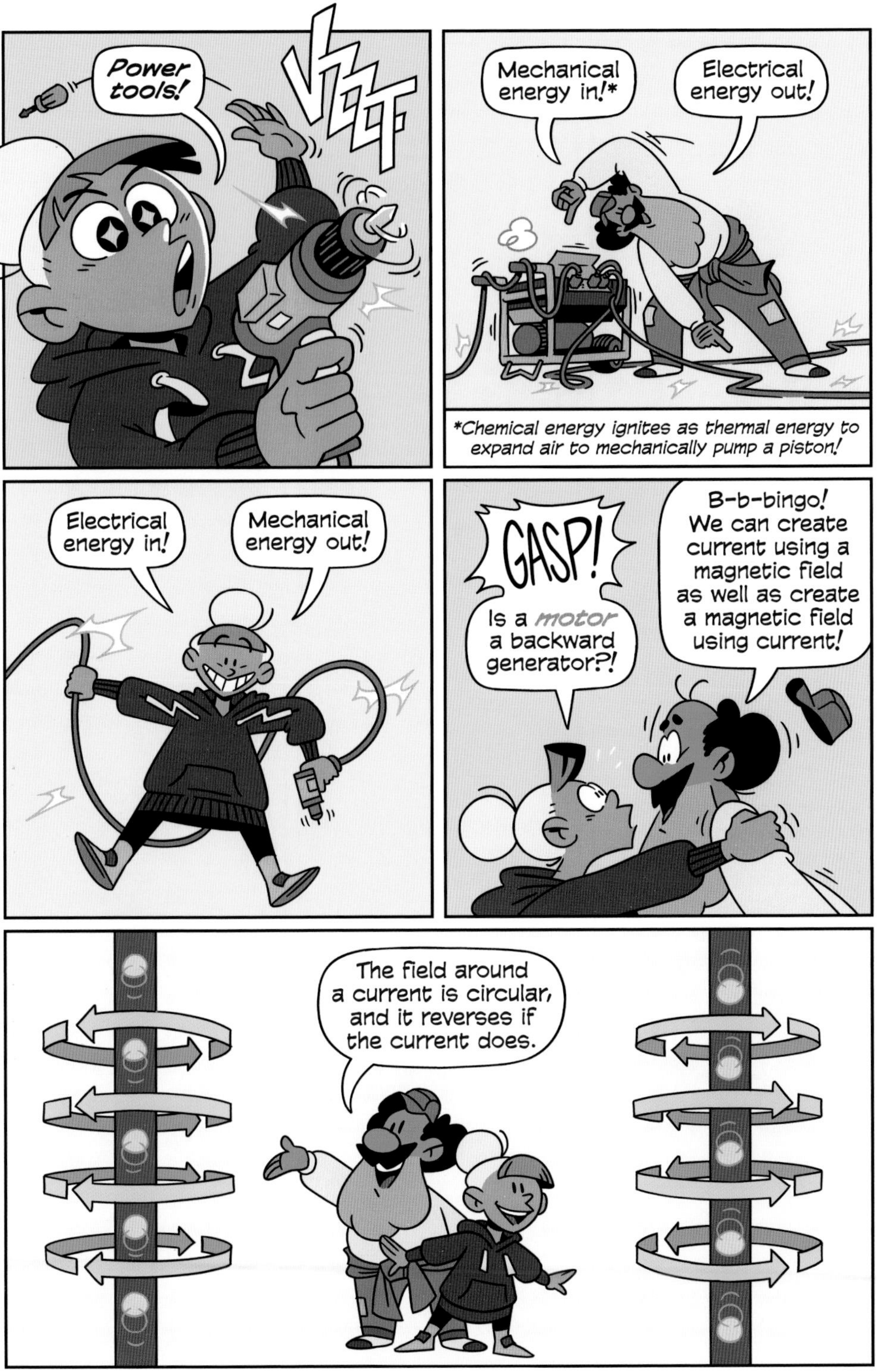
Power tools!
VZZZT
Mechanical energy in!*
Electrical energy out!
*Chemical energy ignites as thermal energy to expand air to mechanically pump a piston!
Electrical energy in!
Mechanical energy out!
GASP!
Is a motor a backward generator?!
B-b-bingo! We can create current using a magnetic field as well as create a magnetic field using current!
The field around a current is circular, and it reverses if the current does.

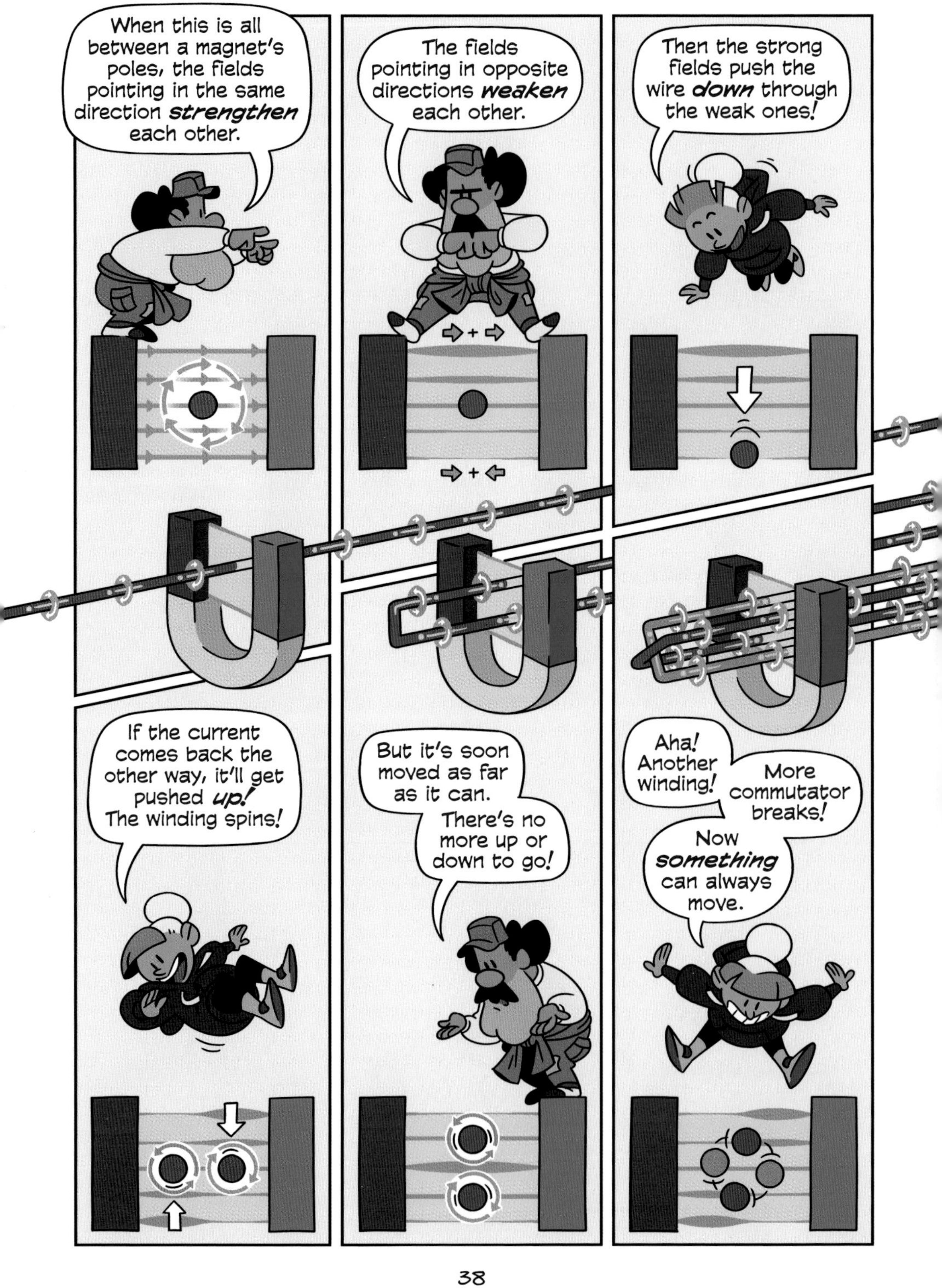
When this is all between a magnet's poles, the fields pointing in the same direction *strengthen* each other.
The fields pointing in opposite directions *weaken* each other.
Then the strong fields push the wire *down* through the weak ones!
If the current comes back the other way, it'll get pushed *up!* The winding spins!
But it's soon moved as far as it can.
There's no more up or down to go!
Aha! Another winding!
More commutator breaks!
Now *something* can always move.

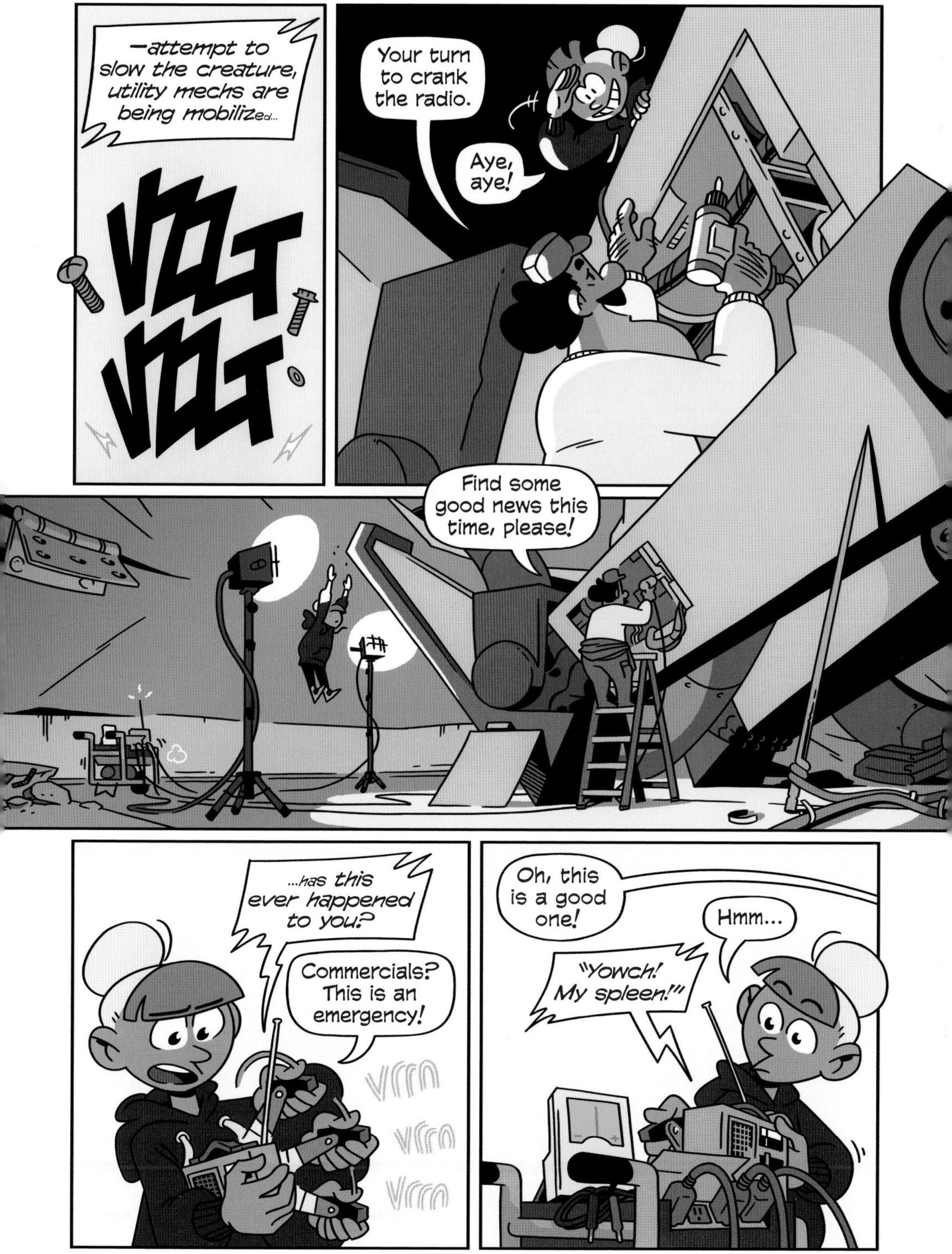
—attempt to slow the creature, utility mechs are being mobilized...
VZZT VZZT
Your turn to crank the radio.
Aye, aye!
Find some good news this time, please!
...has this ever happened to you?
Commercials? This is an emergency!
vrrn vrrn vrrn
Oh, this is a good one!
Hmm...
"Yowch! My spleen!"

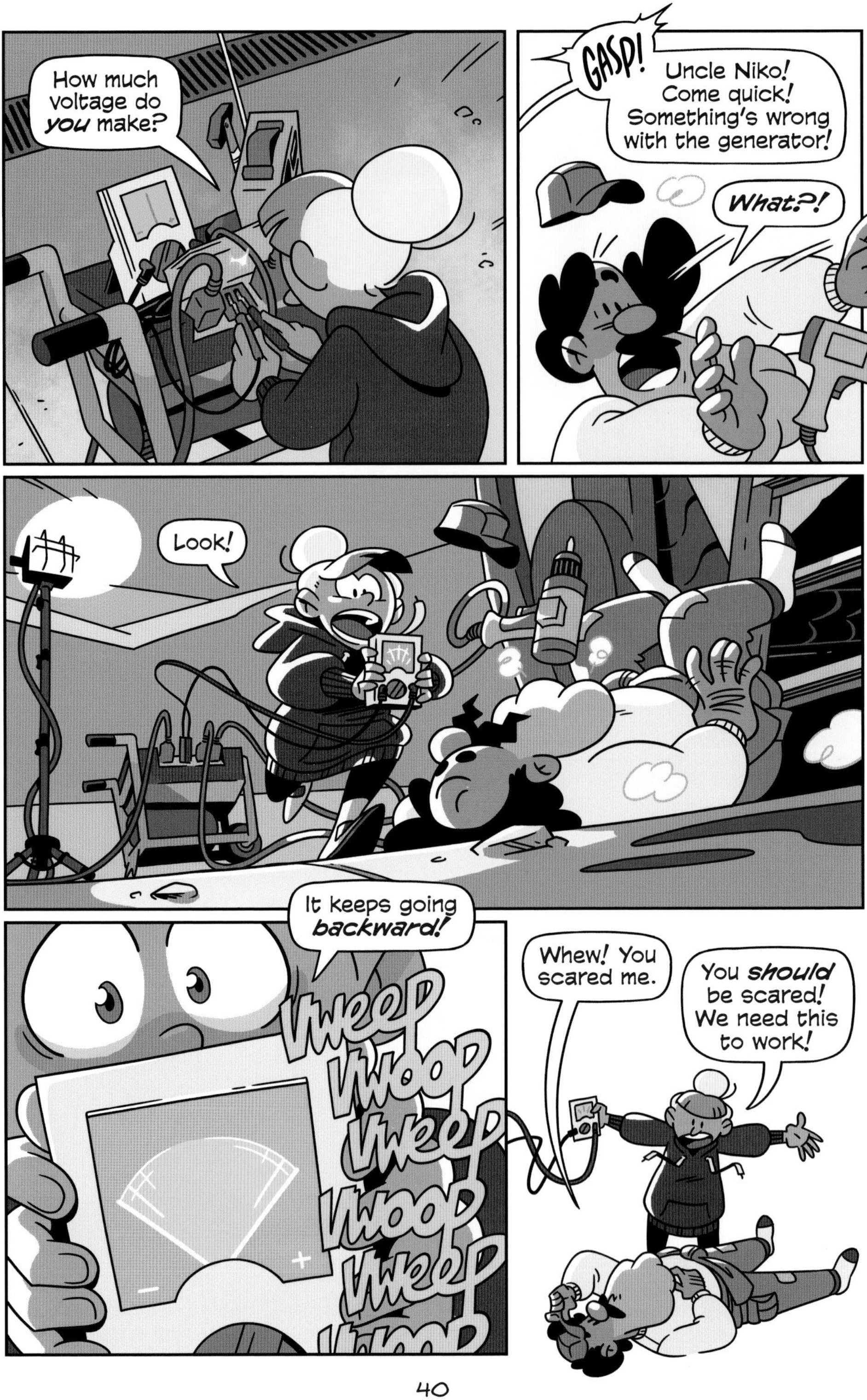
How much voltage do *you* make?
GASP!
Uncle Niko! Come quick! Something's wrong with the generator!
What?!
Look!
It keeps going *backward!*
VWEEP VWOOP VWEEP VWOOP VWEEP
Whew! You scared me.
You *should* be scared! We need this to work!

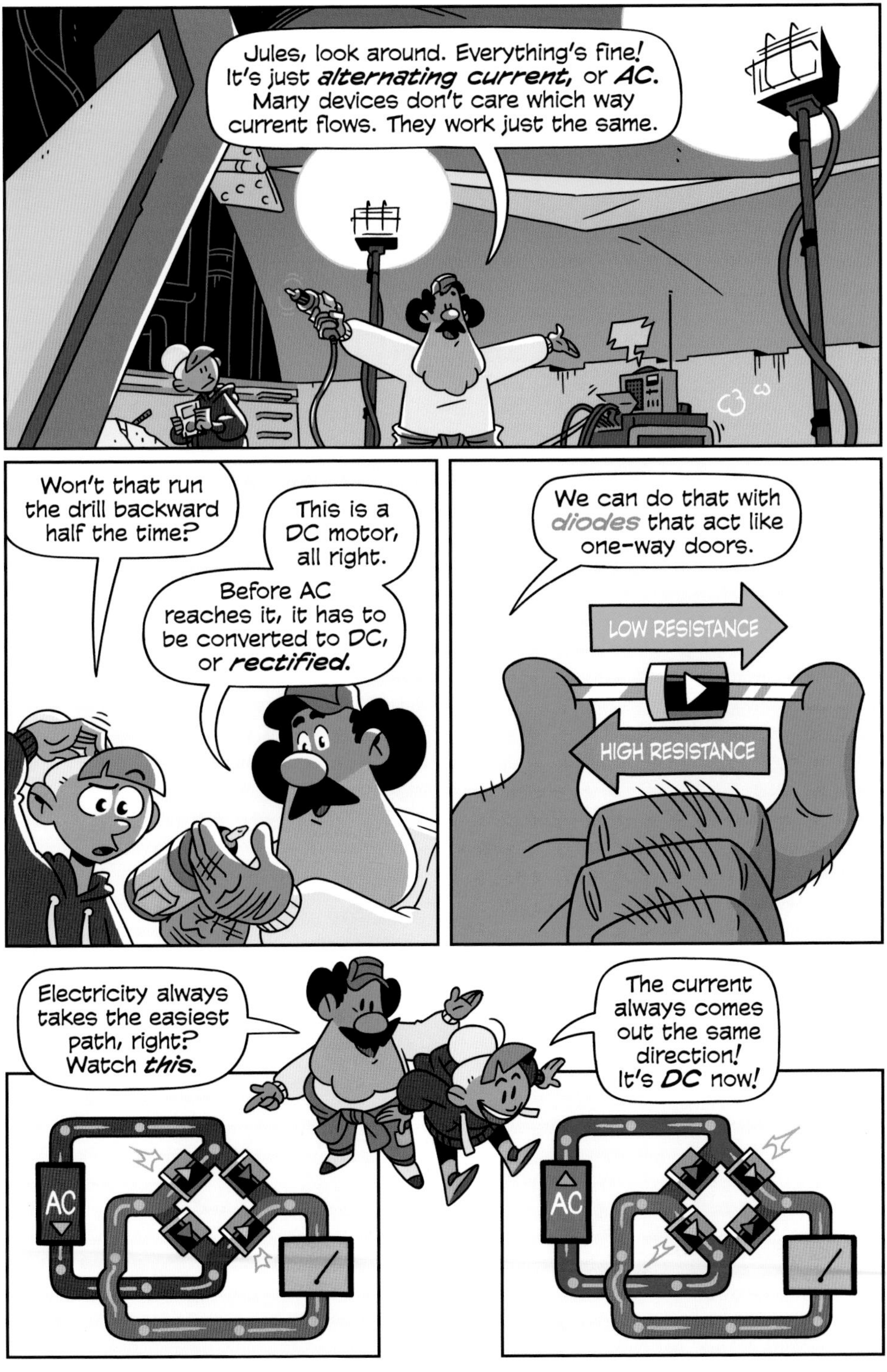
Jules, look around. Everything's fine! It's just *alternating current,* or *AC.* Many devices don't care which way current flows. They work just the same.
Won't that run the drill backward half the time?
This is a DC motor, all right.
Before AC reaches it, it has to be converted to DC, or *rectified.*
We can do that with *diodes* that act like one-way doors.
LOW RESISTANCE
HIGH RESISTANCE
Electricity always takes the easiest path, right? Watch *this.*
The current always comes out the same direction! It's *DC* now!
AC
AC

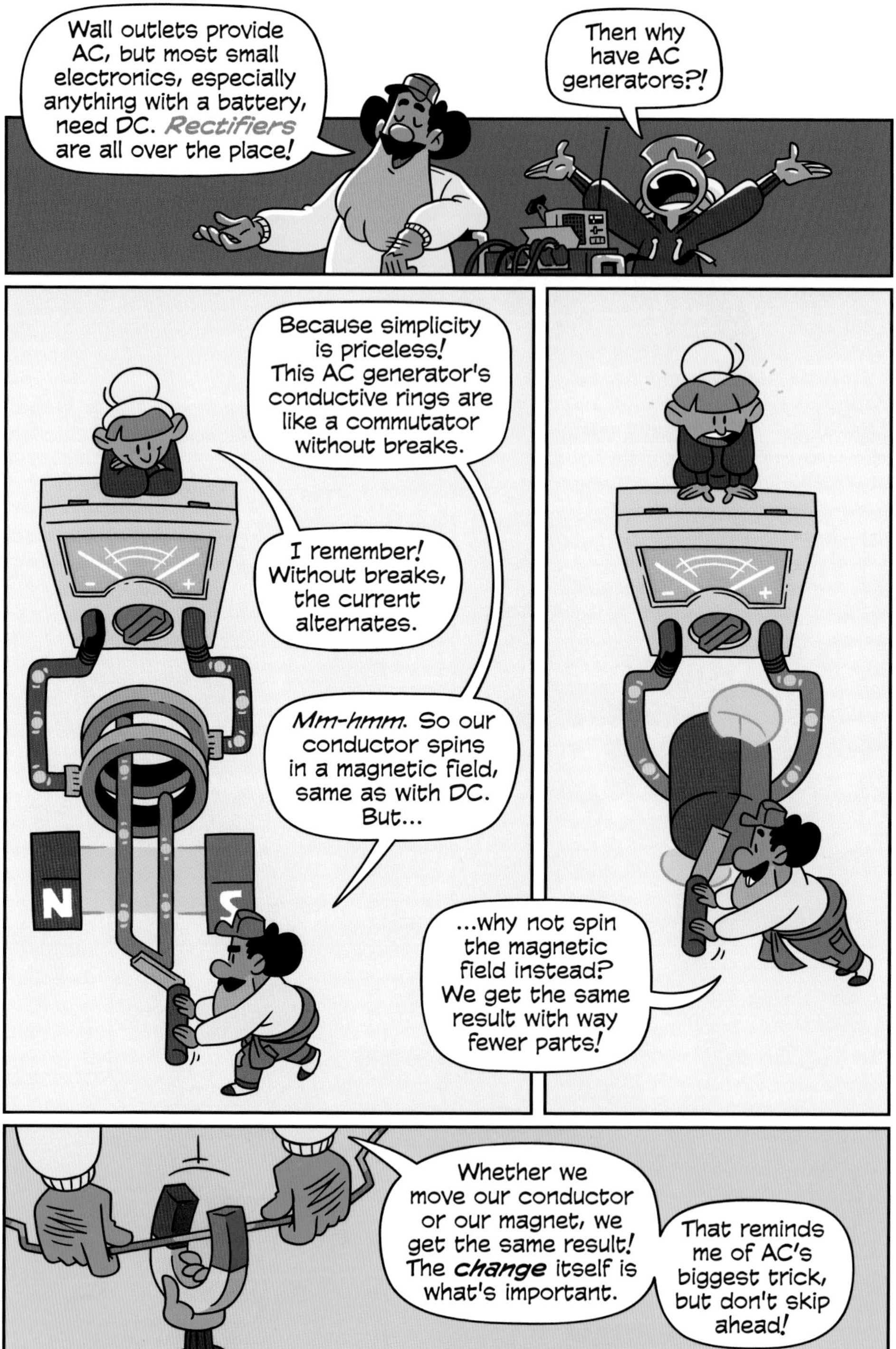
Wall outlets provide AC, but most small electronics, especially anything with a battery, need DC. Rectifiers are all over the place!
Then why have AC generators?!
Because simplicity is priceless! This AC generator's conductive rings are like a commutator without breaks.
I remember! Without breaks, the current alternates.
Mm-hmm. So our conductor spins in a magnetic field, same as with DC. But...
N
S
...why not spin the magnetic field instead? We get the same result with way fewer parts!
Whether we move our conductor or our magnet, we get the same result! The ***change*** itself is what's important.
That reminds me of AC's biggest trick, but don't skip ahead!

Motors and generators have two key parts: the *stator*, which stays still, and the *rotor*, which rotates.

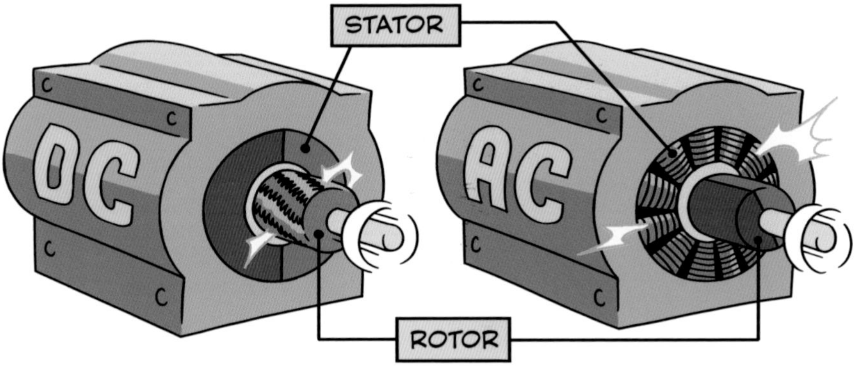
STATOR
DC
AC
ROTOR

Our DC machines have all had magnetized stators and electrified rotors. AC has the opposite. This is more durable and uses fewer parts.

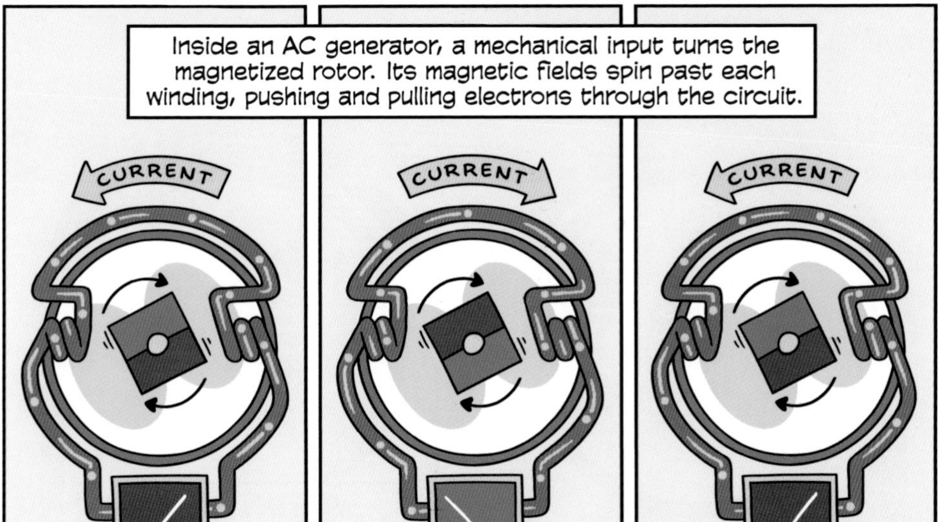
Inside an AC generator, a mechanical input turns the magnetized rotor. Its magnetic fields spin past each winding, pushing and pulling electrons through the circuit.
CURRENT
VOLTAGE
CURRENT
VOLTAGE
CURRENT
VOLTAGE

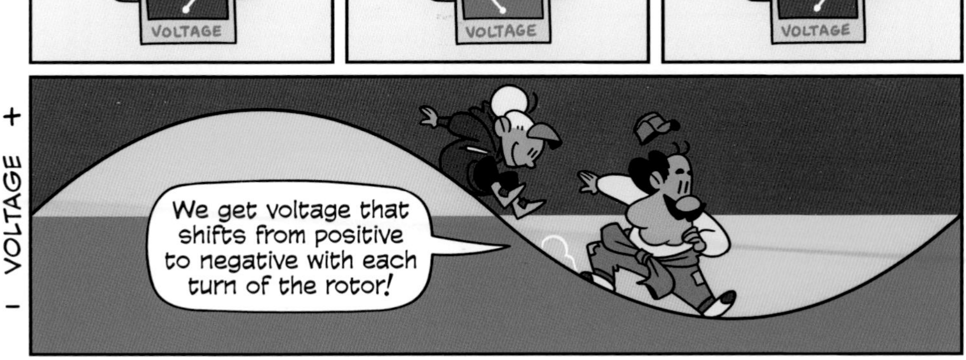
+
VOLTAGE
–
We get voltage that shifts from positive to negative with each turn of the rotor!

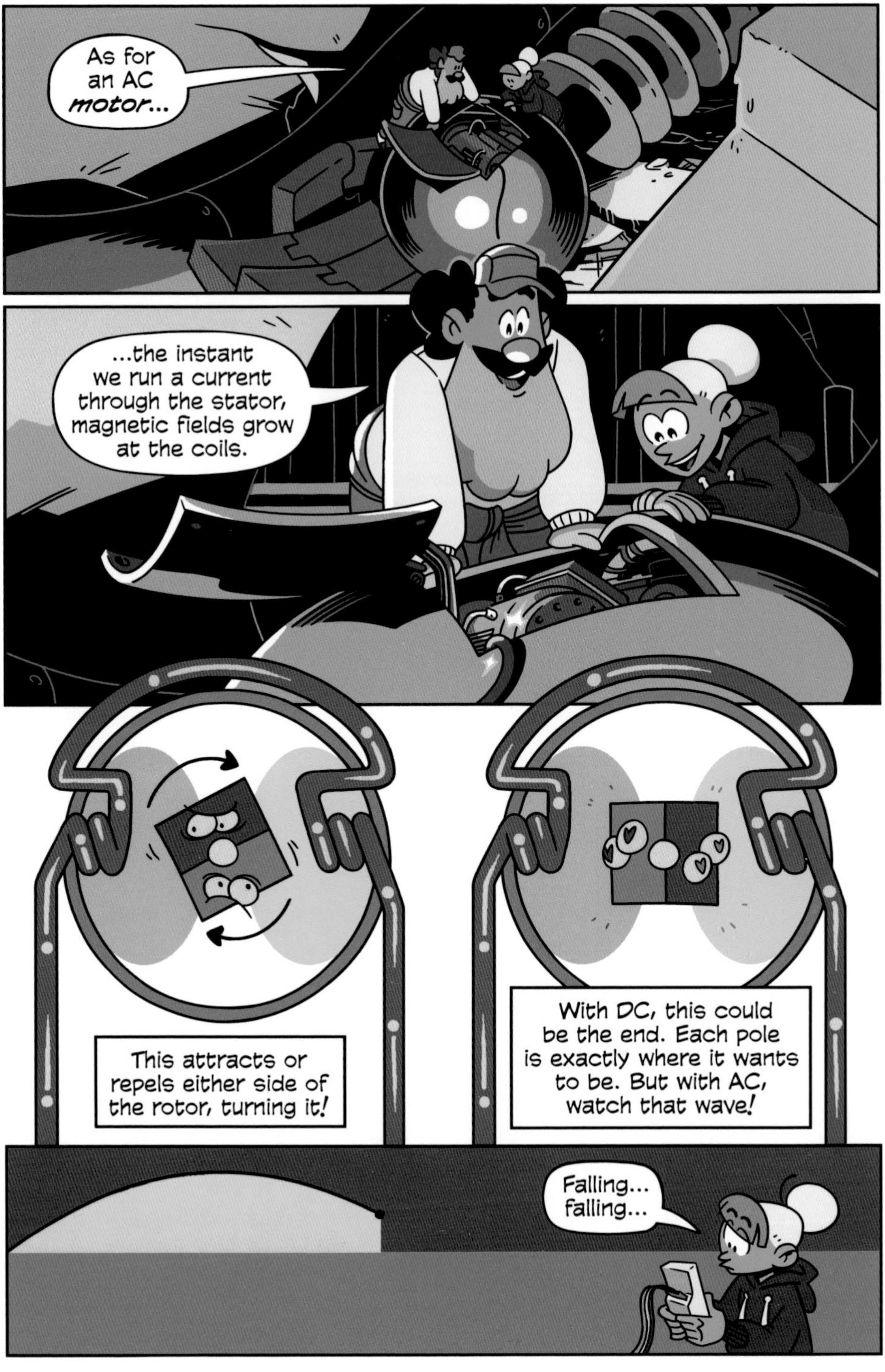
As for an AC *motor*...
...the instant we run a current through the stator, magnetic fields grow at the coils.
This attracts or repels either side of the rotor, turning it!
With DC, this could be the end. Each pole is exactly where it wants to be. But with AC, watch that wave!
– VOLTAGE +
Falling... falling...

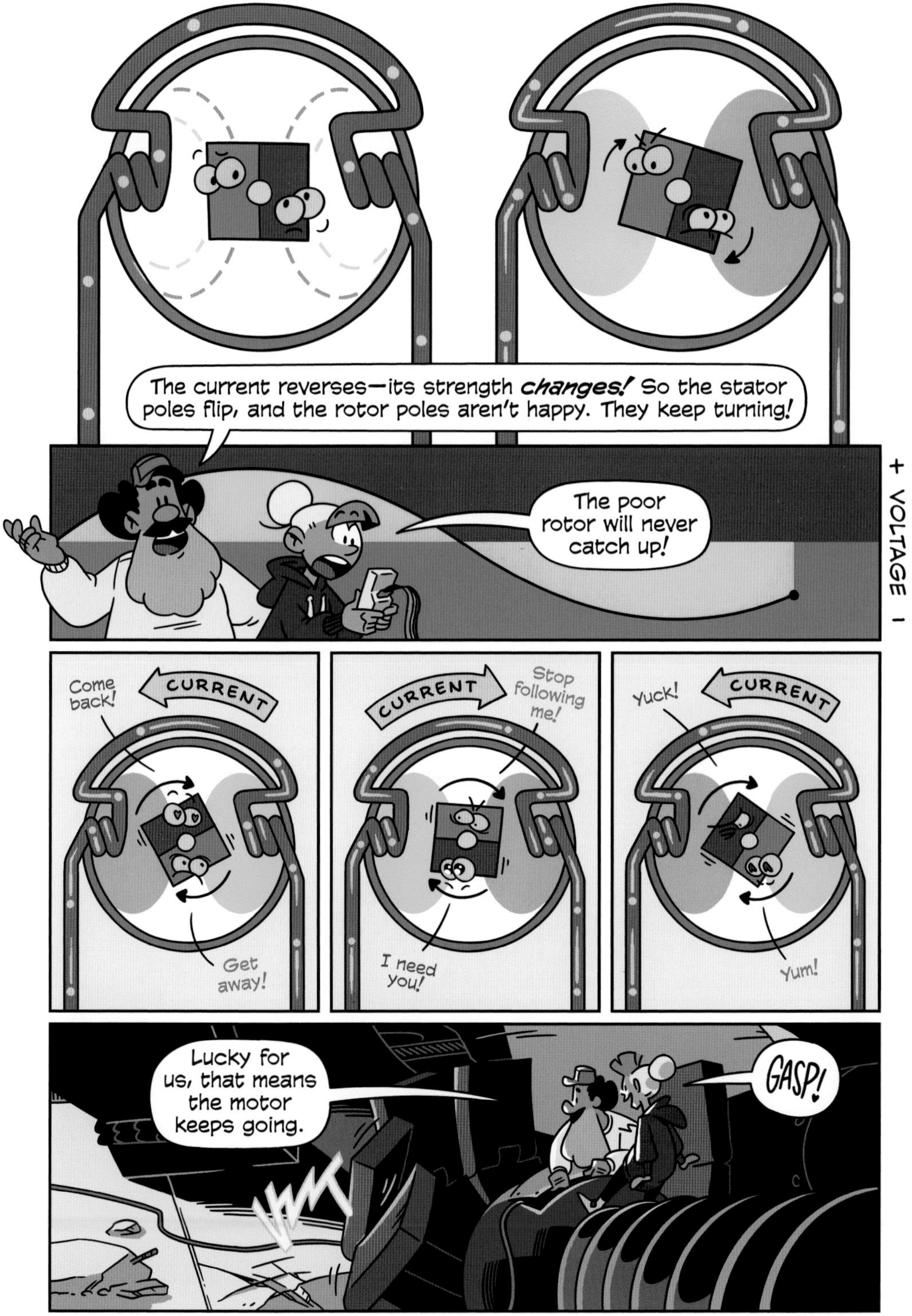
The current reverses—its strength ***changes!*** So the stator poles flip, and the rotor poles aren't happy. They keep turning!
The poor rotor will never catch up!
+ VOLTAGE -
Come back!
CURRENT
Get away!
CURRENT
Stop following me!
I need you!
Yuck!
CURRENT
Yum!
Lucky for us, that means the motor keeps going.
GASP!

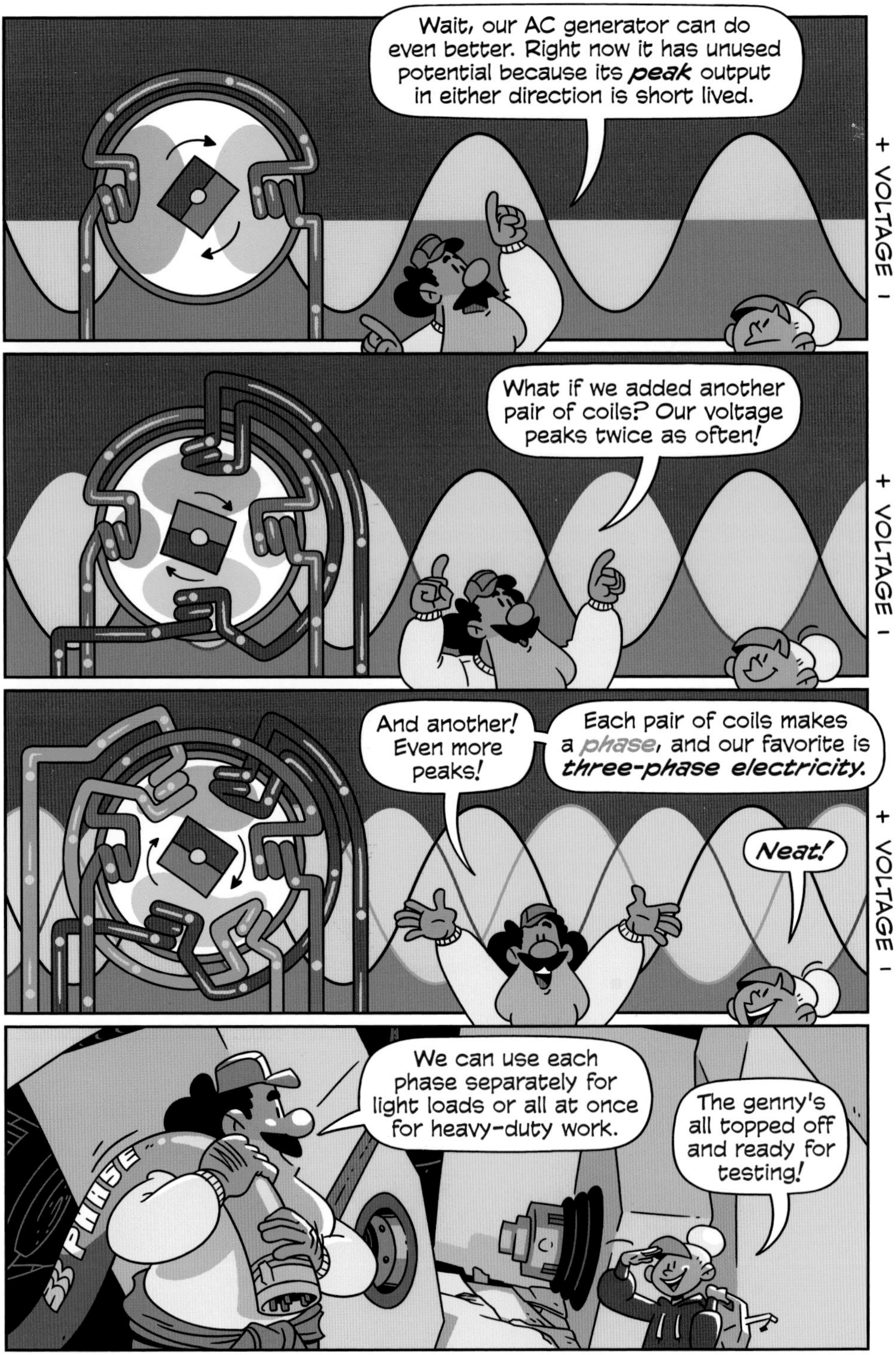
Wait, our AC generator can do even better. Right now it has unused potential because its *peak* output in either direction is short lived.
+ VOLTAGE –
What if we added another pair of coils? Our voltage peaks twice as often!
+ VOLTAGE –
And another! Even more peaks!
Each pair of coils makes a *phase*, and our favorite is ***three-phase electricity.***
Neat!
+ VOLTAGE –
We can use each phase separately for light loads or all at once for heavy-duty work.
PHASE
The genny's all topped off and ready for testing!

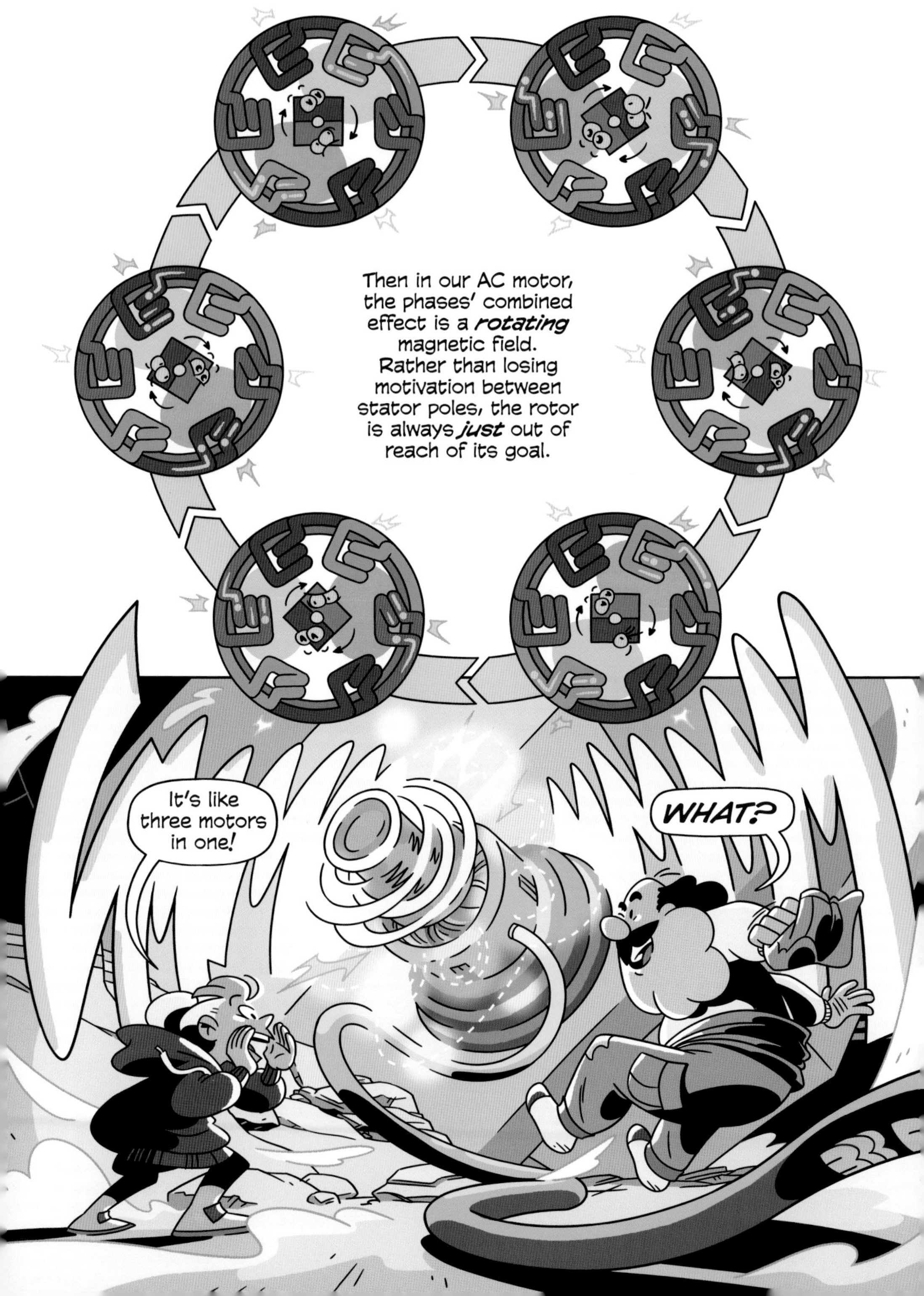
Then in our AC motor, the phases' combined effect is a *rotating* magnetic field. Rather than losing motivation between stator poles, the rotor is always *just* out of reach of its goal.
It's like three motors in one!
WHAT?

Plating secured, checkup complete!

Good! Just one more thing, then.

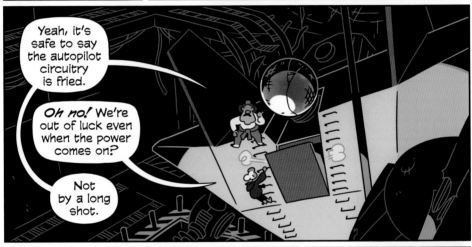

Yeah, it's safe to say the autopilot circuitry is fried.

Oh no! We're out of luck even when the power comes on?

Not by a long shot.

Looks like the city's hero is coming out of retirement.

The city's hero used to be more flexible. I hope he can build a remote control.

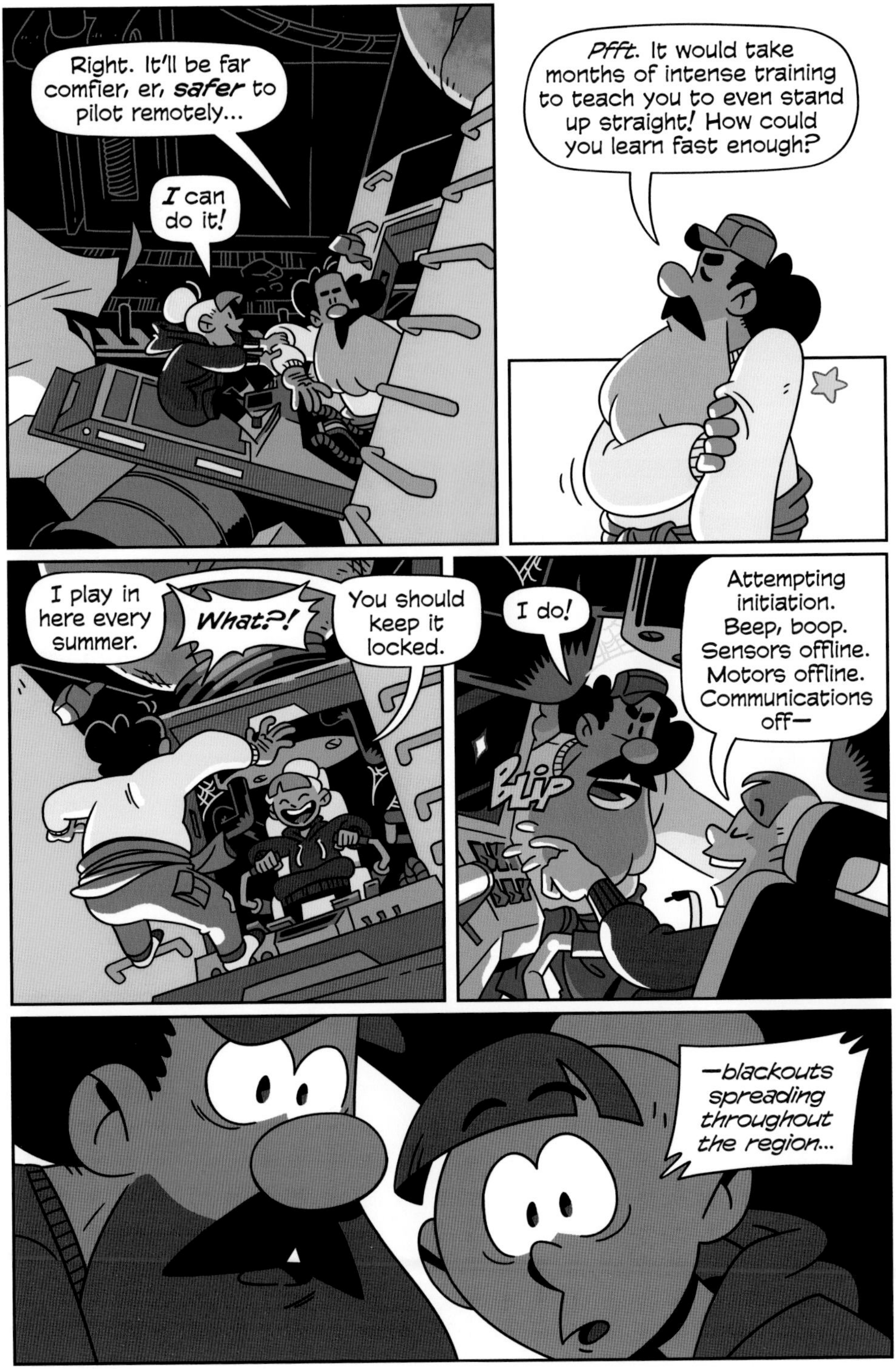

Right. It'll be far comfier, er, *safer* to pilot remotely...
I can do it!
Pfft. It would take months of intense training to teach you to even stand up straight! How could you learn fast enough?
I play in here every summer.
What?!
You should keep it locked.
I do!
Attempting initiation. Beep, boop. Sensors offline. Motors offline. Communications off—
BLIP
—blackouts spreading throughout the region...

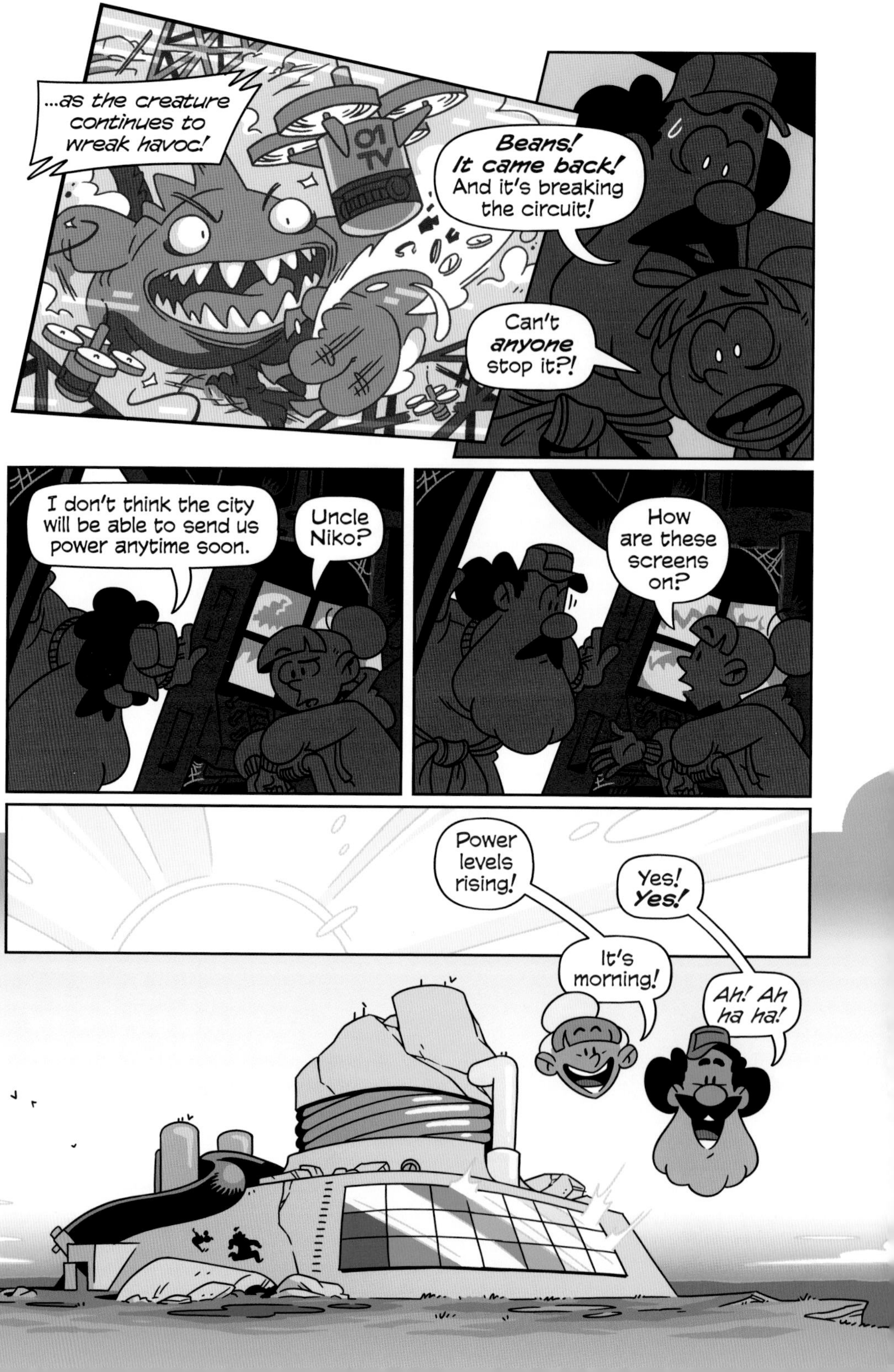

...as the creature continues to wreak havoc!
01 TV
Beans! It came back! And it's breaking the circuit!
Can't anyone stop it?!
I don't think the city will be able to send us power anytime soon.
Uncle Niko?
How are these screens on?
Power levels rising!
Yes! Yes!
It's morning!
Ah! Ah ha ha!

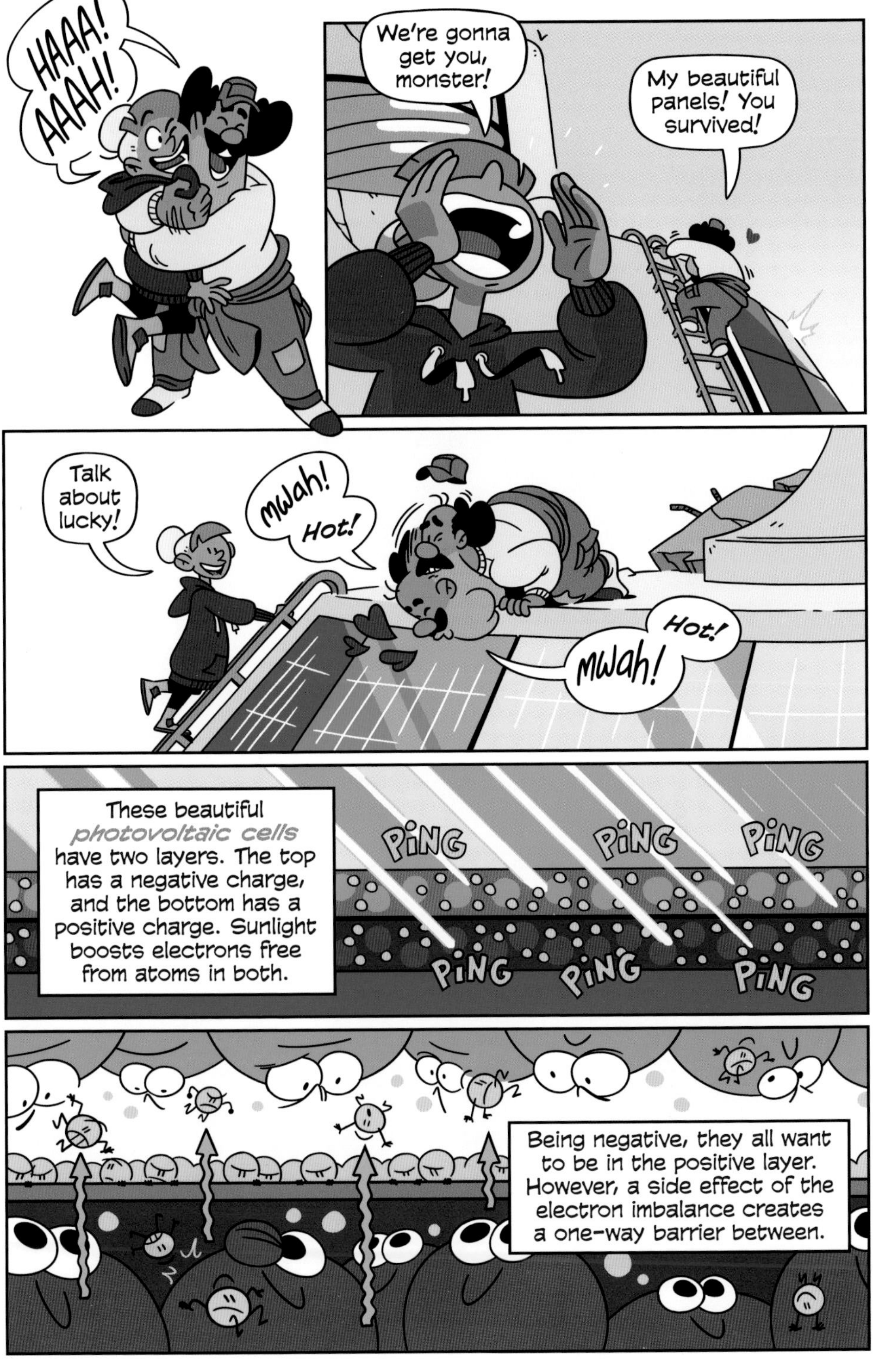
HAAA! AAAH!
We're gonna get you, monster!
My beautiful panels! You survived!
Talk about lucky!
MWAH! Hot!
Hot! MWAH!
These beautiful *photovoltaic cells* have two layers. The top has a negative charge, and the bottom has a positive charge. Sunlight boosts electrons free from atoms in both.
PING
PING
PING
PING
PING
PING
Being negative, they all want to be in the positive layer. However, a side effect of the electron imbalance creates a one-way barrier between.

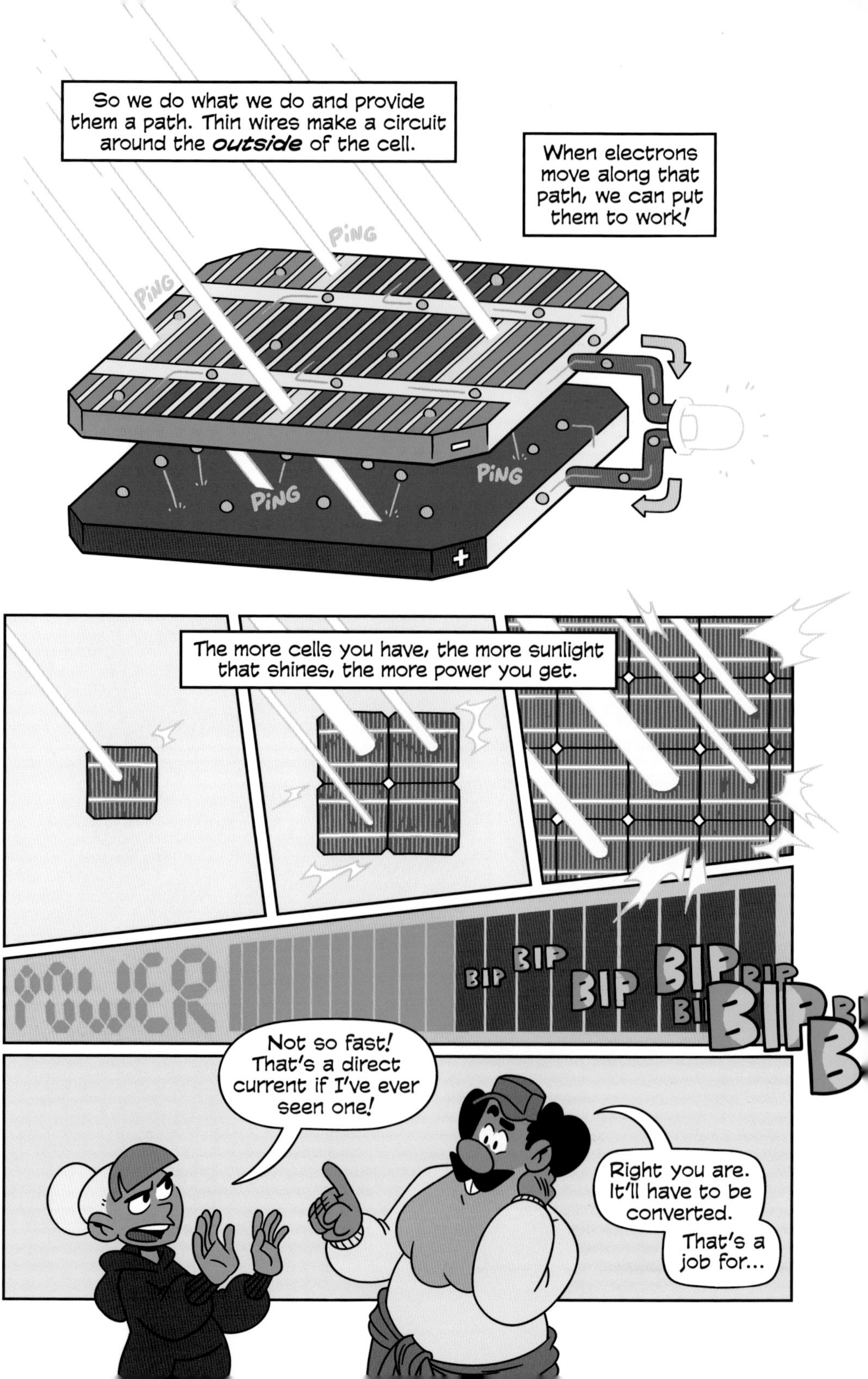

So we do what we do and provide them a path. Thin wires make a circuit around the *outside* of the cell.
When electrons move along that path, we can put them to work!
PING
PING
PING
PING
The more cells you have, the more sunlight that shines, the more power you get.
POWER
BIP BIP BIP BIP
Not so fast! That's a direct current if I've ever seen one!
Right you are. It'll have to be converted.
That's a job for...

...an *inverter!*

Make way—

OOF!

Ow.

Ooh, they're so smart!

Single-phase inverters contain two pairs of switches, mechanical or not, that offer paths in opposite directions.

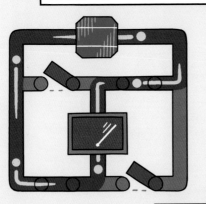

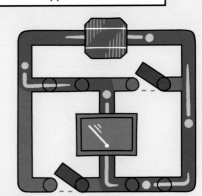

Great! Our DC is already alternating.

VOLTAGE +

This square wave isn't as pretty as our usual one.

Not at all! The voltage shifts instantly from one peak to the opposite, and electronics are sensitive to that sort of thing.

It's a good thing these switches are *ultra fast*. Our electricity's voltage usually cycles 50 or 60 times per second, but these can move more than *10,000* times per second!

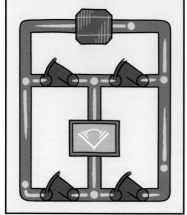

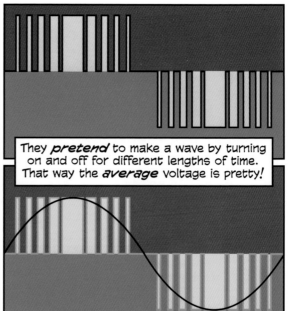

They *pretend* to make a wave by turning on and off for different lengths of time. That way the *average* voltage is pretty!

What are we waiting for? Let's move!

How?

Menlo can't *store* this energy.

They can turn on, but we can't *go* anywhere.

Unless...

Unless?

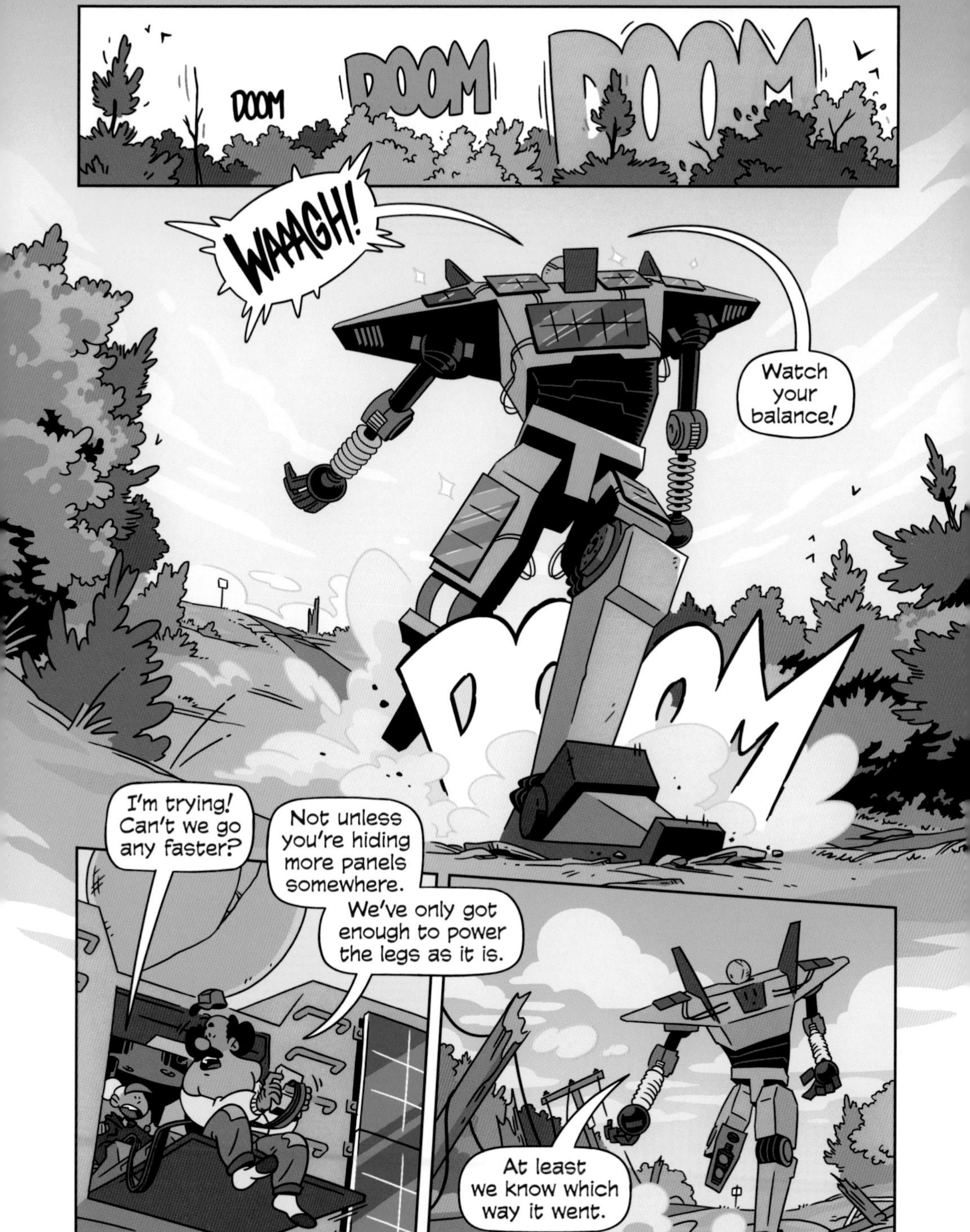

DOOM
DOOM
DOOM
WAAAGH!
Watch your balance!
BOOM
I'm trying! Can't we go any faster?
Not unless you're hiding more panels somewhere.
We've only got enough to power the legs as it is.
At least we know which way it went.

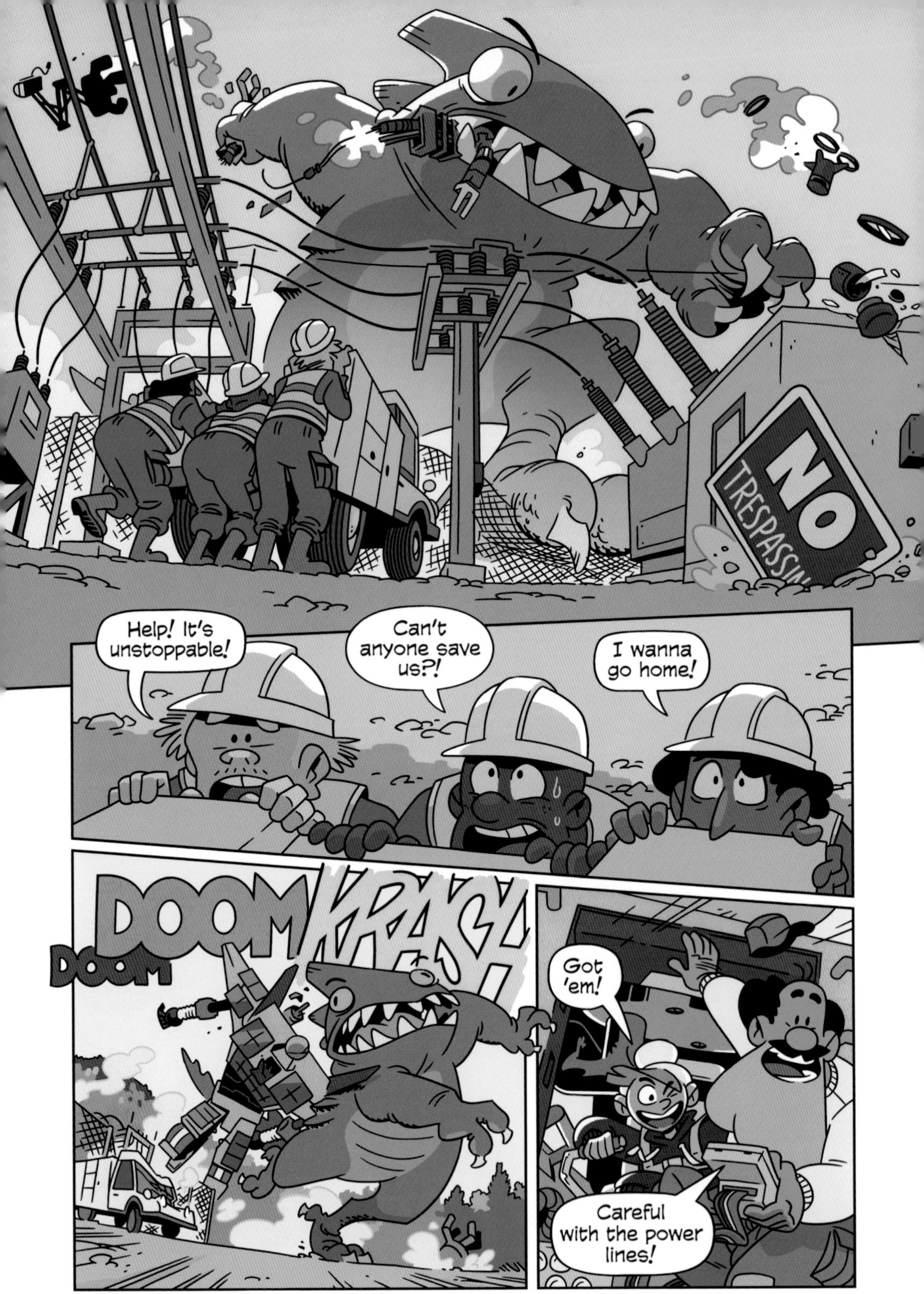
NO TRESPASSIN
Help! It's unstoppable!
Can't anyone save us?!
I wanna go home!
DOOM
DOOM
KRASH
Got 'em!
Careful with the power lines!

That electricity is *extremely* high voltage. We do *not* want it loose.

If the lines are so dangerous, they shouldn't be at face level!

It'll be safer once it runs through a *transformer*, where paired conductive coils work their magic.

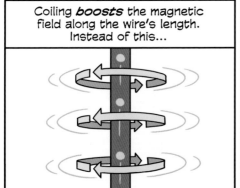

Coiling *boosts* the magnetic field along the wire's length. Instead of this...

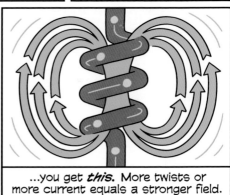

...you get *this*. More twists or more current equals a stronger field.

We can use that field to cause a current! Put one coil next to another, run AC through the first, and *induce* AC in the second! It's a magnetic circuit!

Shut your face! It's transmitting electricity *wirelessly!*

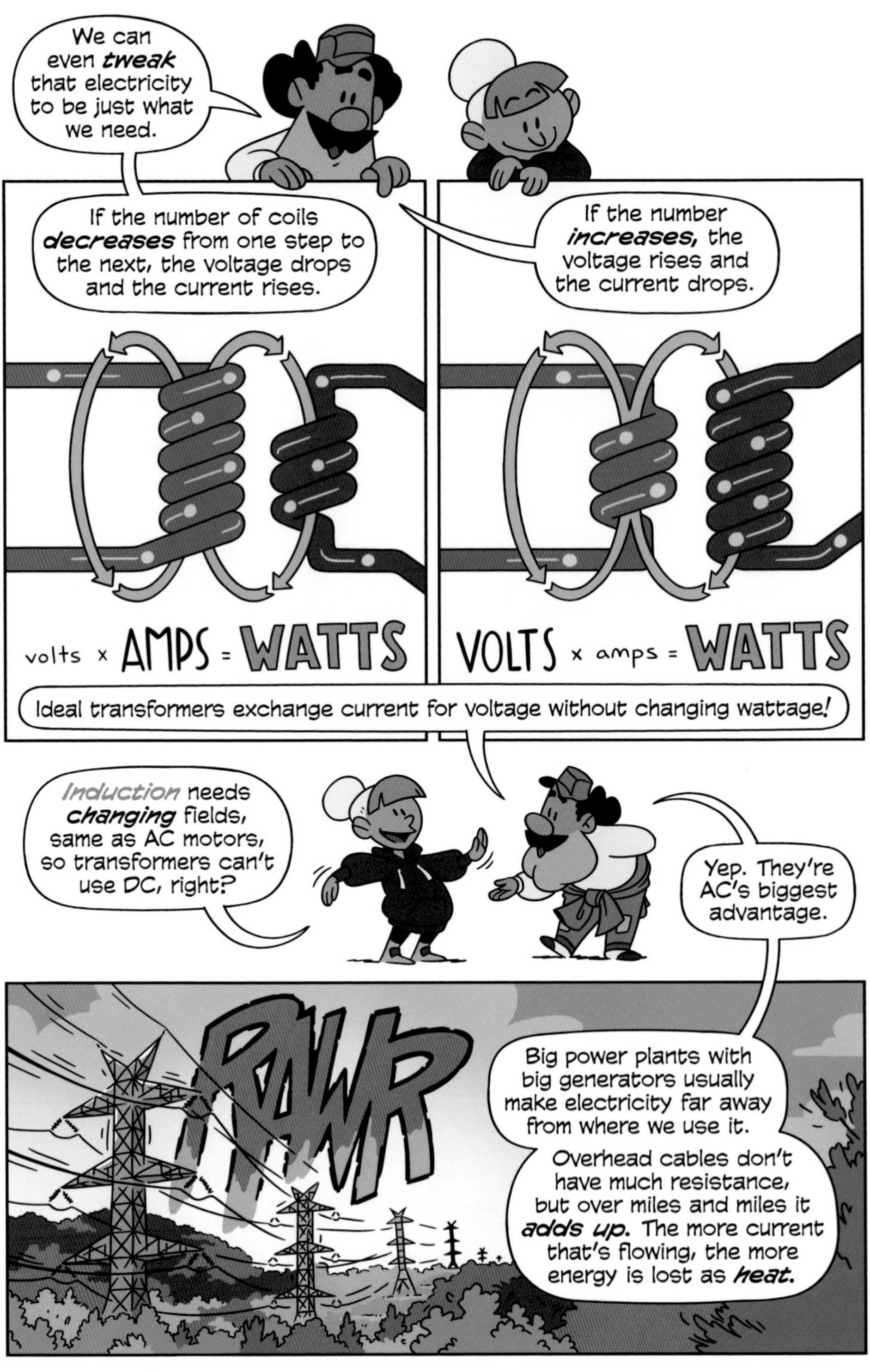
We can even *tweak* that electricity to be just what we need.
If the number of coils *decreases* from one step to the next, the voltage drops and the current rises.
If the number *increases,* the voltage rises and the current drops.
volts x AMPS = WATTS
VOLTS x amps = WATTS
Ideal transformers exchange current for voltage without changing wattage!
Induction needs *changing* fields, same as AC motors, so transformers can't use DC, right?
Yep. They're AC's biggest advantage.
RAWR
Big power plants with big generators usually make electricity far away from where we use it.
Overhead cables don't have much resistance, but over miles and miles it *adds up.* The more current that's flowing, the more energy is lost as *heat.*

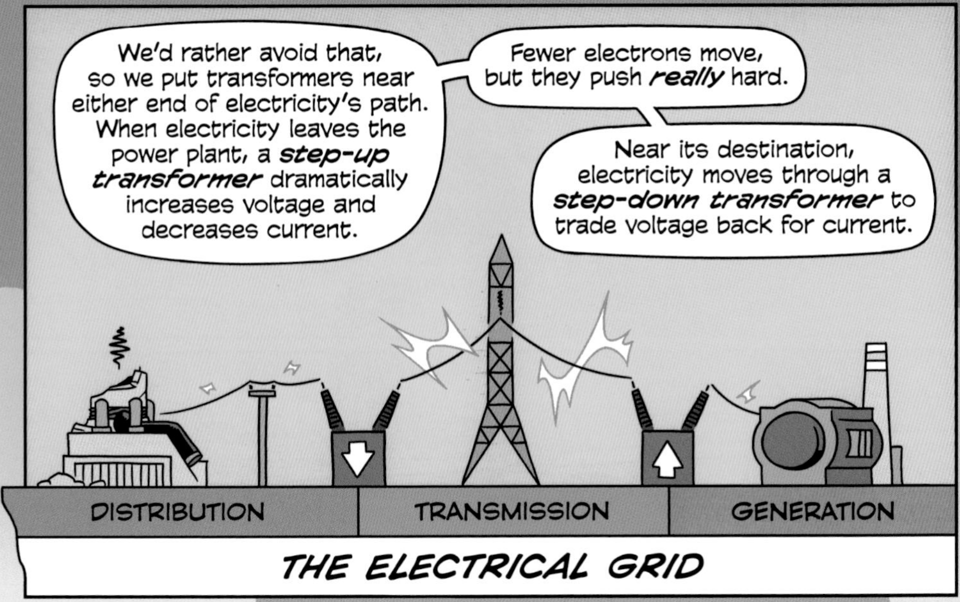
We'd rather avoid that, so we put transformers near either end of electricity's path. When electricity leaves the power plant, a ***step-up transformer*** dramatically increases voltage and decreases current.
Fewer electrons move, but they push ***really*** hard.
Near its destination, electricity moves through a ***step-down transformer*** to trade voltage back for current.
DISTRIBUTION
TRANSMISSION
GENERATION
THE ELECTRICAL GRID

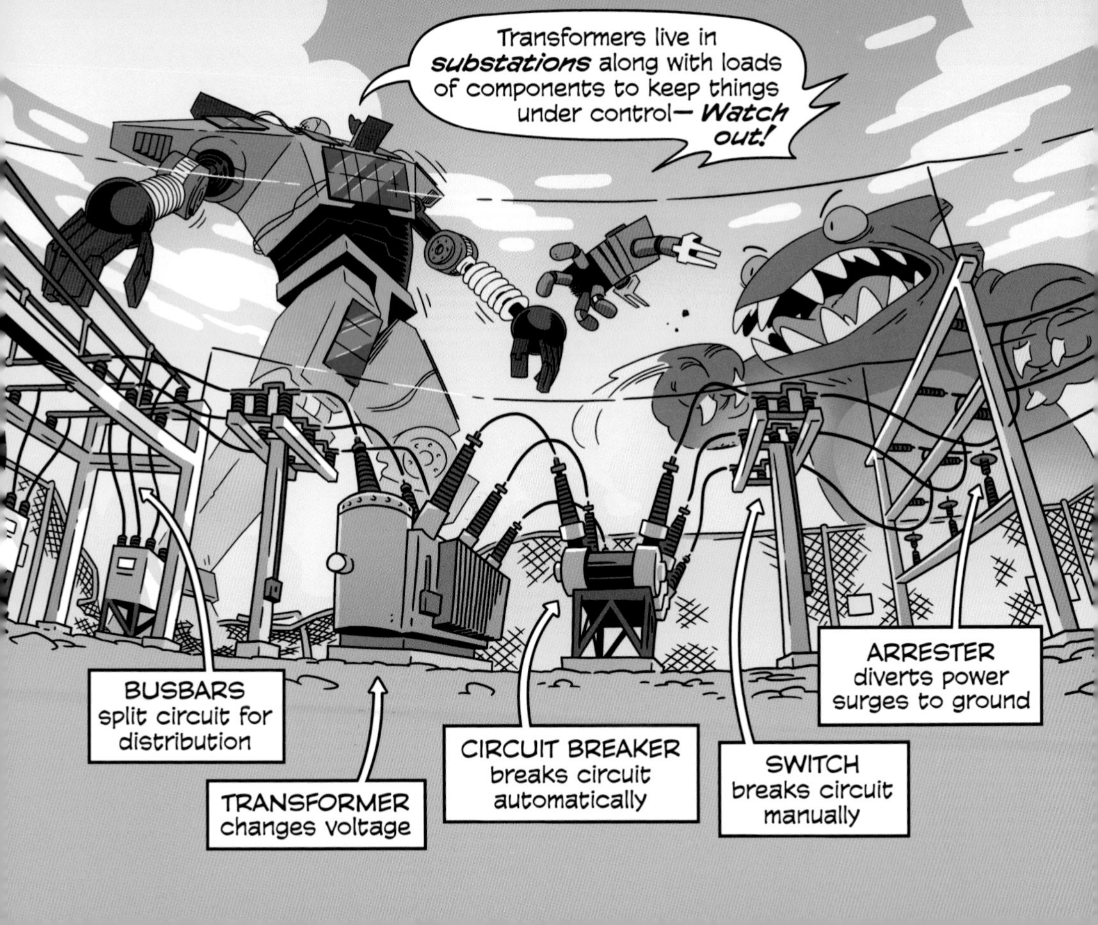
Transformers live in ***substations*** along with loads of components to keep things under control— ***Watch out!***
BUSBARS split circuit for distribution
TRANSFORMER changes voltage
CIRCUIT BREAKER breaks circuit automatically
SWITCH breaks circuit manually
ARRESTER diverts power surges to ground

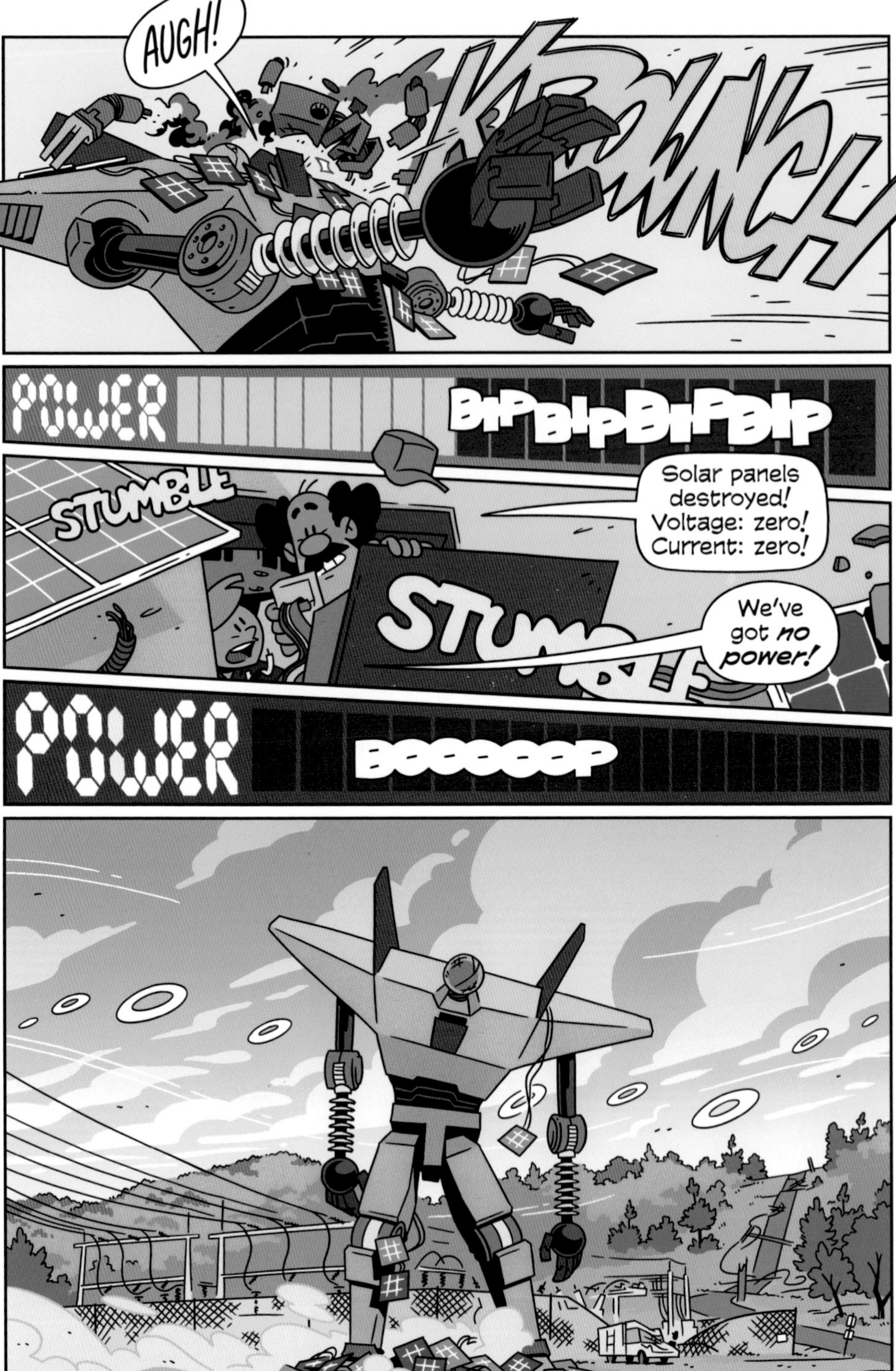
AUGH!
KRUNCH
POWER
BIPBIPBIPBIP
STUMBLE
Solar panels destroyed! Voltage: zero! Current: zero!
STUMBLE
We've got *no power!*
POWER
BOOOOOOP

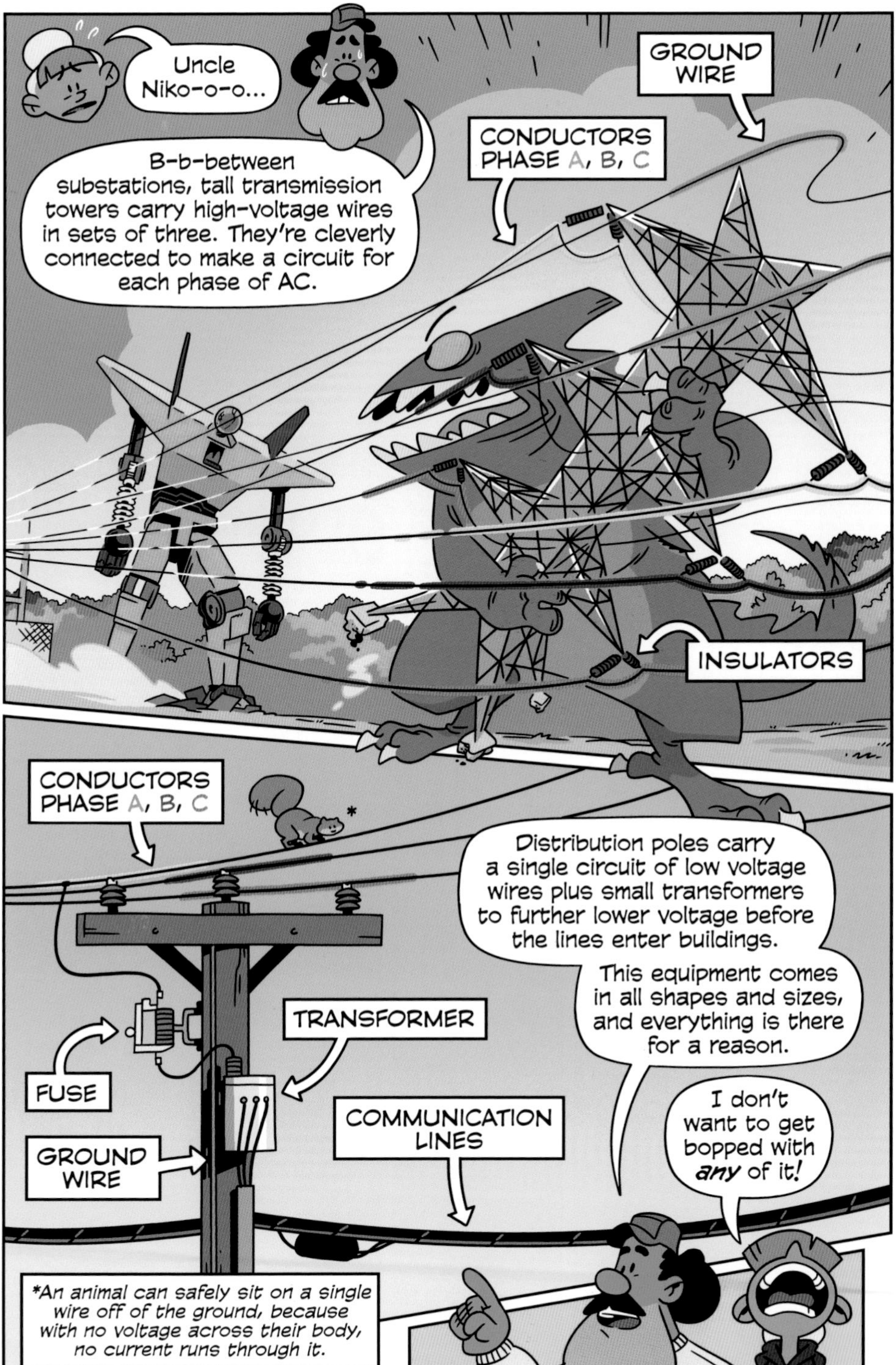
Uncle Niko-o-o...
B-b-between substations, tall transmission towers carry high-voltage wires in sets of three. They're cleverly connected to make a circuit for each phase of AC.
GROUND WIRE
CONDUCTORS PHASE A, B, C
INSULATORS
CONDUCTORS PHASE A, B, C
*
Distribution poles carry a single circuit of low voltage wires plus small transformers to further lower voltage before the lines enter buildings.
This equipment comes in all shapes and sizes, and everything is there for a reason.
TRANSFORMER
FUSE
GROUND WIRE
COMMUNICATION LINES
I don't want to get bopped with *any* of it!
*An animal can safely sit on a single wire off of the ground, because with no voltage across their body, no current runs through it.

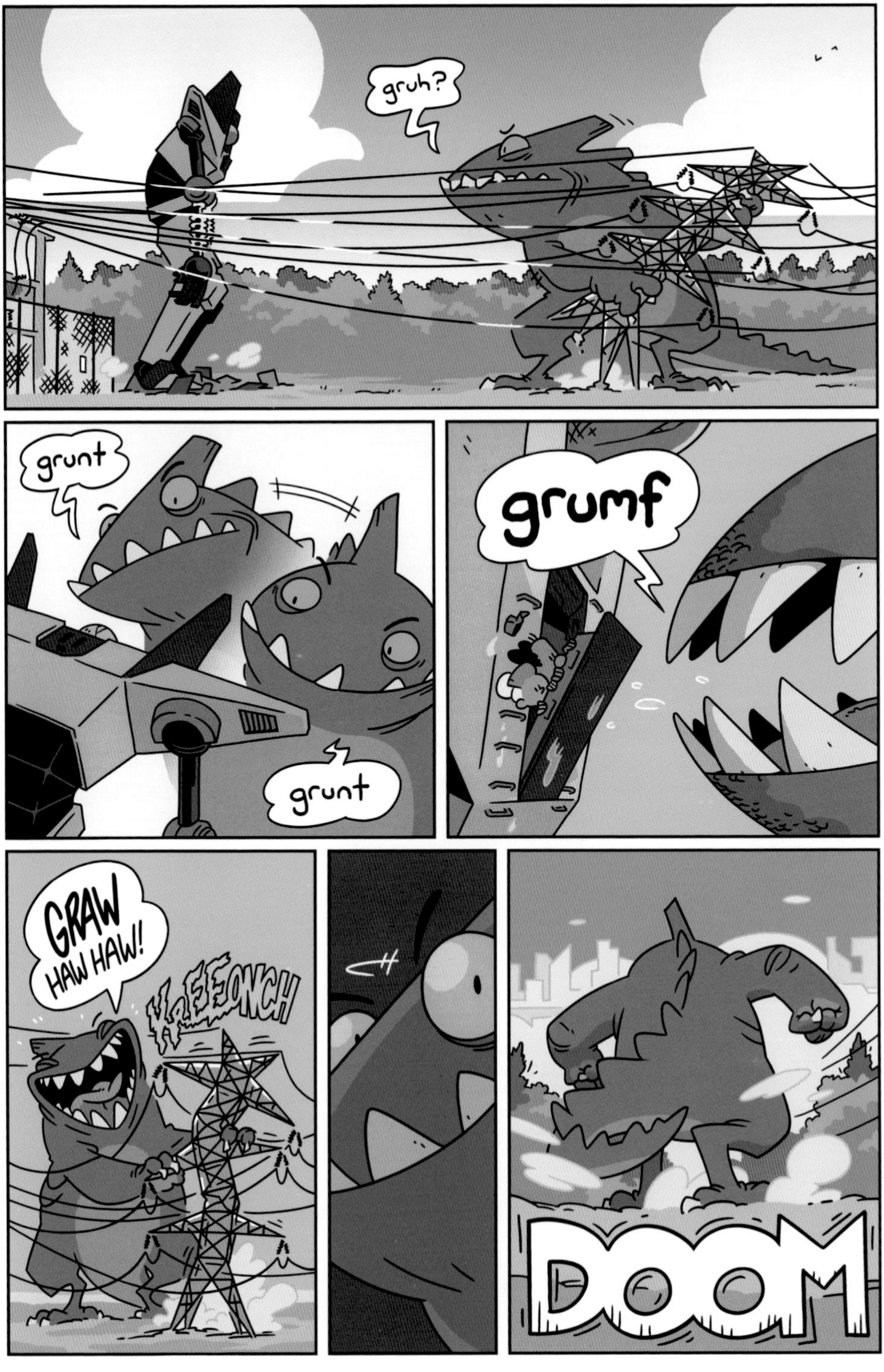
gruh?
grunt
grunt
grumf
GRAW HAW HAW!
KREEONCH
DOOM

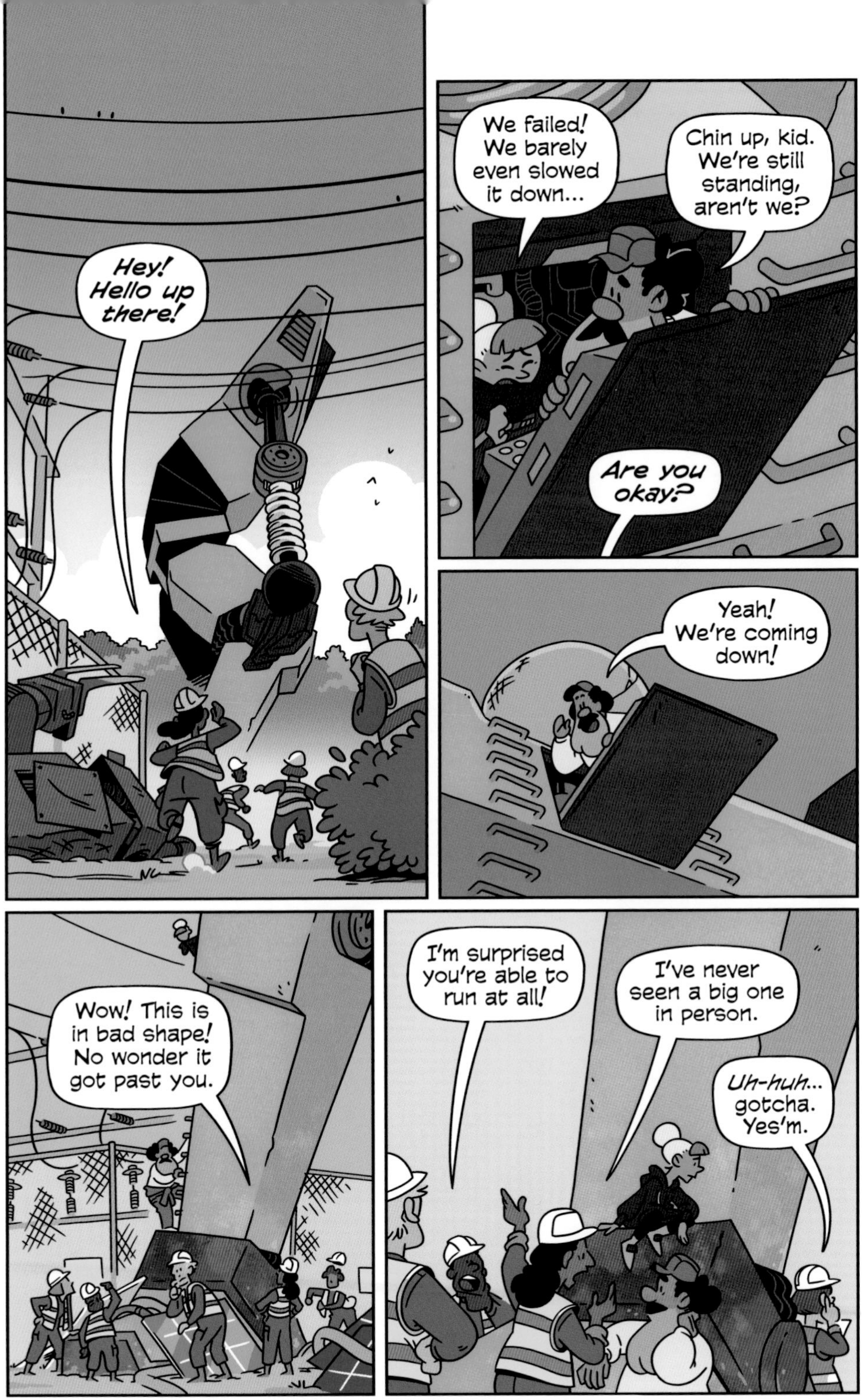
Hey! Hello up there!
We failed! We barely even slowed it down...
Chin up, kid. We're still standing, aren't we?
Are you okay?
Yeah! We're coming down!
Wow! This is in bad shape! No wonder it got past you.
I'm surprised you're able to run at all!
I've never seen a big one in person.
Uh-huh... gotcha. Yes'm.

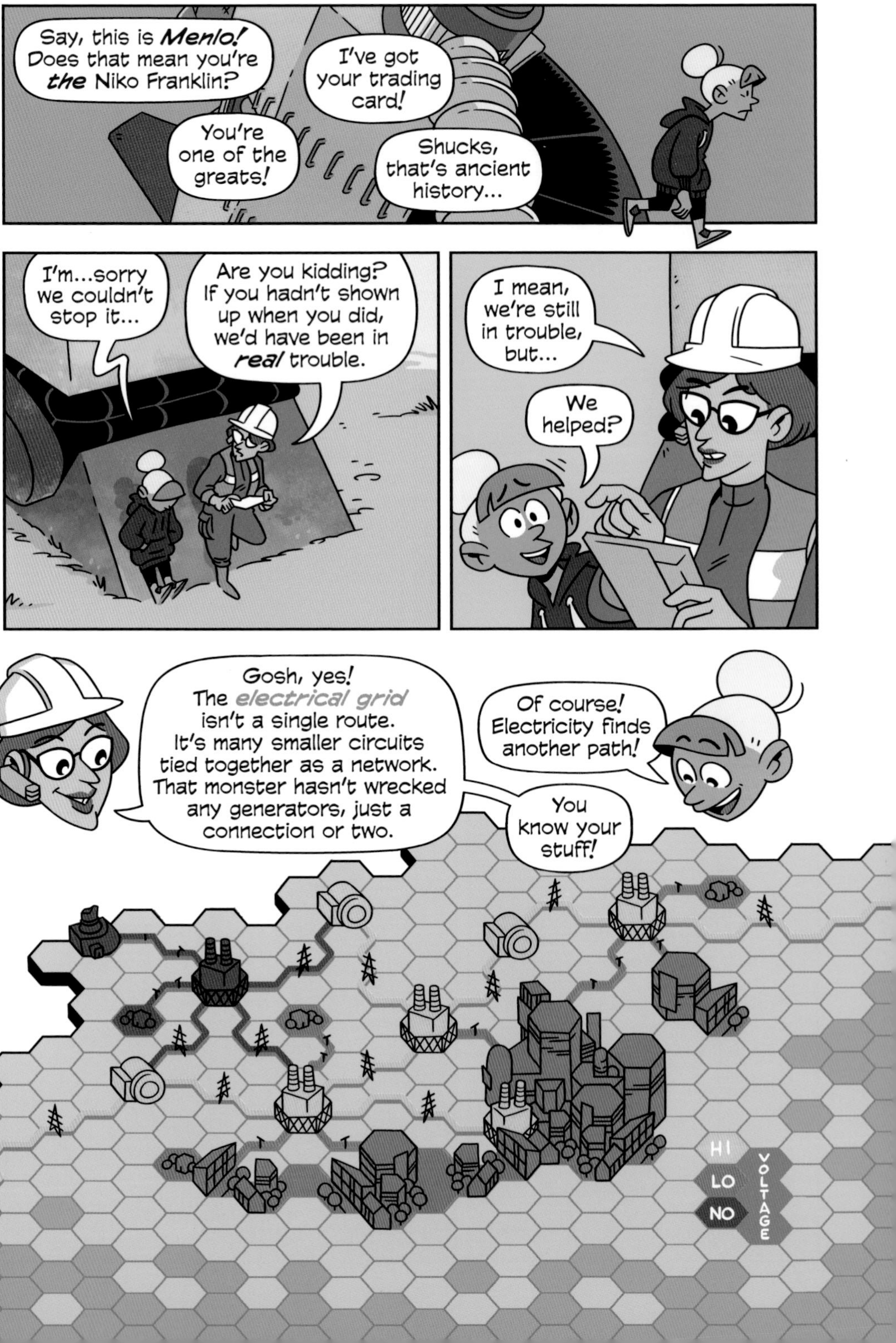
Say, this is *Menlo!* Does that mean you're *the* Niko Franklin?
I've got your trading card!
You're one of the greats!
Shucks, that's ancient history...
I'm...sorry we couldn't stop it...
Are you kidding? If you hadn't shown up when you did, we'd have been in *real* trouble.
I mean, we're still in trouble, but...
We helped?
Gosh, yes! The *electrical grid* isn't a single route. It's many smaller circuits tied together as a network. That monster hasn't wrecked any generators, just a connection or two.
Of course! Electricity finds another path!
You know your stuff!
HI
LO
NO
VOLTAGE

You see, the grid needs to be *balanced*. Generators provide *exactly* as much electricity as is being used at that moment.

Imagine generation and usage, supply and demand, playing *tug-of-war*. The game keeps going as long as each pulls *just as hard* as the other.

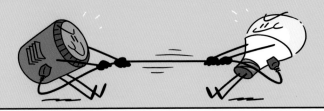

If the *generator* supplies more energy and pulls too hard, the user can't handle it.

And if the *user* demands more energy and pulls harder, it's game over for generation.

Now, excess supply is one thing. It's not hard to slow or shut down generators. Excess demand, though, that's tougher.

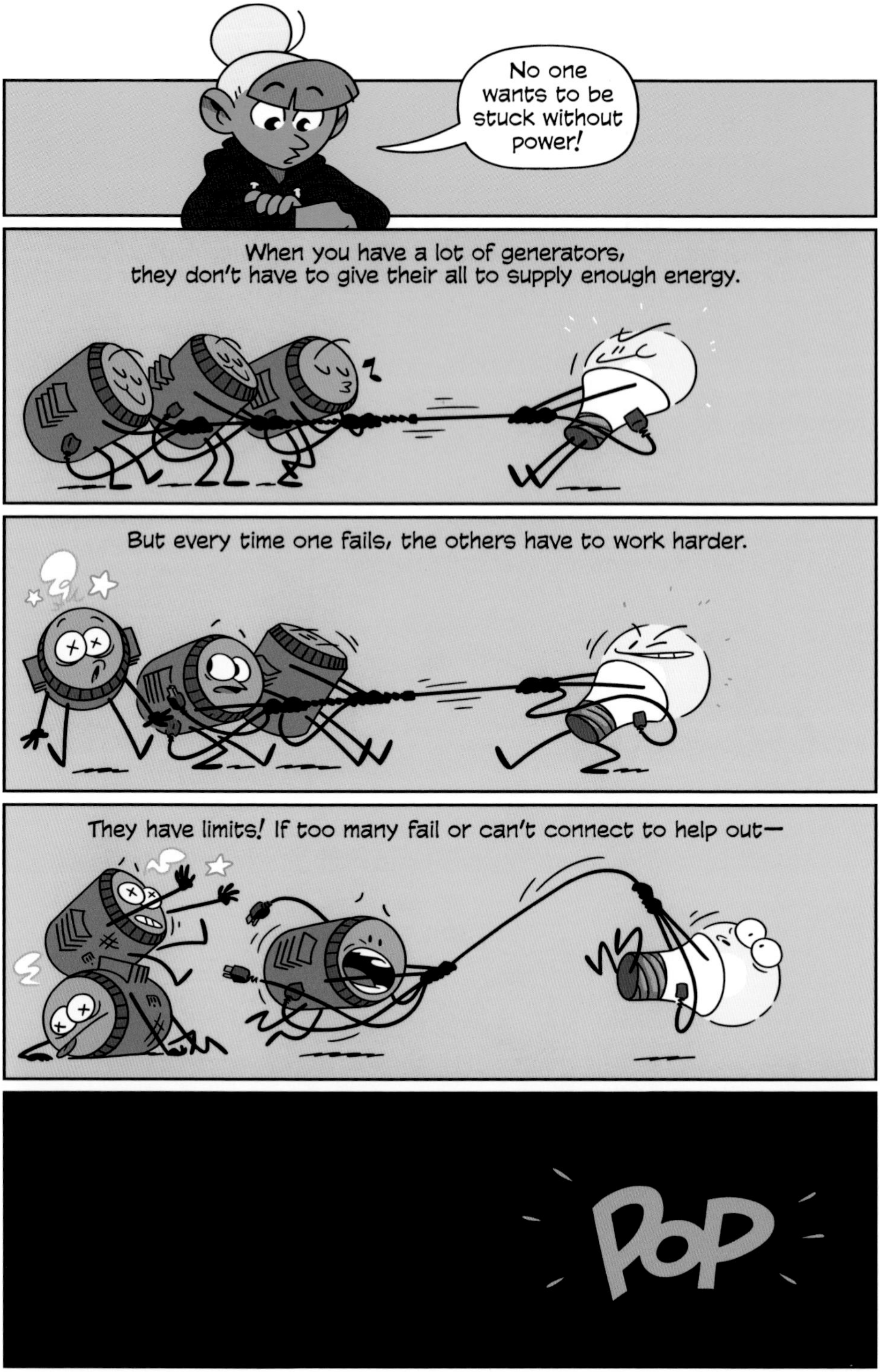
No one wants to be stuck without power!
When you have a lot of generators, they don't have to give their all to supply enough energy.
But every time one fails, the others have to work harder.
They have limits! If too many fail or can't connect to help out—
POP

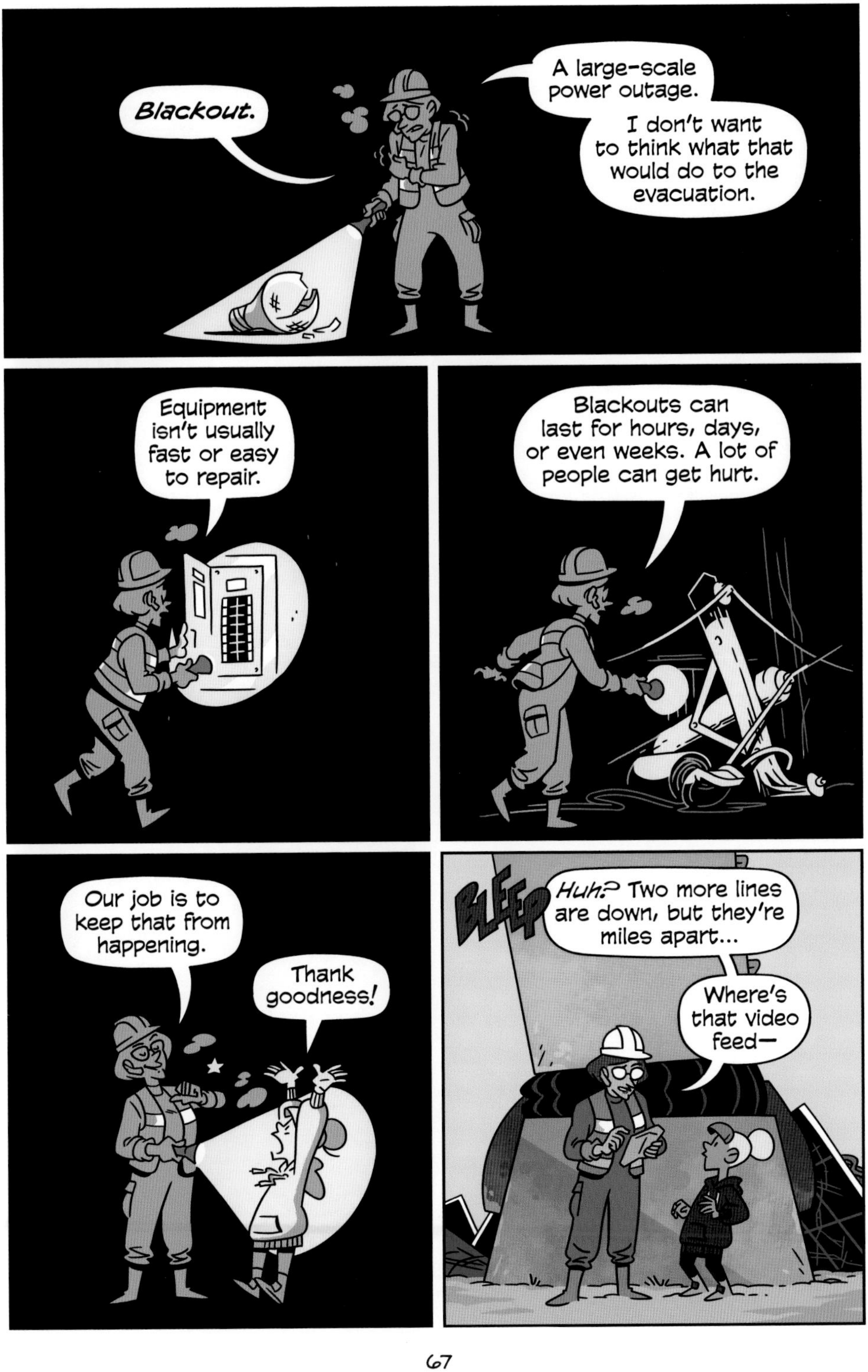
Blackout.
A large-scale power outage.
I don't want to think what that would do to the evacuation.
Equipment isn't usually fast or easy to repair.
Blackouts can last for hours, days, or even weeks. A lot of people can get hurt.
Our job is to keep that from happening.
Thank goodness!
BLEEP
Huh? Two more lines are down, but they're miles apart...
Where's that video feed—

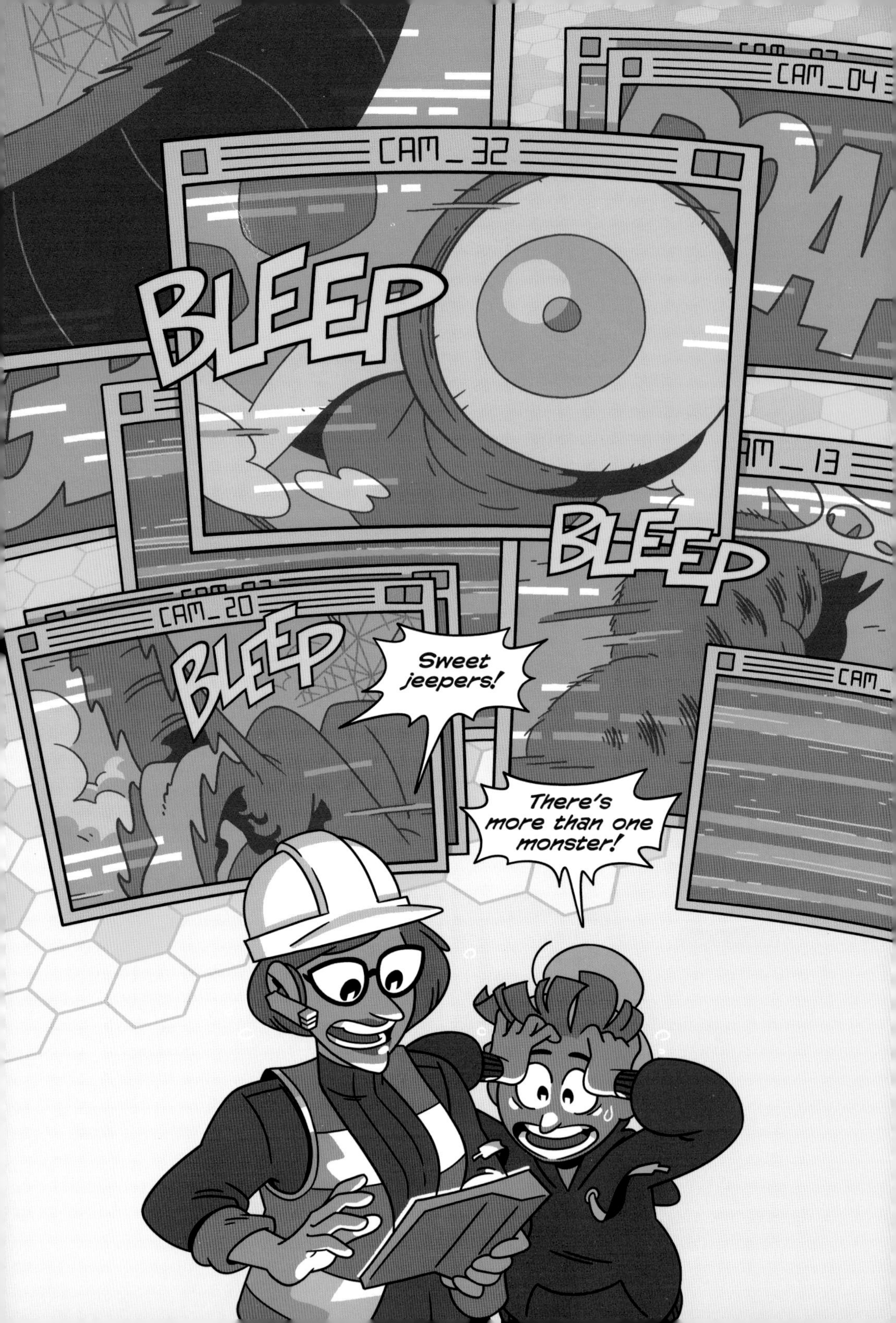
CAM_04
CAM_32
BLEEP
CAM_13
BLEEP
CAM_20
BLEEP
Sweet jeepers!
There's more than one monster!

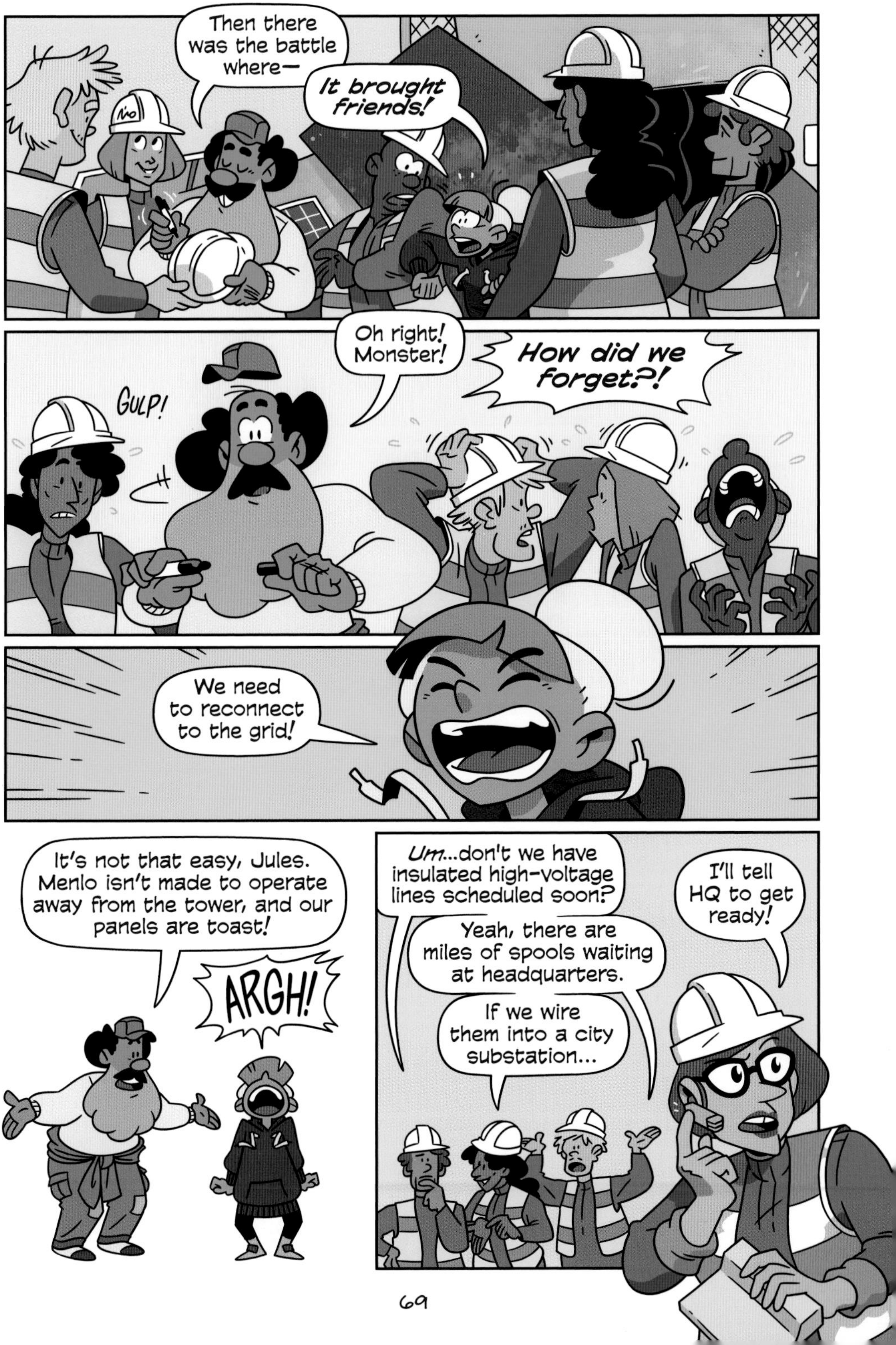
Then there was the battle where—
It brought friends!
Oh right! Monster!
How did we forget?!
GULP!
We need to reconnect to the grid!
It's not that easy, Jules. Menlo isn't made to operate away from the tower, and our panels are toast!
ARGH!
Um...don't we have insulated high-voltage lines scheduled soon?
Yeah, there are miles of spools waiting at headquarters.
If we wire them into a city substation...
I'll tell HQ to get ready!

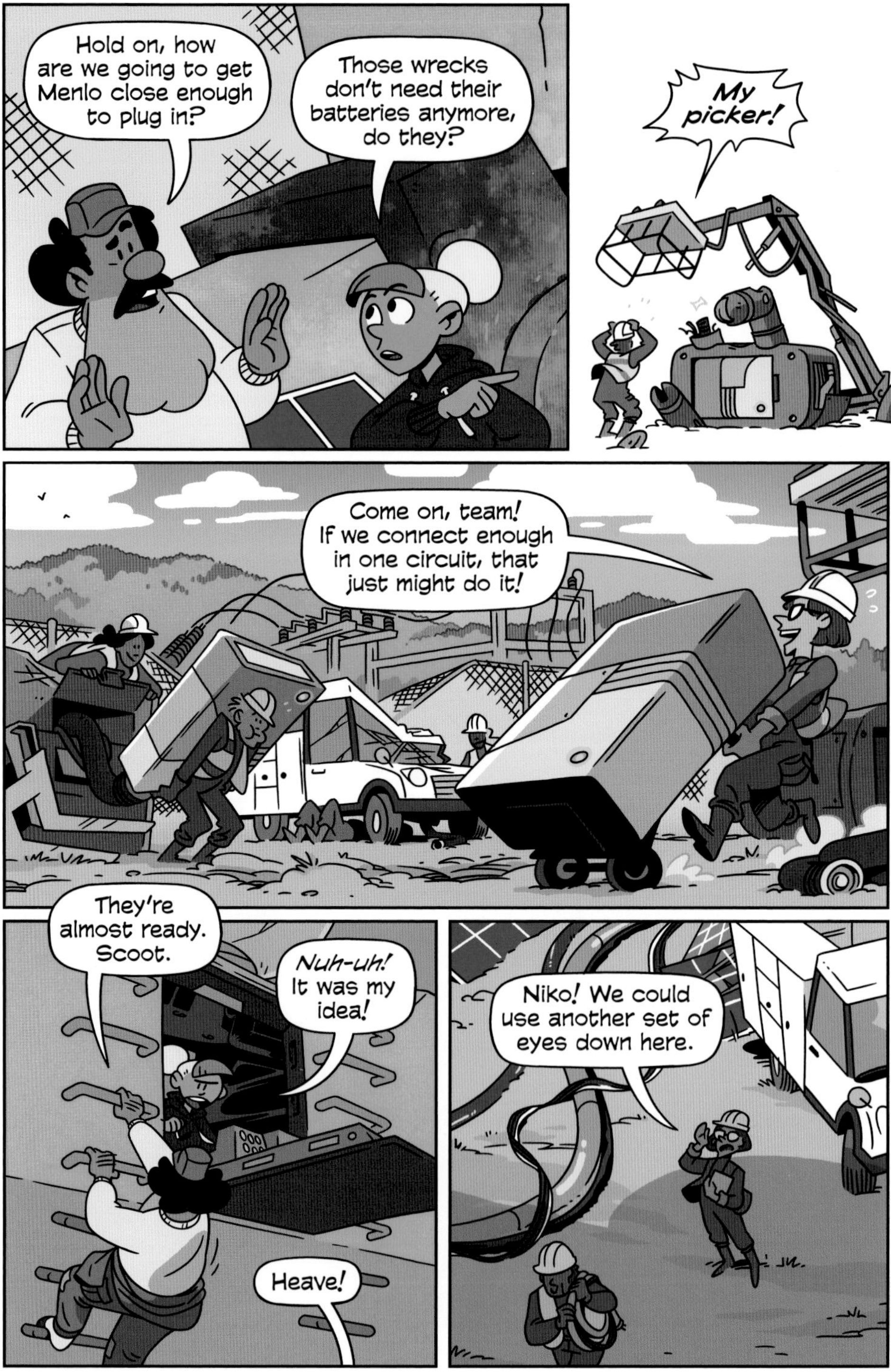
Hold on, how are we going to get Menlo close enough to plug in?
Those wrecks don't need their batteries anymore, do they?
My picker!
Come on, team! If we connect enough in one circuit, that just might do it!
They're almost ready. Scoot.
Nuh-uh! It was my idea!
Heave!
Niko! We could use another set of eyes down here.

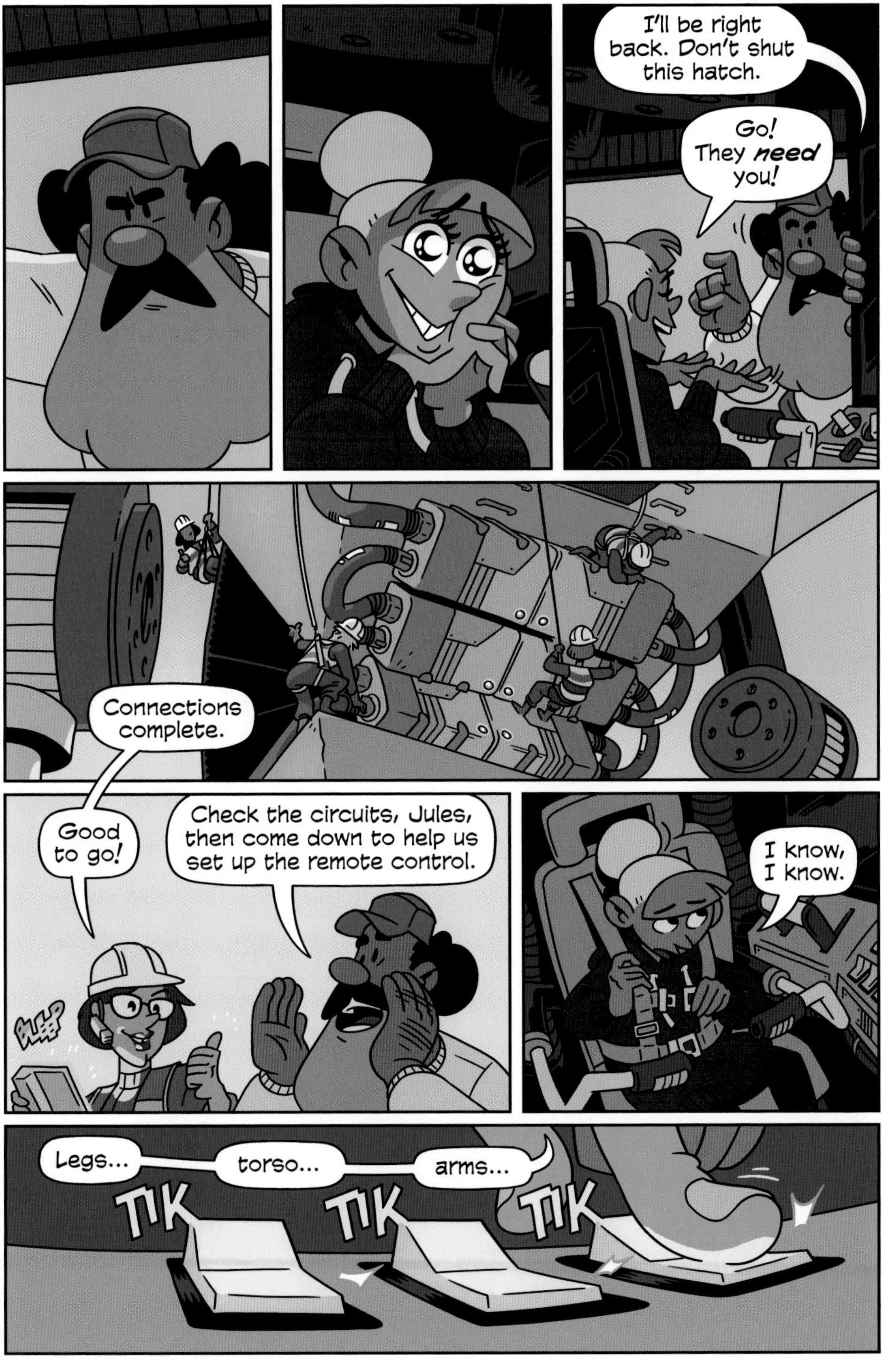
I'll be right back. Don't shut this hatch.
Go! They *need* you!
Connections complete.
Good to go!
Check the circuits, Jules, then come down to help us set up the remote control.
BLEEP
I know, I know.
Legs...
torso...
arms...
TIK
TIK
TIK

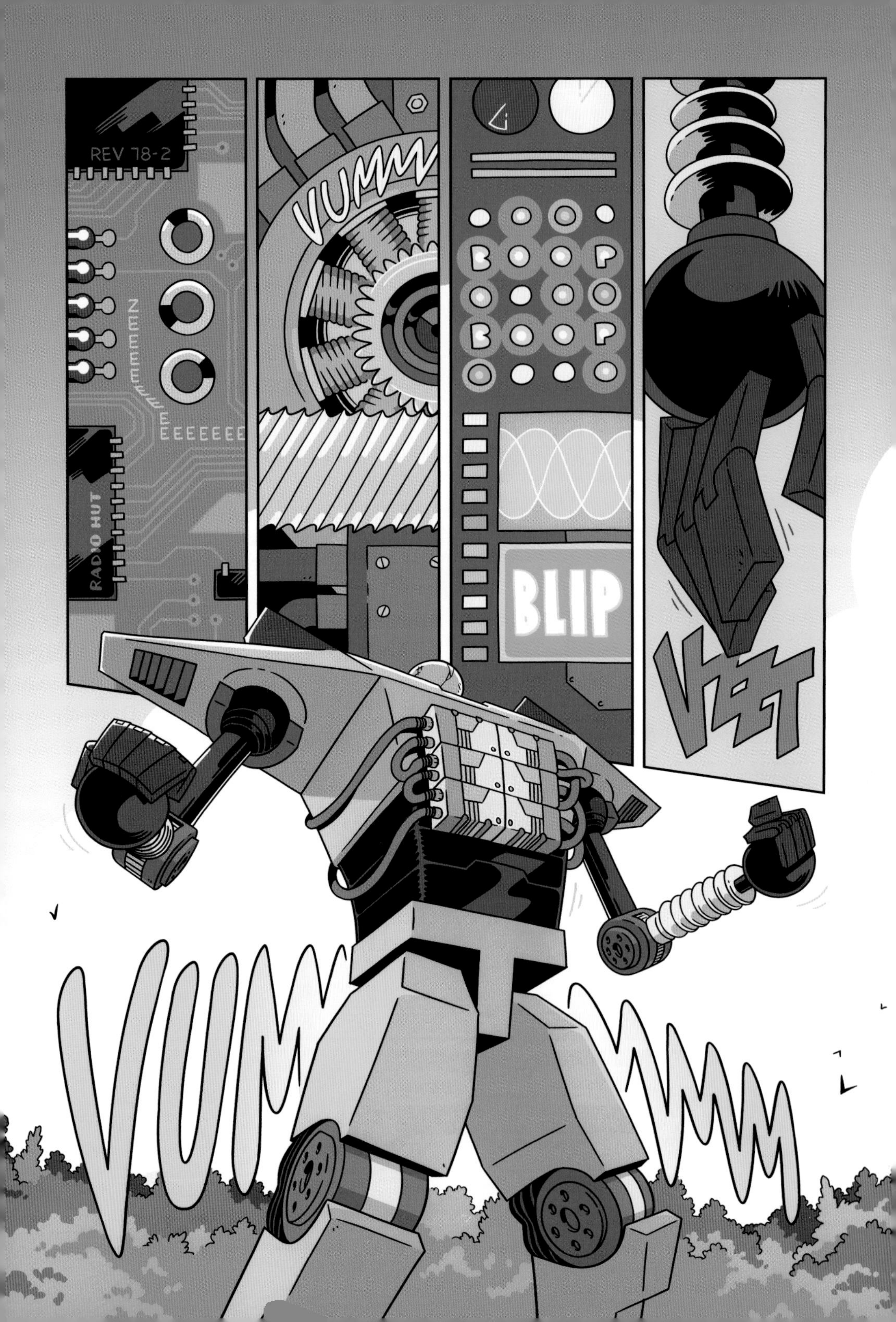
REV 78-2
RADIO HUT
VUMM
BLIP

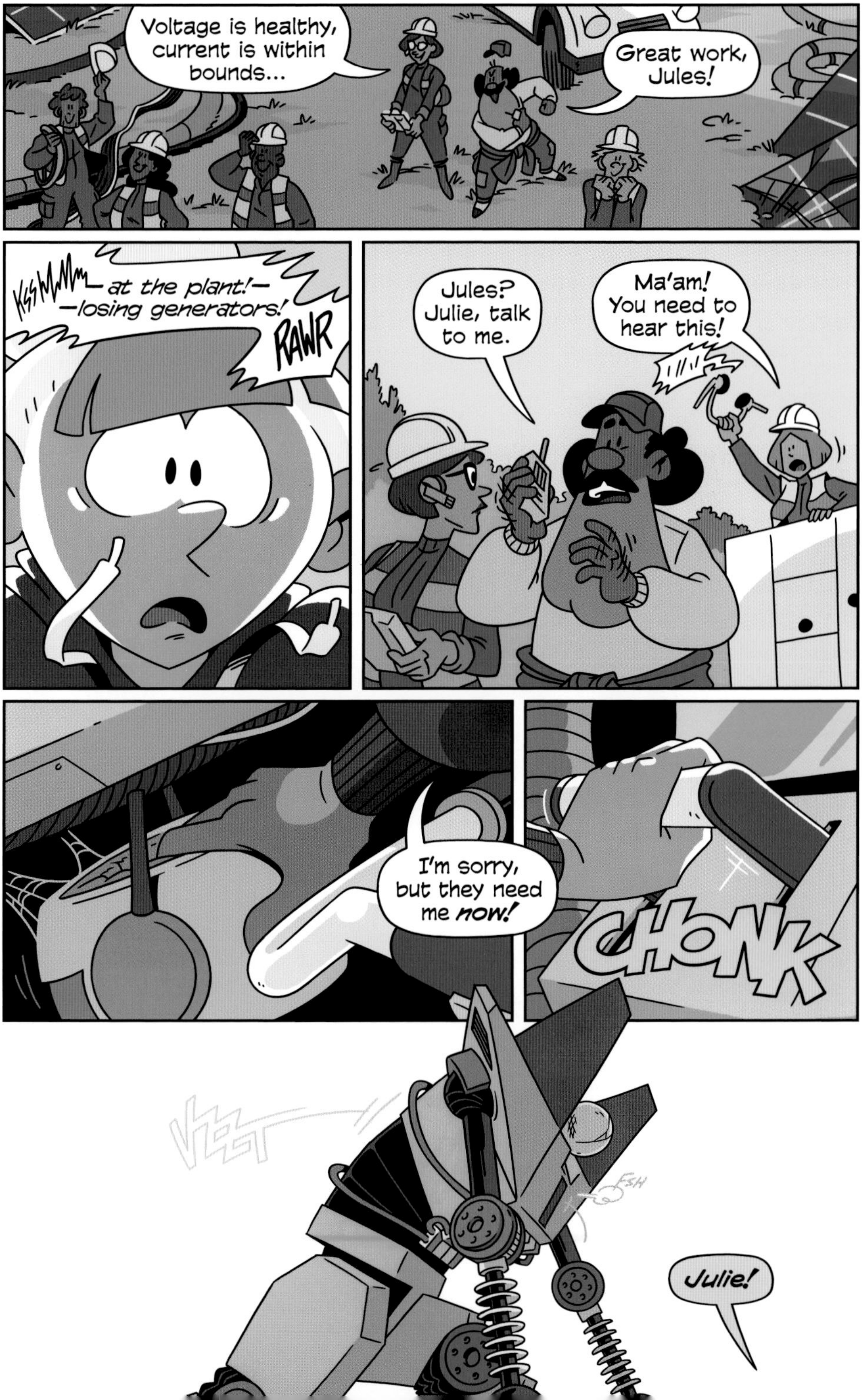
Voltage is healthy, current is within bounds...
Great work, Jules!
KSSHWMM —at the plant!—
—losing generators!
RAWR
Jules? Julie, talk to me.
Ma'am! You need to hear this!
I'm sorry, but they need me *NOW!*
CHONK
VZZT
FSH
Julie!

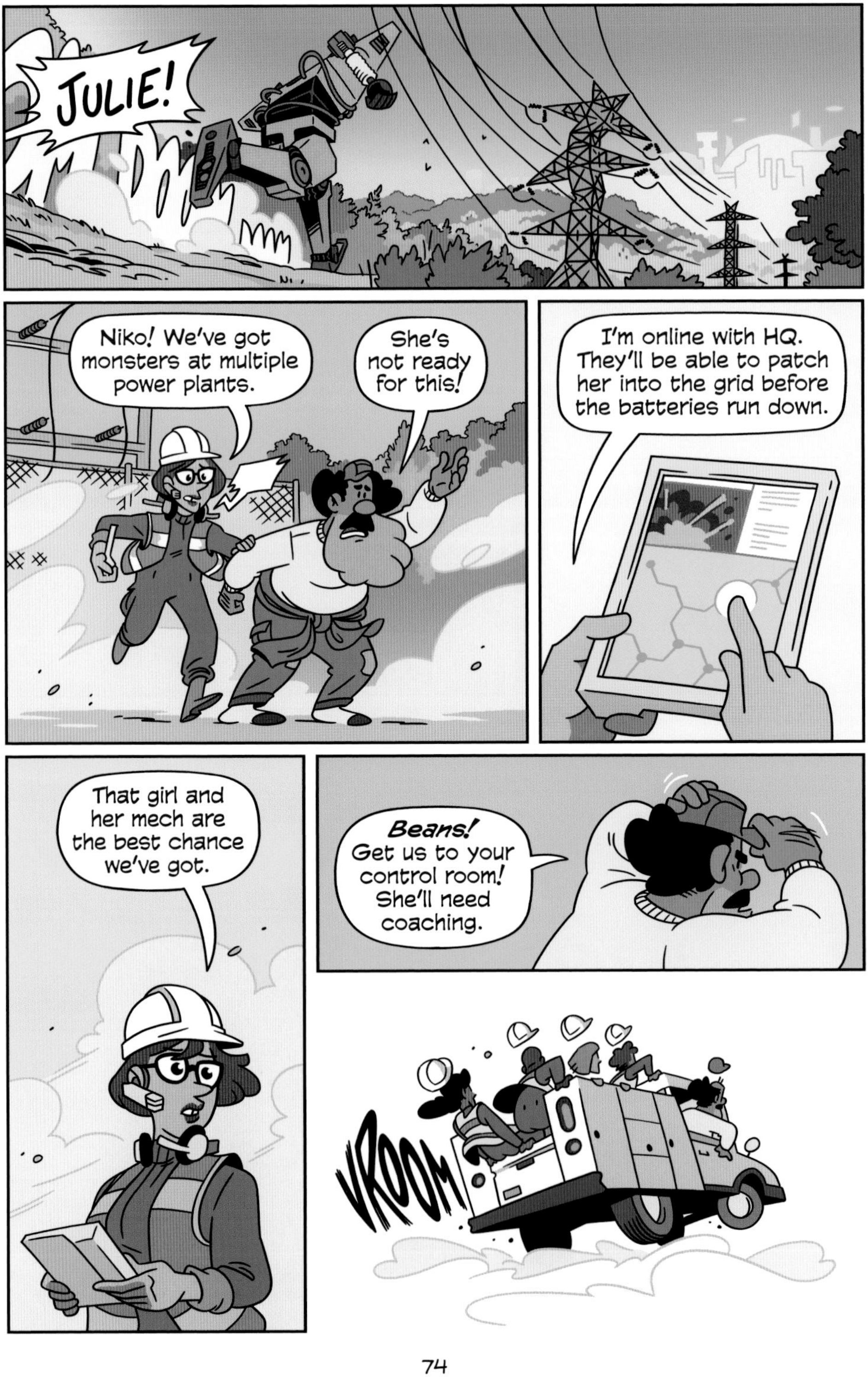
JULIE!
Niko! We've got monsters at multiple power plants.
She's not ready for this!
I'm online with HQ. They'll be able to patch her into the grid before the batteries run down.
That girl and her mech are the best chance we've got.
Beans! Get us to your control room! She'll need coaching.
VROOM

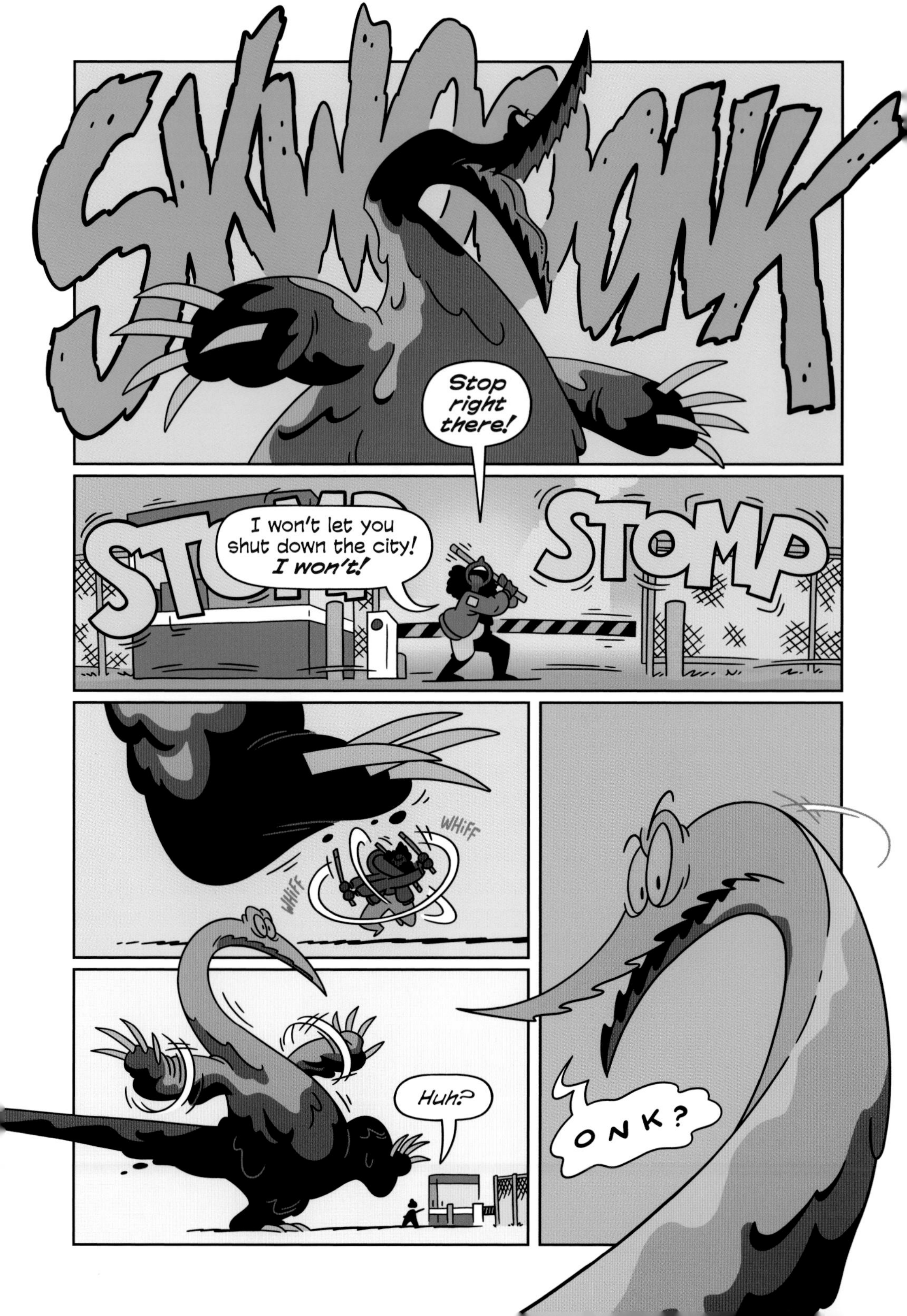
SKWOOONK
Stop right there!
STOMP
I won't let you shut down the city! *I won't!*
STOMP
WHiFF
WHiFF
Huh?
ONK?

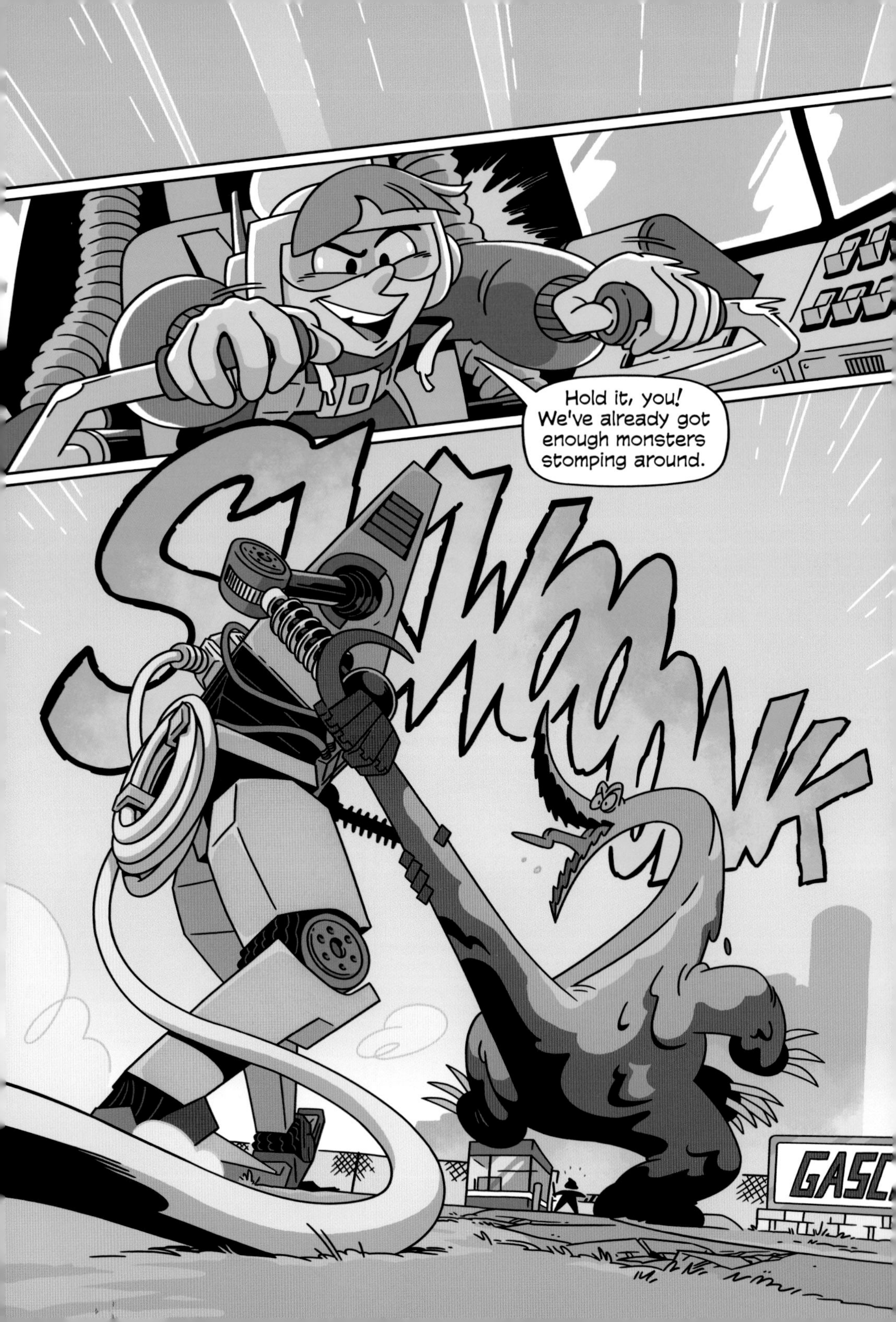
Hold it, you! We've already got enough monsters stomping around.
SHWOONK
GASC

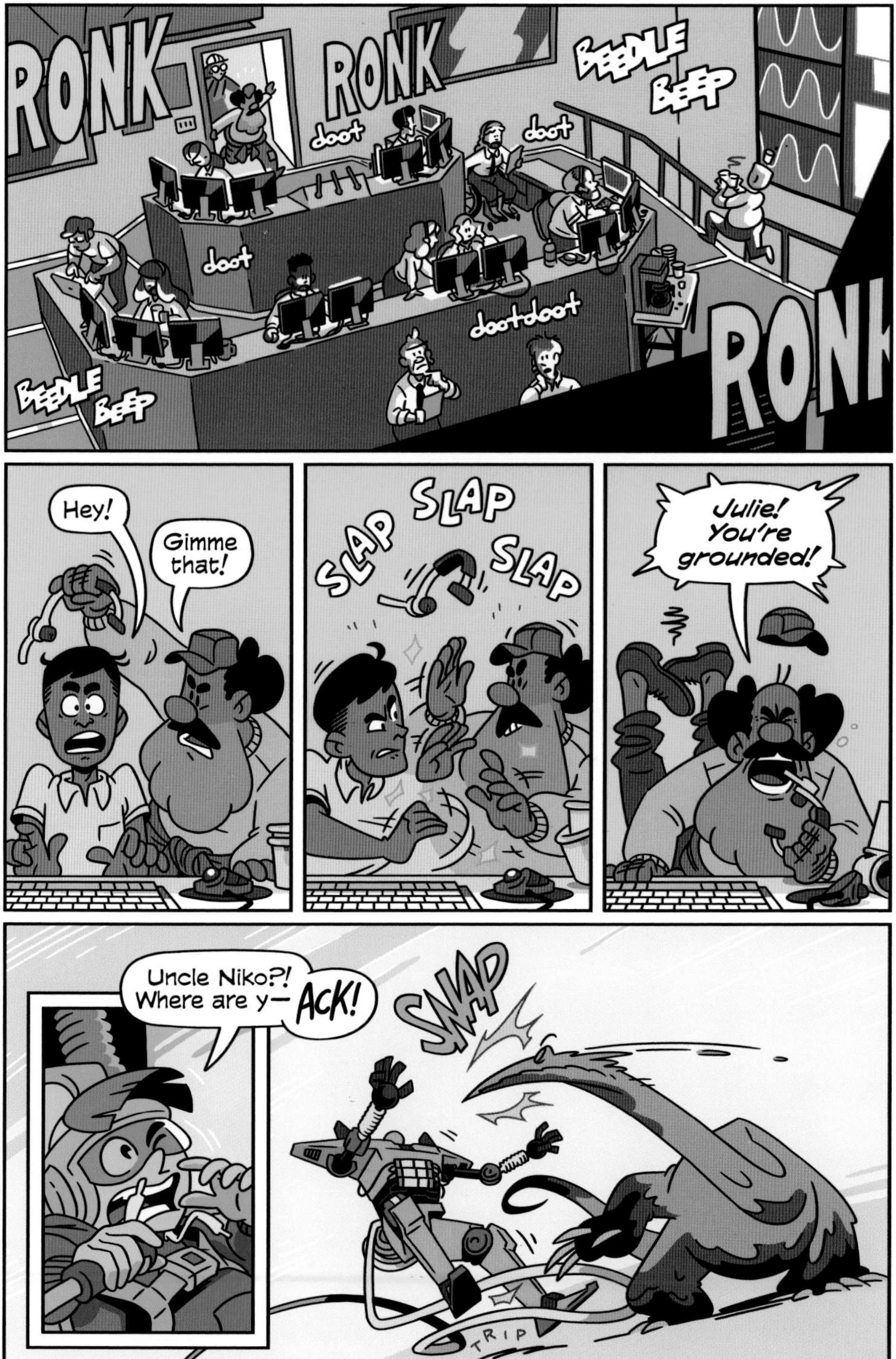
RONK
RONK
BEEDLE BEEP
doot
doot
doot
dootdoot
BEEDLE BEEP
RONK
Hey!
Gimme that!
SLAP
SLAP
SLAP
Julie! You're grounded!
Uncle Niko?! Where are y—ACK!
SNAP
TRIP

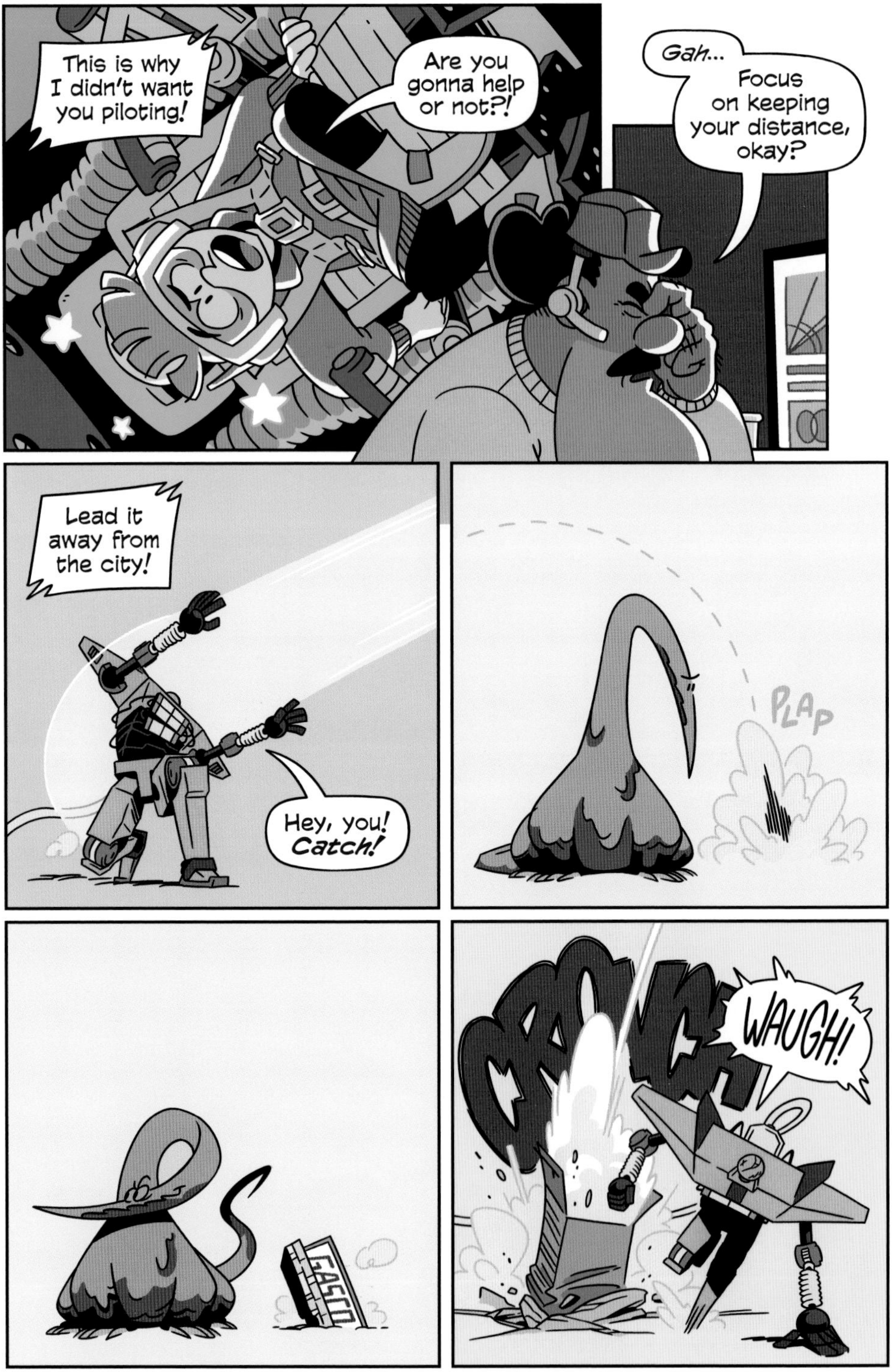
This is why I didn't want you piloting!
Are you gonna help or not?!
Gah... Focus on keeping your distance, okay?
Lead it away from the city!
Hey, you! Catch!
PLAP
GASCO
WAUGH!

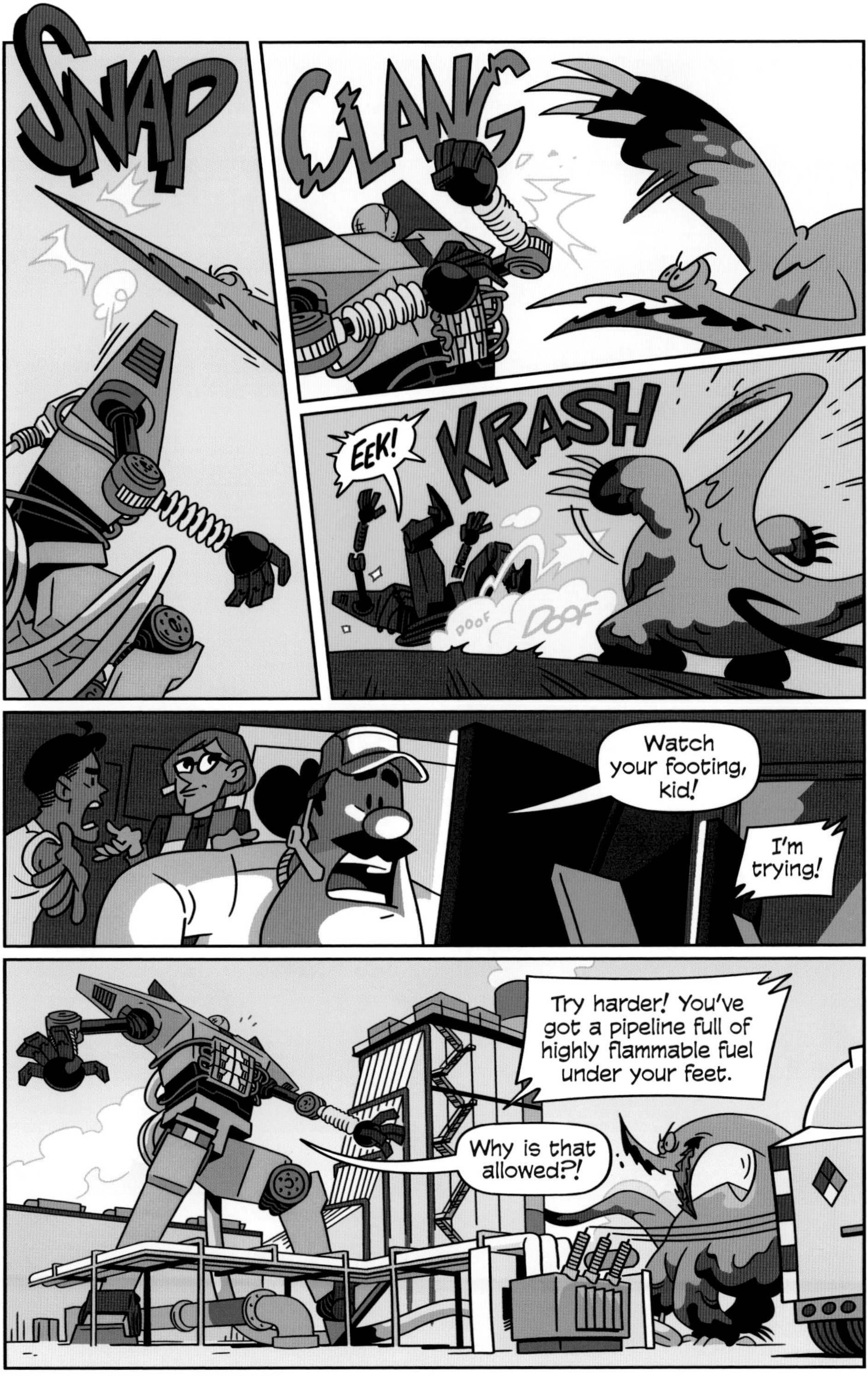
SNAP
CLANG
EEK!
KRASH
DOOF
DOOF
Watch your footing, kid!
I'm trying!
Try harder! You've got a pipeline full of highly flammable fuel under your feet.
Why is that allowed?!

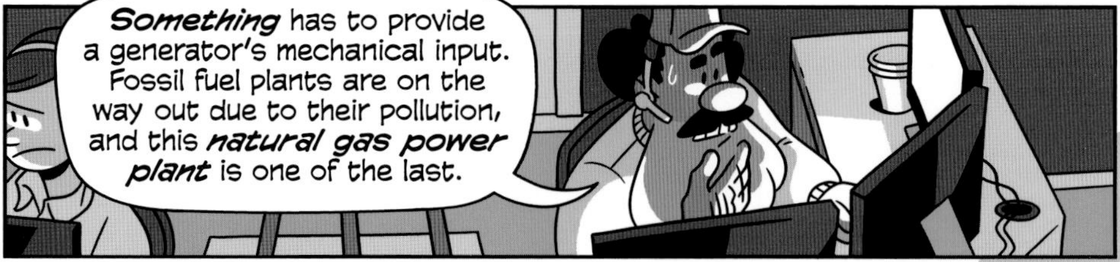

Something has to provide a generator's mechanical input. Fossil fuel plants are on the way out due to their pollution, and this ***natural gas power plant*** is one of the last.

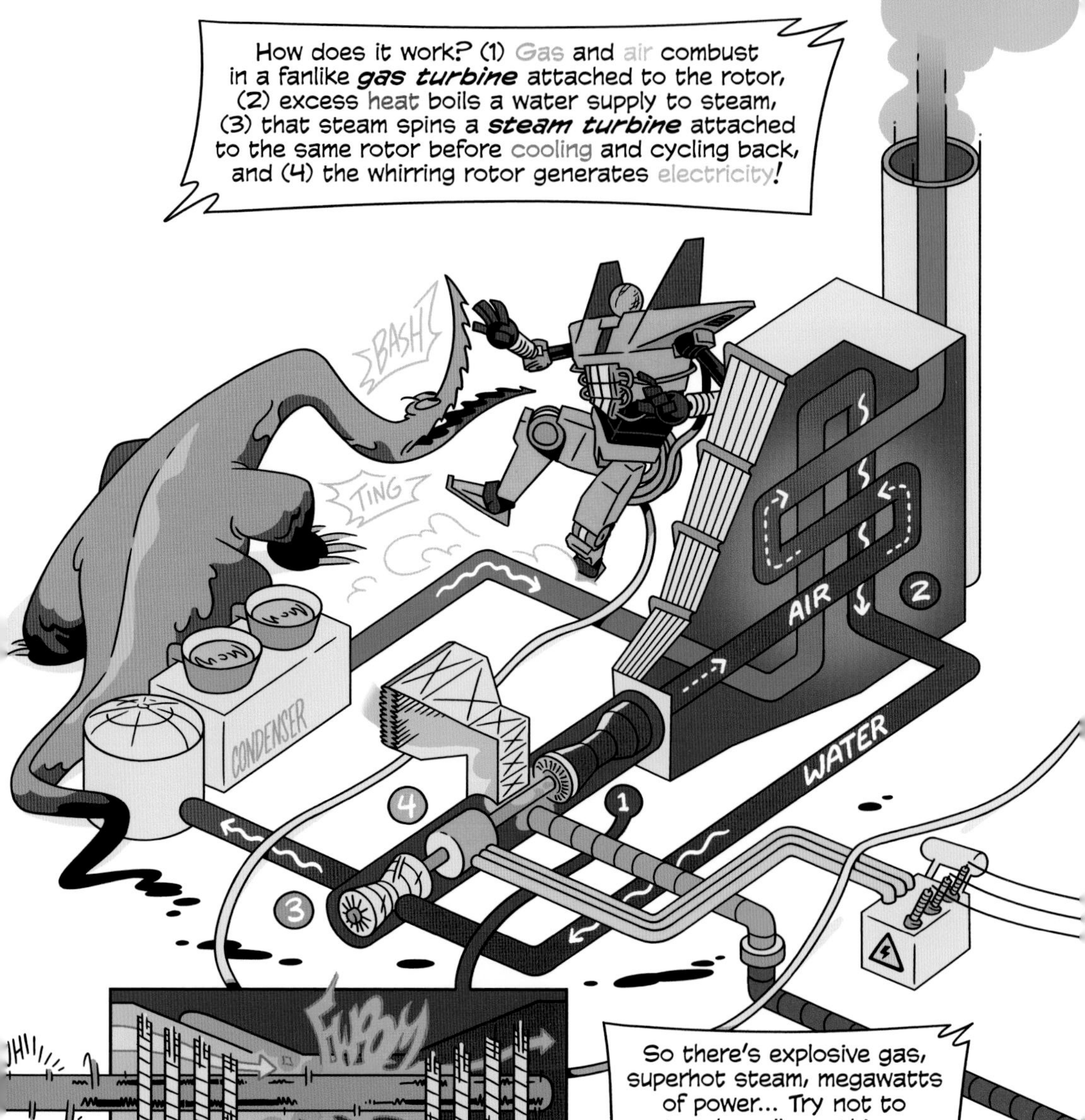

How does it work? (1) Gas and air combust in a fanlike ***gas turbine*** attached to the rotor, (2) excess heat boils a water supply to steam, (3) that steam spins a ***steam turbine*** attached to the same rotor before cooling and cycling back, and (4) the whirring rotor generates electricity!
BASH
TING
AIR
2
WATER
CONDENSER
1
4
3
GAS TURBINE
So there's explosive gas, superhot steam, megawatts of power... Try not to touch, well, anything.

You'll find that regardless of its source, a lot of grid electricity spends time as thermal energy. Steam *turbines* are used to convert it further.

CHEMICAL   THERMAL   MECHANICAL   ELECTRICAL

Steam enters the machine's narrow end hot and full of thermal energy. Blades sticking out of the rotor will make that energy *mechanical*.

WRRRRRRRN

SPIN

Some, shaped like scoops, will *catch* the steam, spinning like a waterwheel.

Others, shaped like wings, will *split* it and spin into the lower pressure zone.

BLADES

ROTOR

SPIN

The steam expands as it loses energy, so to give it space, the turbine is bigger toward the back.

Whew! By the end, the steam isn't hot enough to be useful. Its next stop is a *condenser*, where it cools by contact with air or other water to once again become liquid itself. Now it's ready to be boiled again!

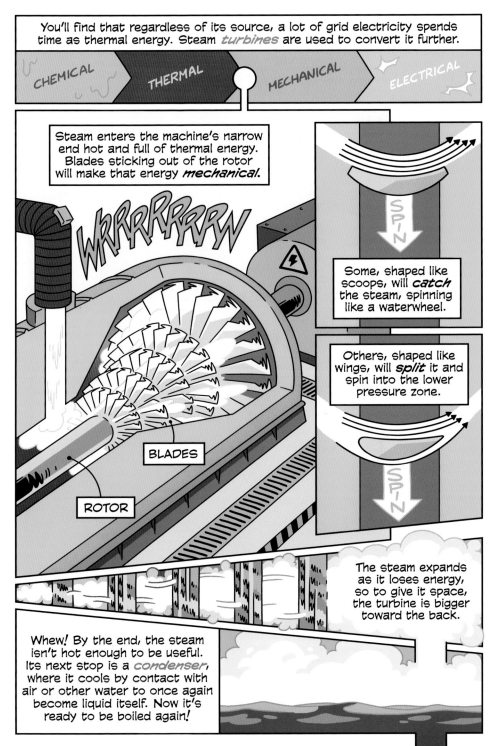

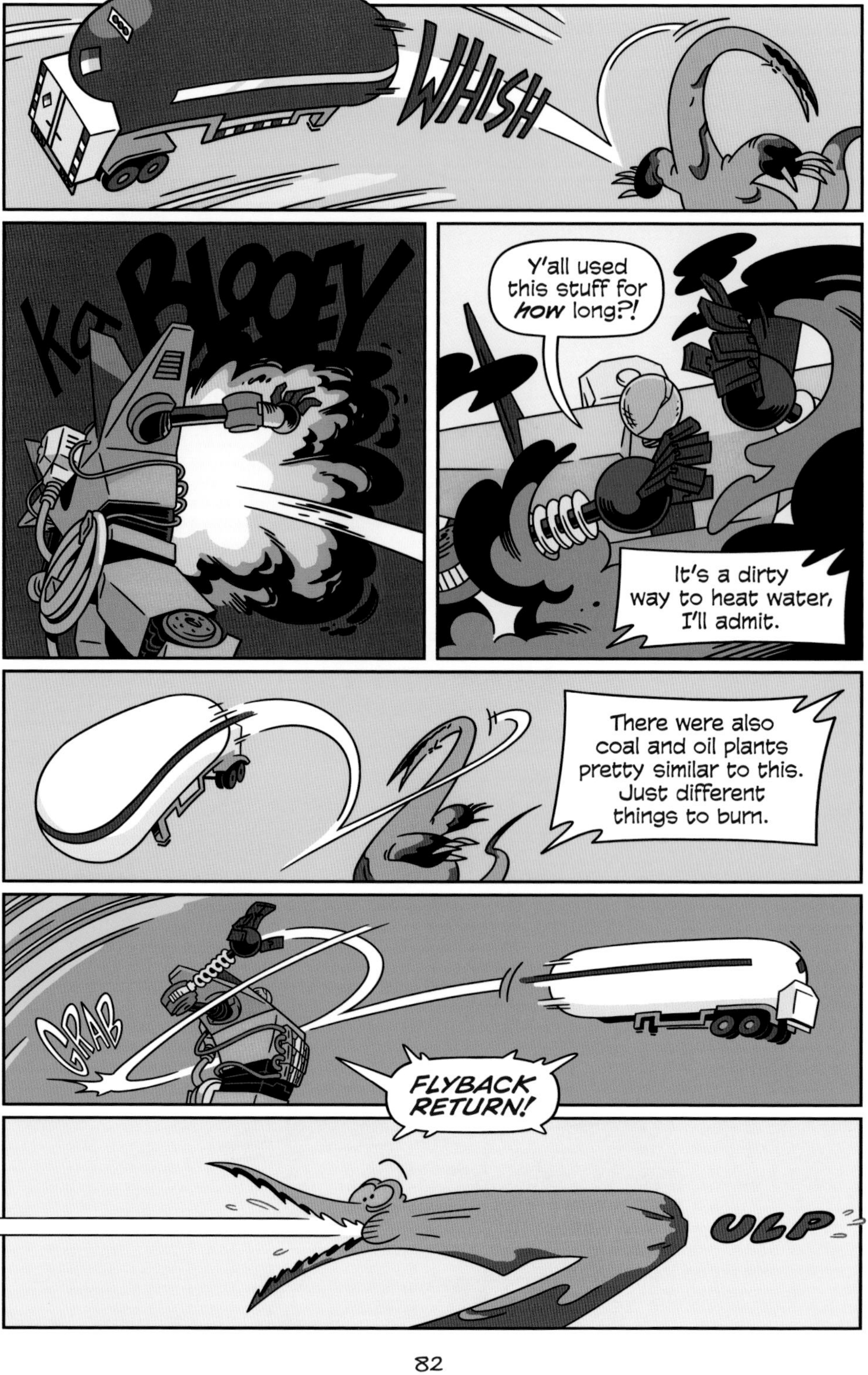
WHISH
KA-BLOOEY
Y'all used this stuff for *how* long?!
It's a dirty way to heat water, I'll admit.
There were also coal and oil plants pretty similar to this. Just different things to burn.
GRAB
FLYBACK RETURN!
ULP

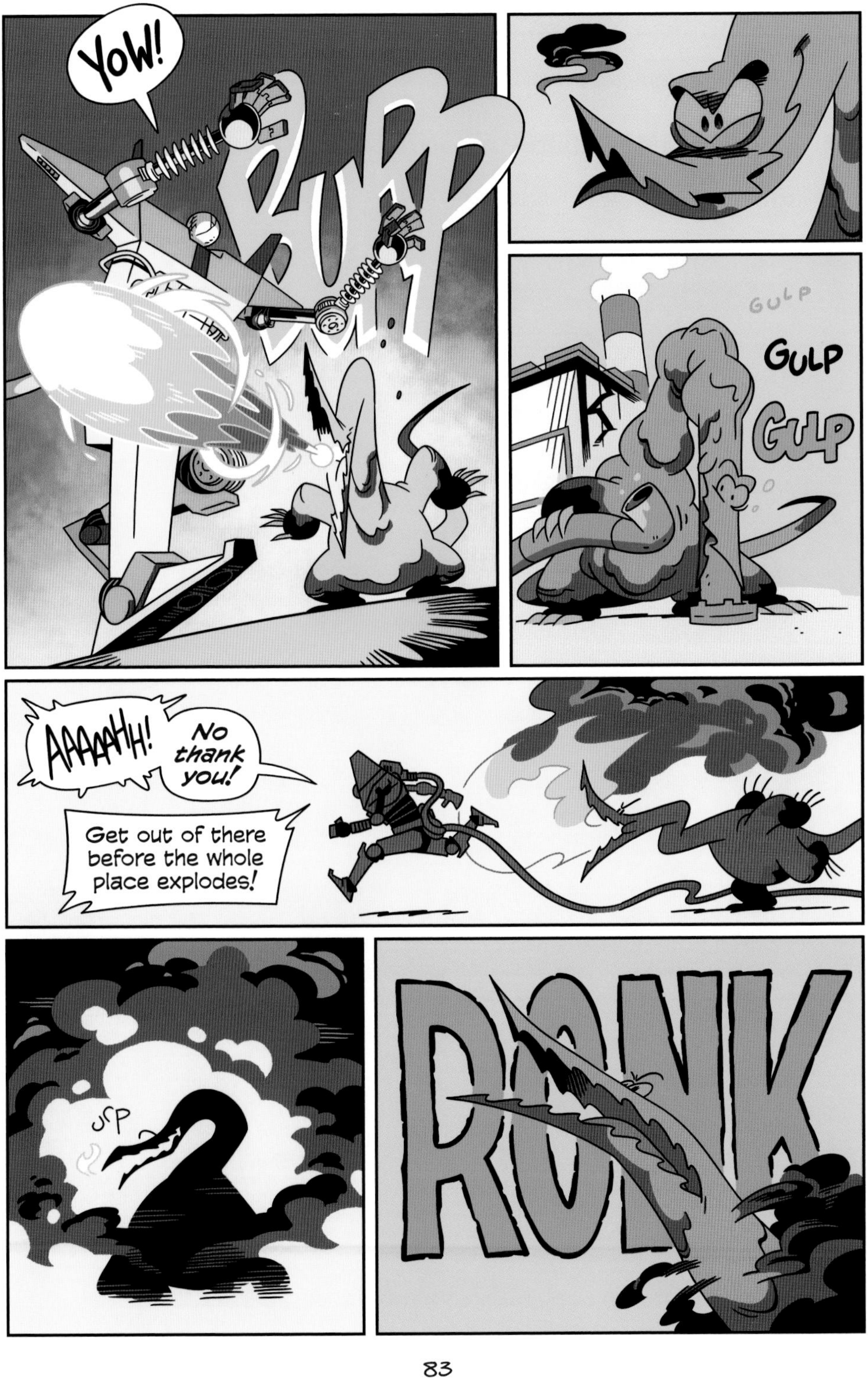
YOW!
BURP
GULP
GULP
GULP
AAAAAHH!
No thank you!
Get out of there before the whole place explodes!
URP
RONK

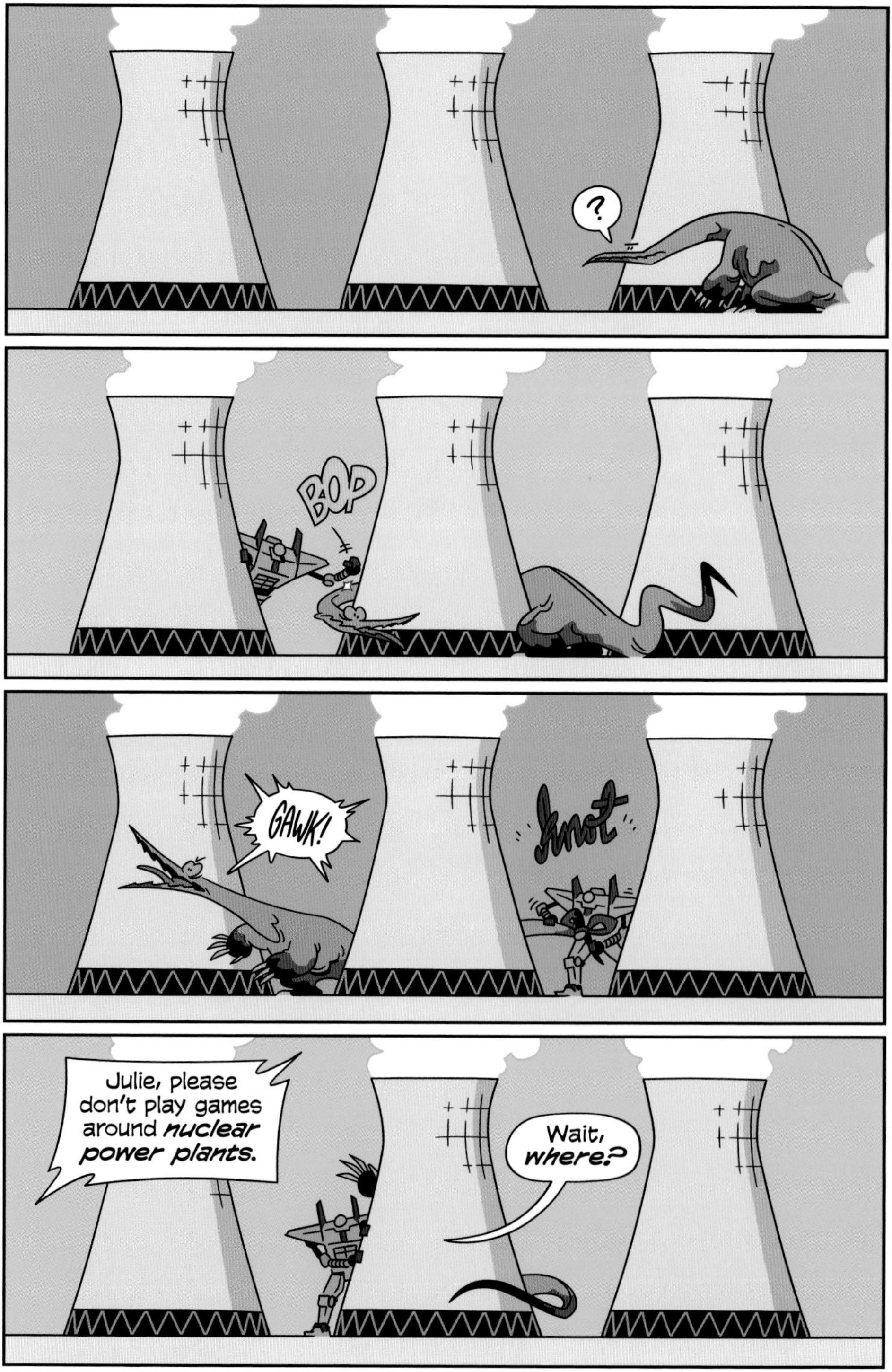
?
BOP
GAWK!
knot
Julie, please don't play games around *nuclear power plants.*
Wait, *where?*

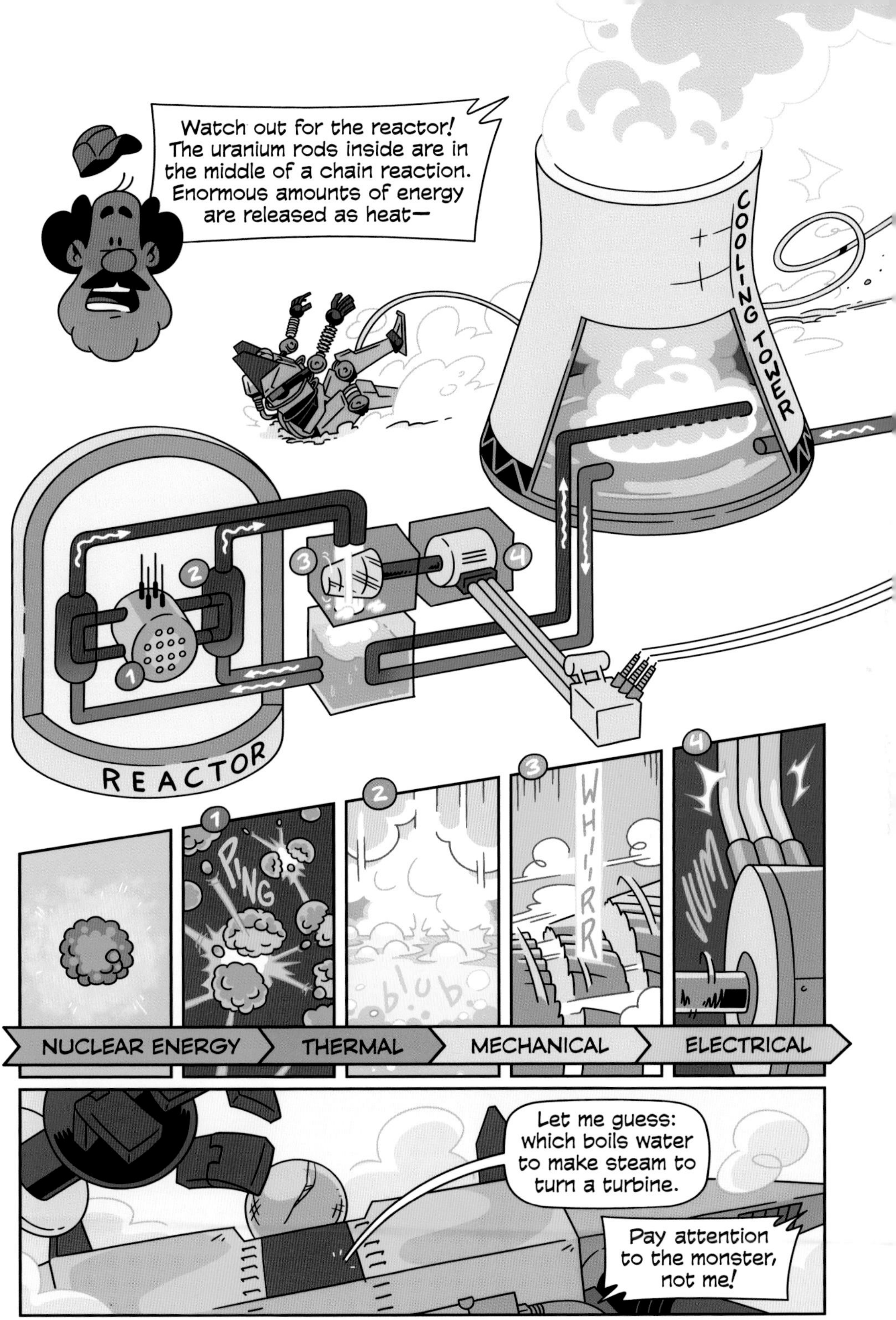
Watch out for the reactor! The uranium rods inside are in the middle of a chain reaction. Enormous amounts of energy are released as heat—
COOLING TOWER
REACTOR
1
2
3
4
PING
blub
WHIRR
VUM
NUCLEAR ENERGY
THERMAL
MECHANICAL
ELECTRICAL
Let me guess: which boils water to make steam to turn a turbine.
Pay attention to the monster, not me!

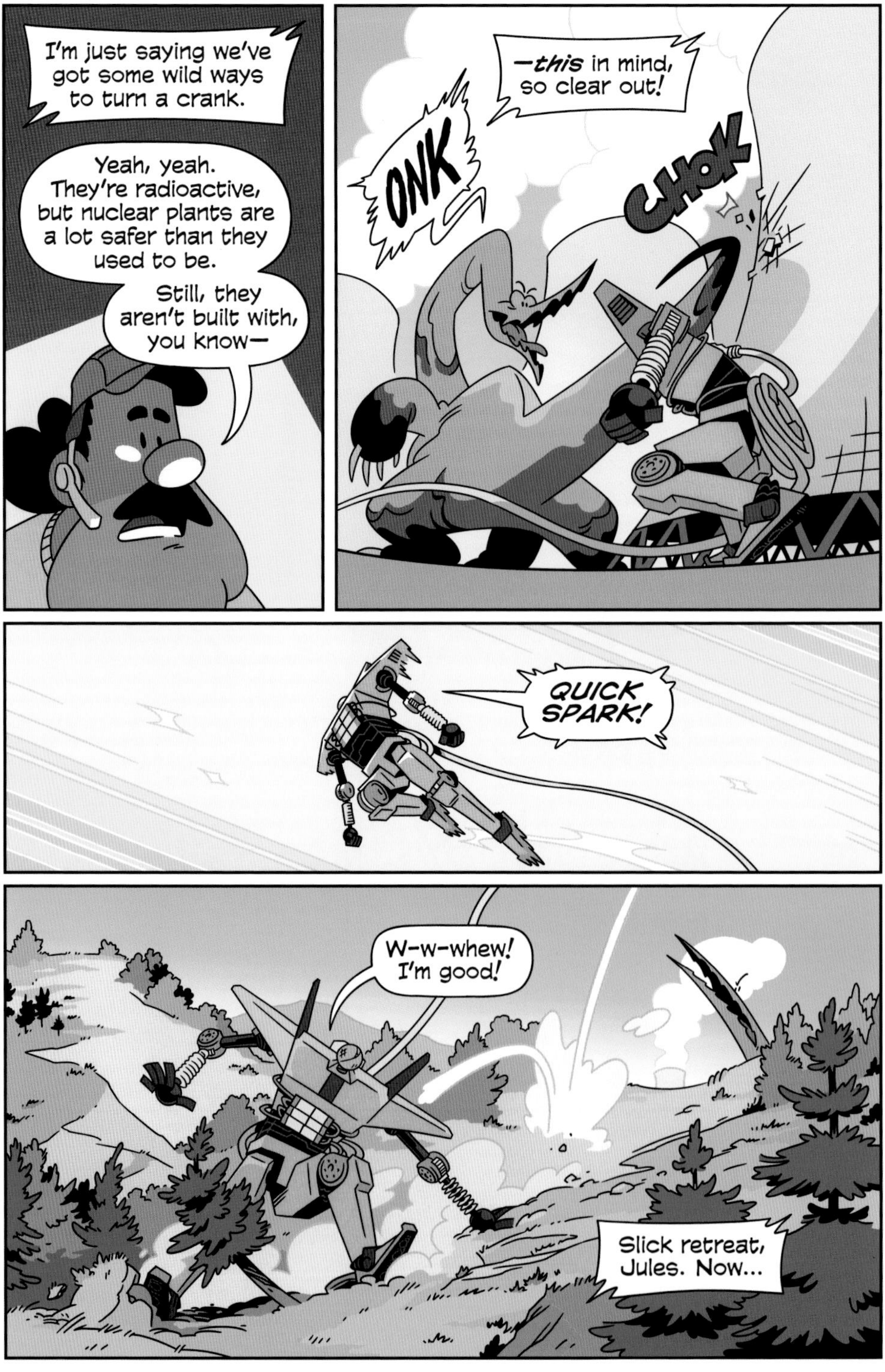
I'm just saying we've got some wild ways to turn a crank.
Yeah, yeah. They're radioactive, but nuclear plants are a lot safer than they used to be.
Still, they aren't built with, you know—
—this in mind, so clear out!
ONK
CHOK
QUICK SPARK!
W-w-whew! I'm good!
Slick retreat, Jules. Now...

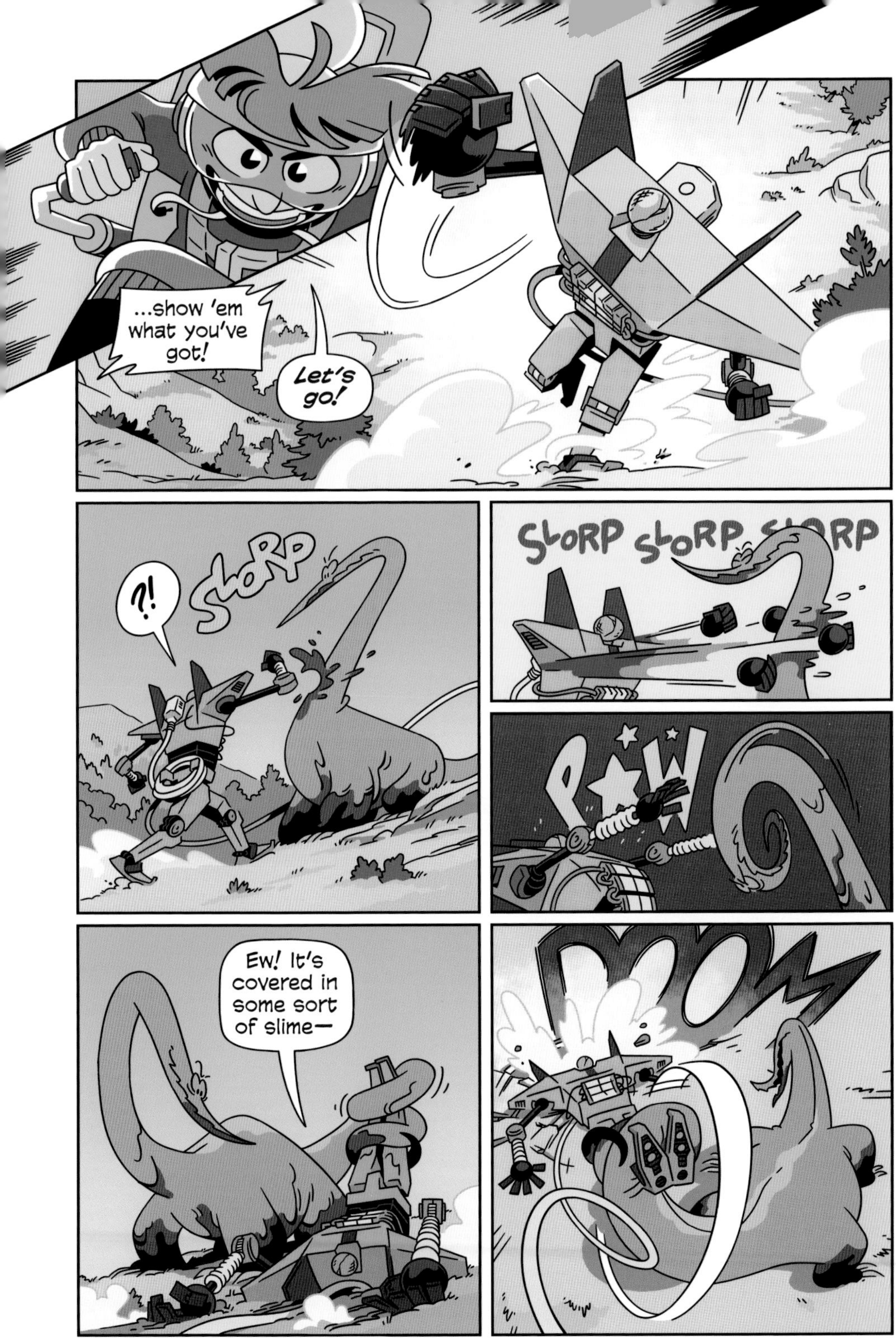

...show 'em what you've got!
Let's go!
?!
SLORP
SLORP SLORP SLORP
POW
Ew! It's covered in some sort of slime—
BOOM

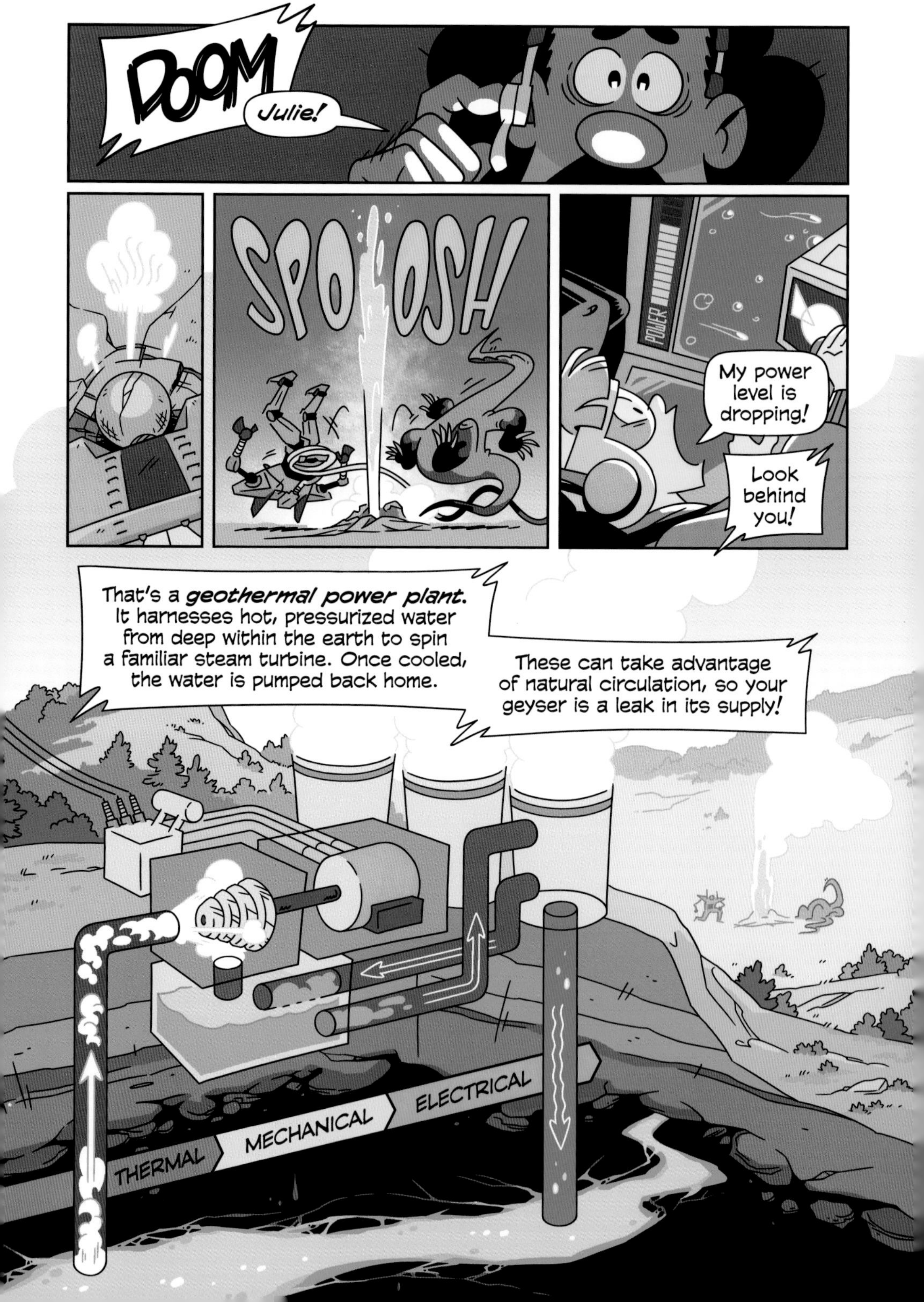
DOOM
Julie!
SPOOSH
POWER
My power level is dropping!
Look behind you!
That's a *geothermal power plant*. It harnesses hot, pressurized water from deep within the earth to spin a familiar steam turbine. Once cooled, the water is pumped back home.
These can take advantage of natural circulation, so your geyser is a leak in its supply!
THERMAL
MECHANICAL
ELECTRICAL

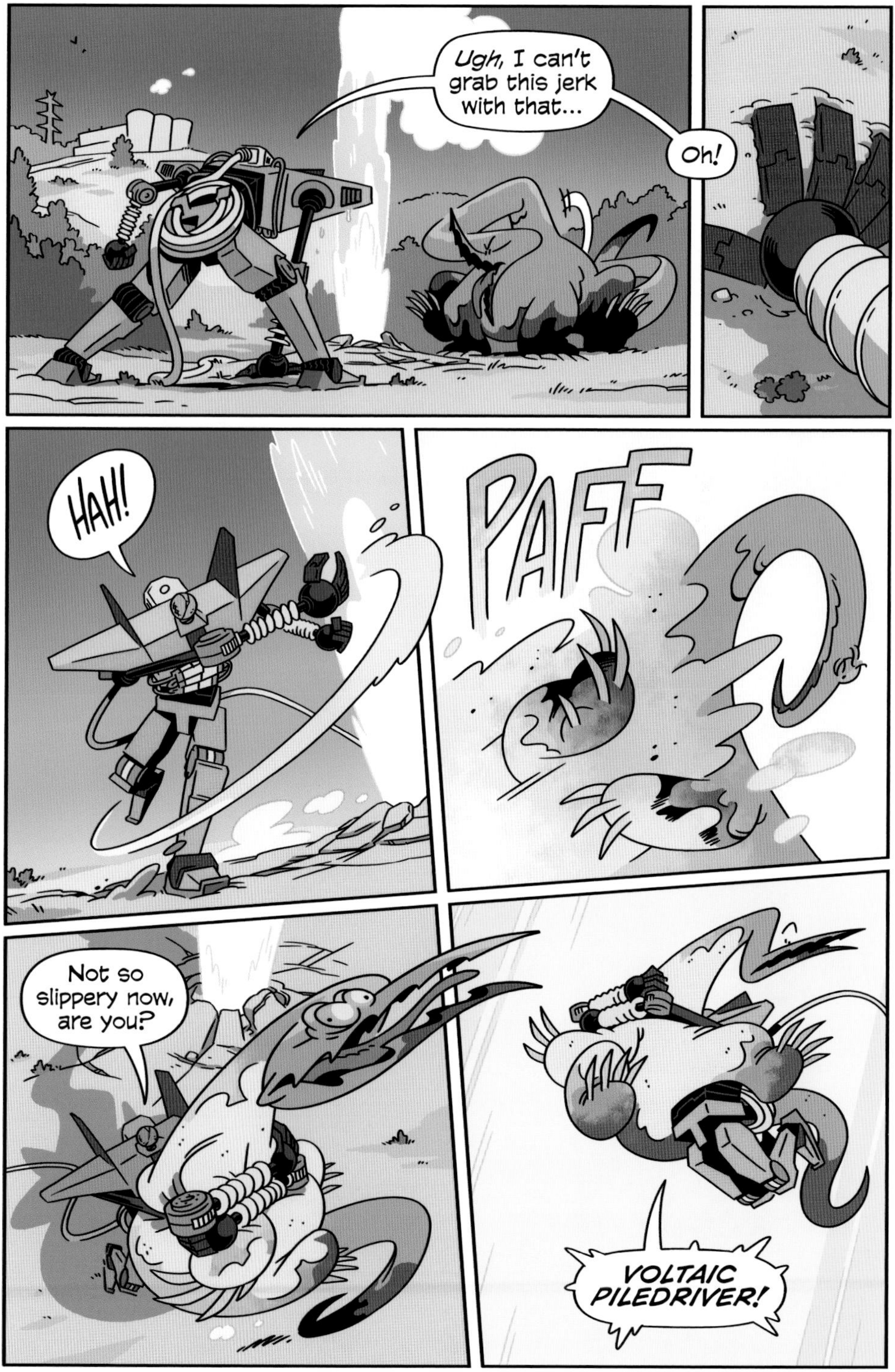
Ugh, I can't grab this jerk with that...
Oh!
HAH!
PAFF
Not so slippery now, are you?
VOLTAIC PILEDRIVER!

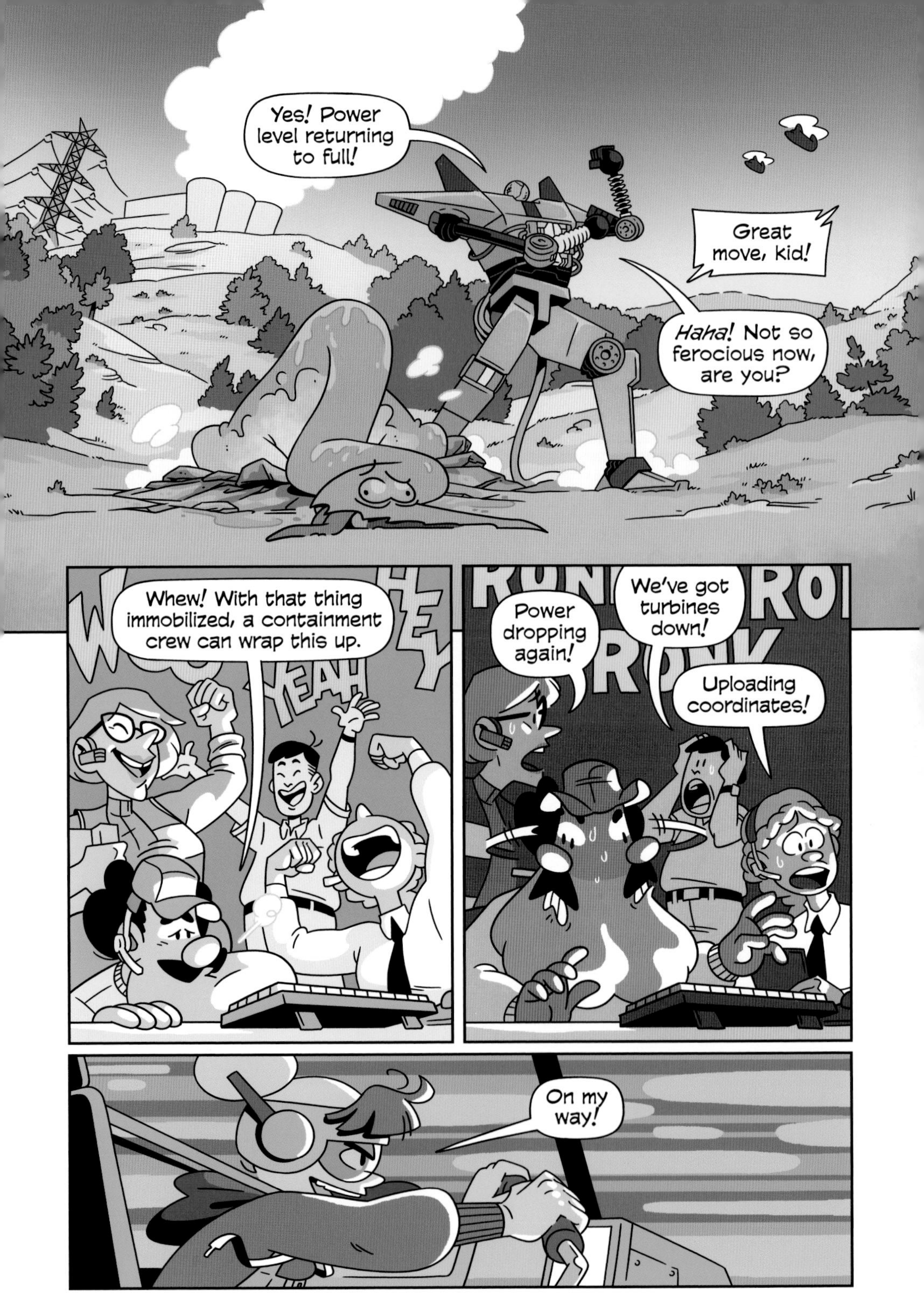
Yes! Power level returning to full!
Great move, kid!
Haha! Not so ferocious now, are you?
Whew! With that thing immobilized, a containment crew can wrap this up.
YEAH
Power dropping again!
We've got turbines down!
Uploading coordinates!
On my way!

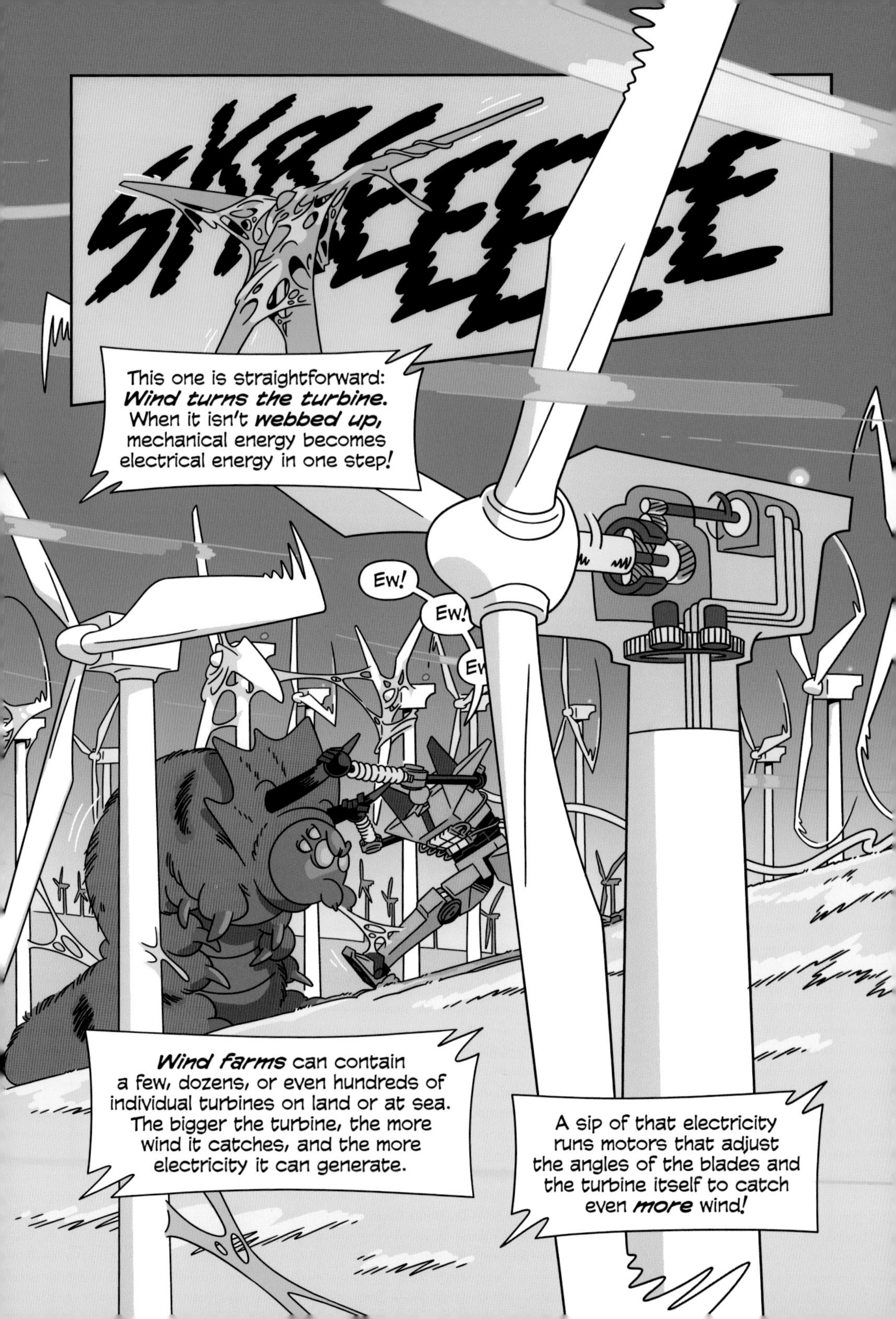
SKREEEEEE
This one is straightforward: ***Wind turns the turbine.*** When it isn't ***webbed up,*** mechanical energy becomes electrical energy in one step!
Ew!
Ew!
Ew
Wind farms can contain a few, dozens, or even hundreds of individual turbines on land or at sea. The bigger the turbine, the more wind it catches, and the more electricity it can generate.
A sip of that electricity runs motors that adjust the angles of the blades and the turbine itself to catch even ***more*** wind!

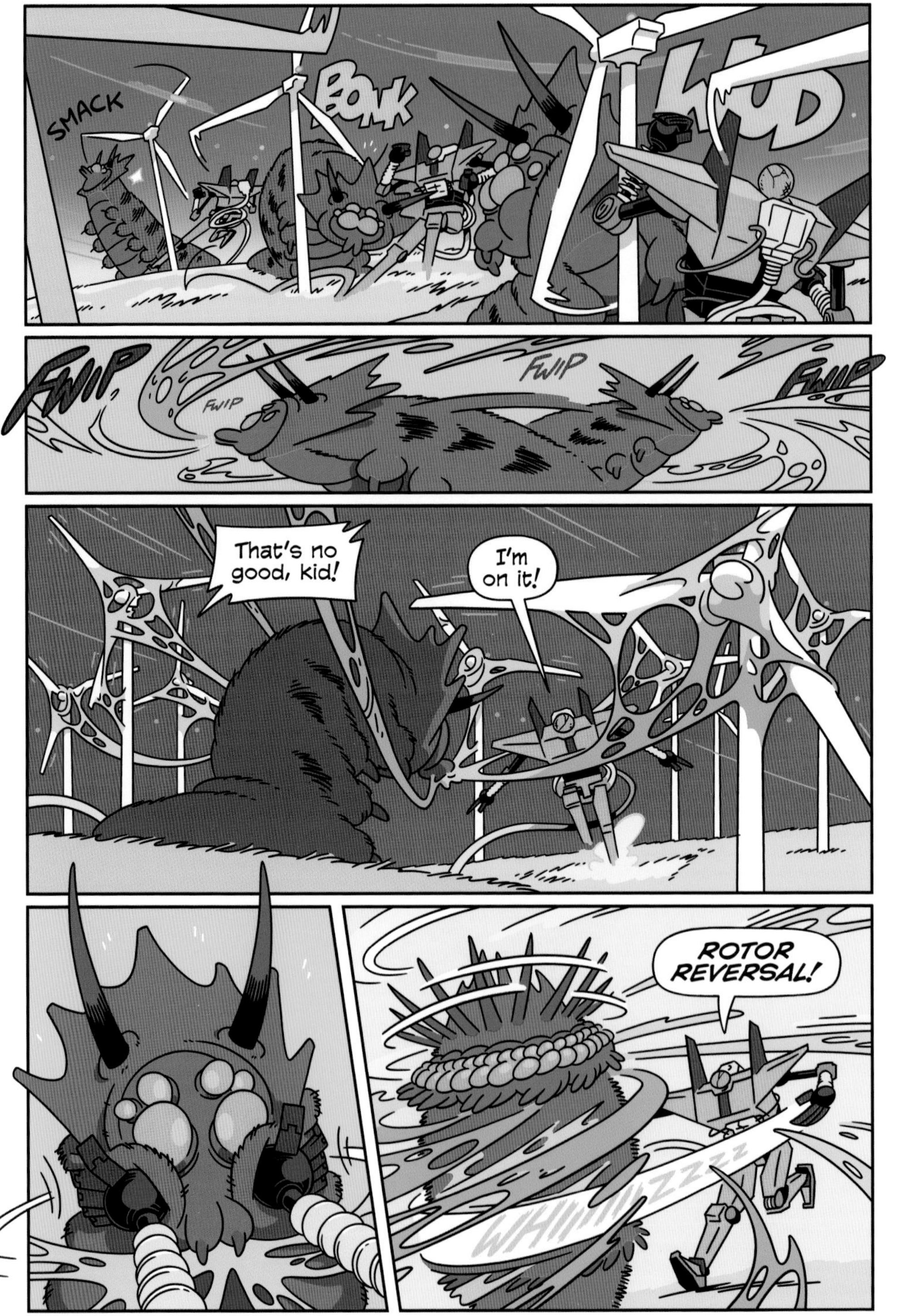
SMACK
BONK
WUD
FWIP
FWIP
FWIP
FWIP
That's no good, kid!
I'm on it!
ROTOR REVERSAL!
WHIIIIIZZZZZ

skitter

That wraps things up here!

Turbines spinning freely! Nice work!

RONK RONK RONK RONK

Beans! They just keep coming!

Point me to 'em!

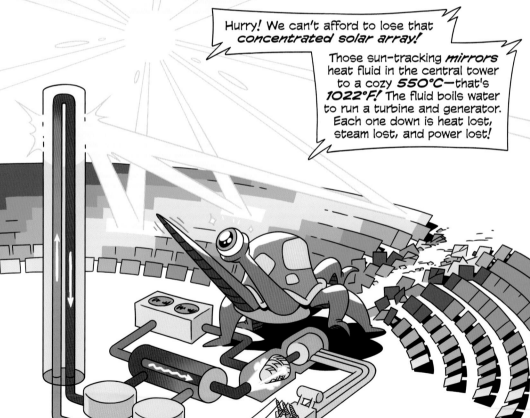

Hurry! We can't afford to lose that *concentrated solar array!*

Those sun-tracking *mirrors* heat fluid in the central tower to a cozy *550°C*—that's *1022°F!* The fluid boils water to run a turbine and generator. Each one down is heat lost, steam lost, and power lost!

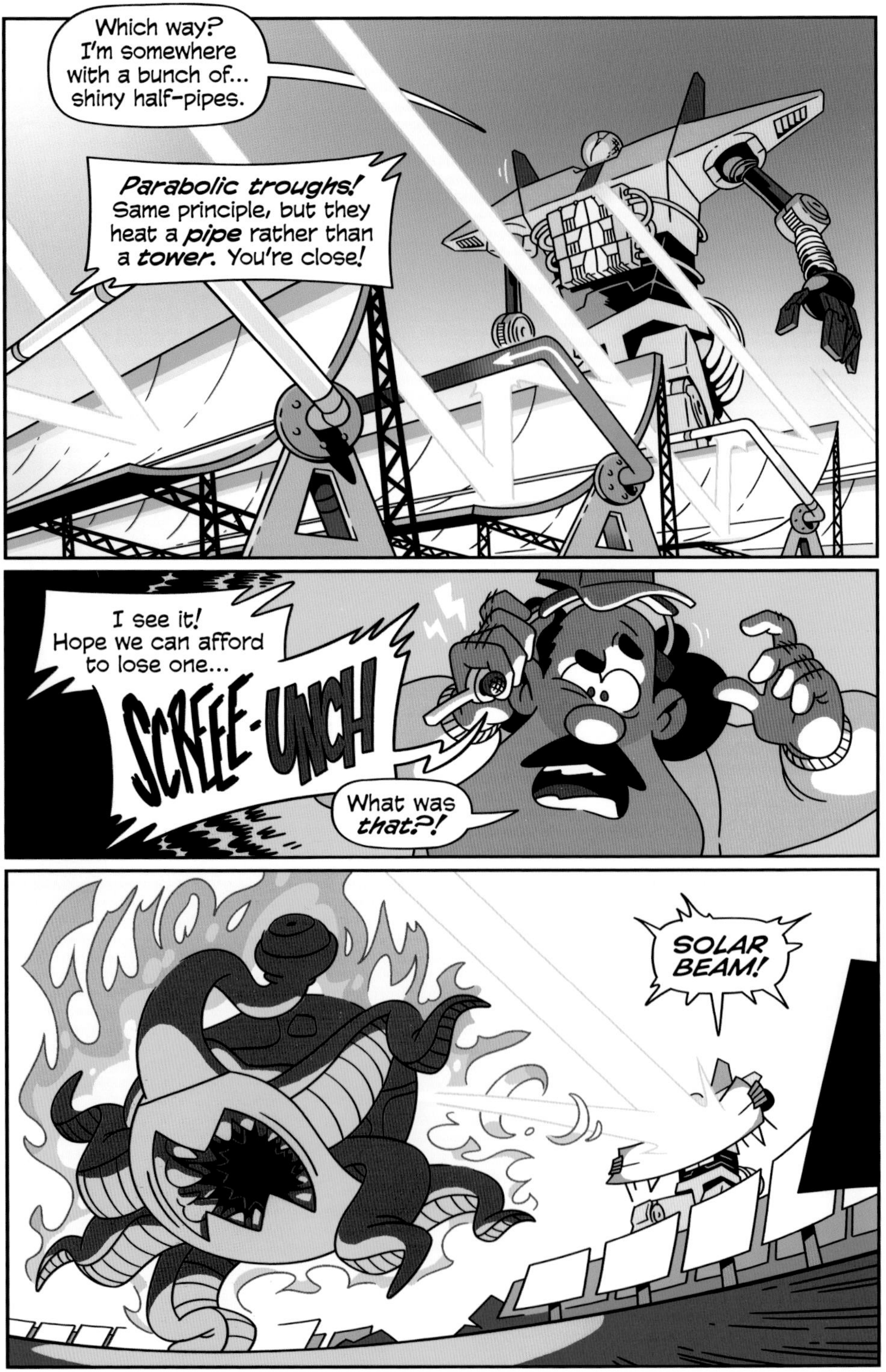
Which way? I'm somewhere with a bunch of... shiny half-pipes.
Parabolic troughs! Same principle, but they heat a *pipe* rather than a *tower*. You're close!
I see it! Hope we can afford to lose one...
SCREEE-UNCH
What was *that?!*
SOLAR BEAM!

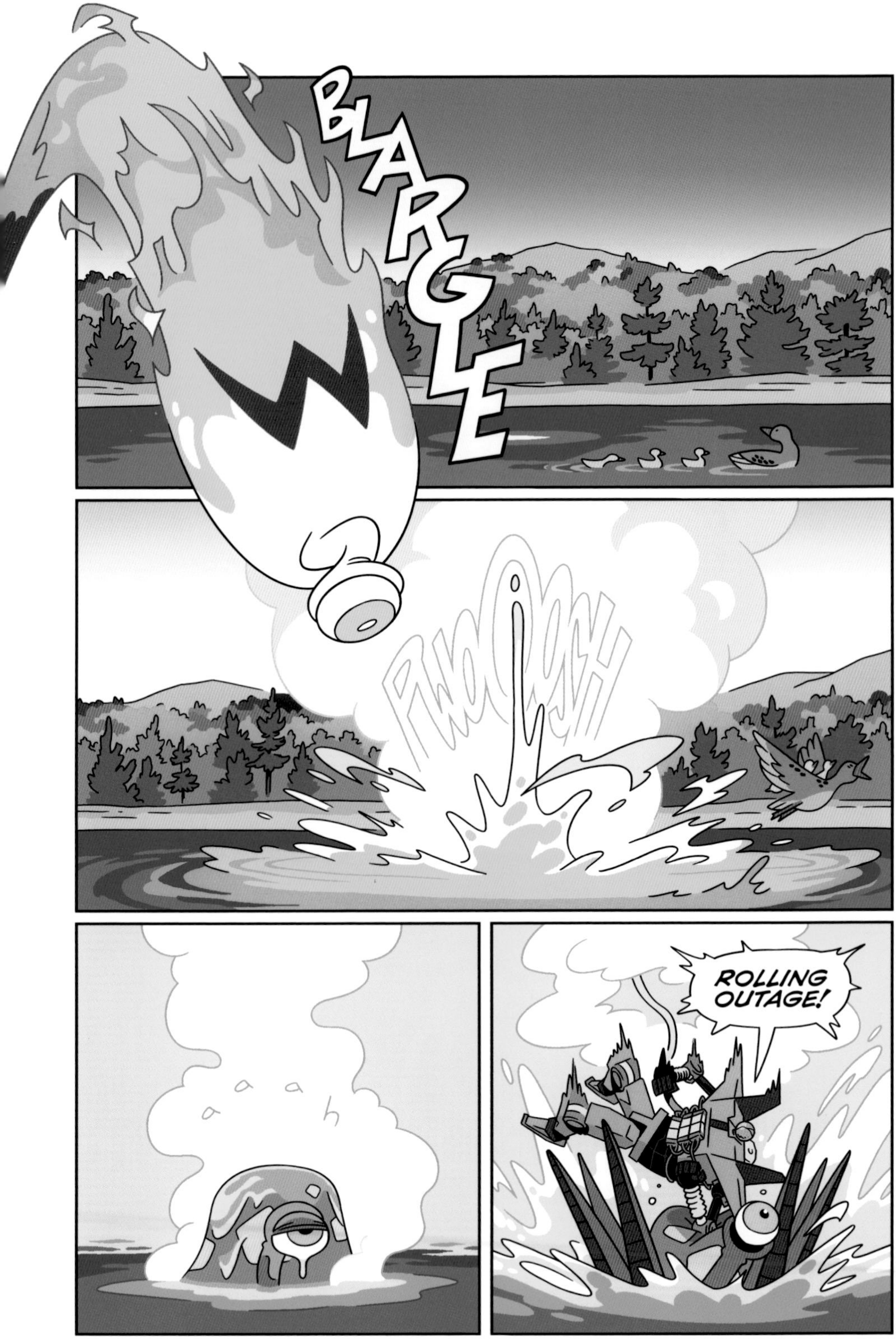
BLARGLE
PWOOOSH
a a a h
ROLLING OUTAGE!

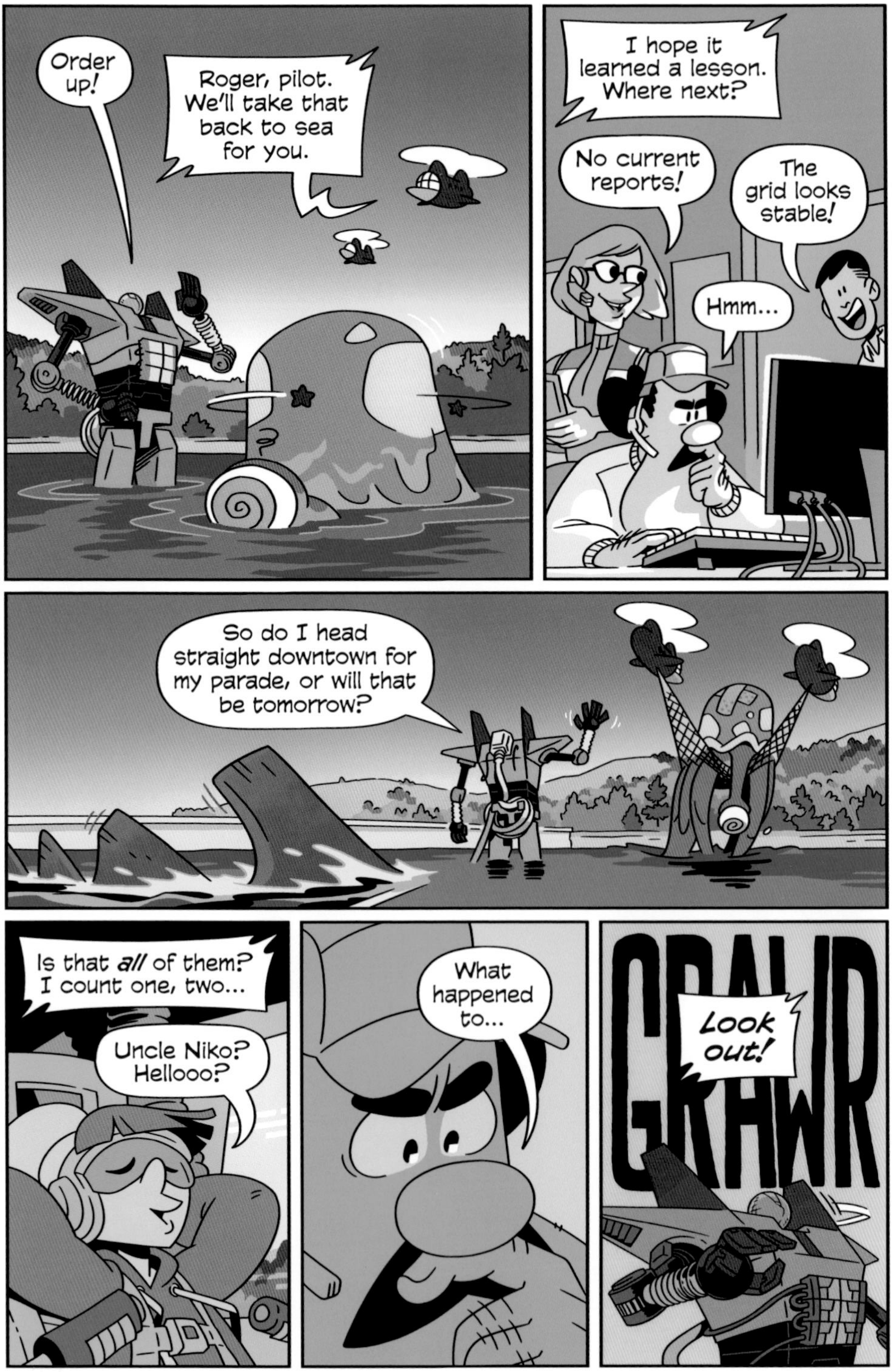
Order up!
Roger, pilot. We'll take that back to sea for you.
I hope it learned a lesson. Where next?
No current reports!
The grid looks stable!
Hmm...
So do I head straight downtown for my parade, or will that be tomorrow?
Is that all of them? I count one, two...
Uncle Niko? Hellooo?
What happened to...
GRAWR
Look out!

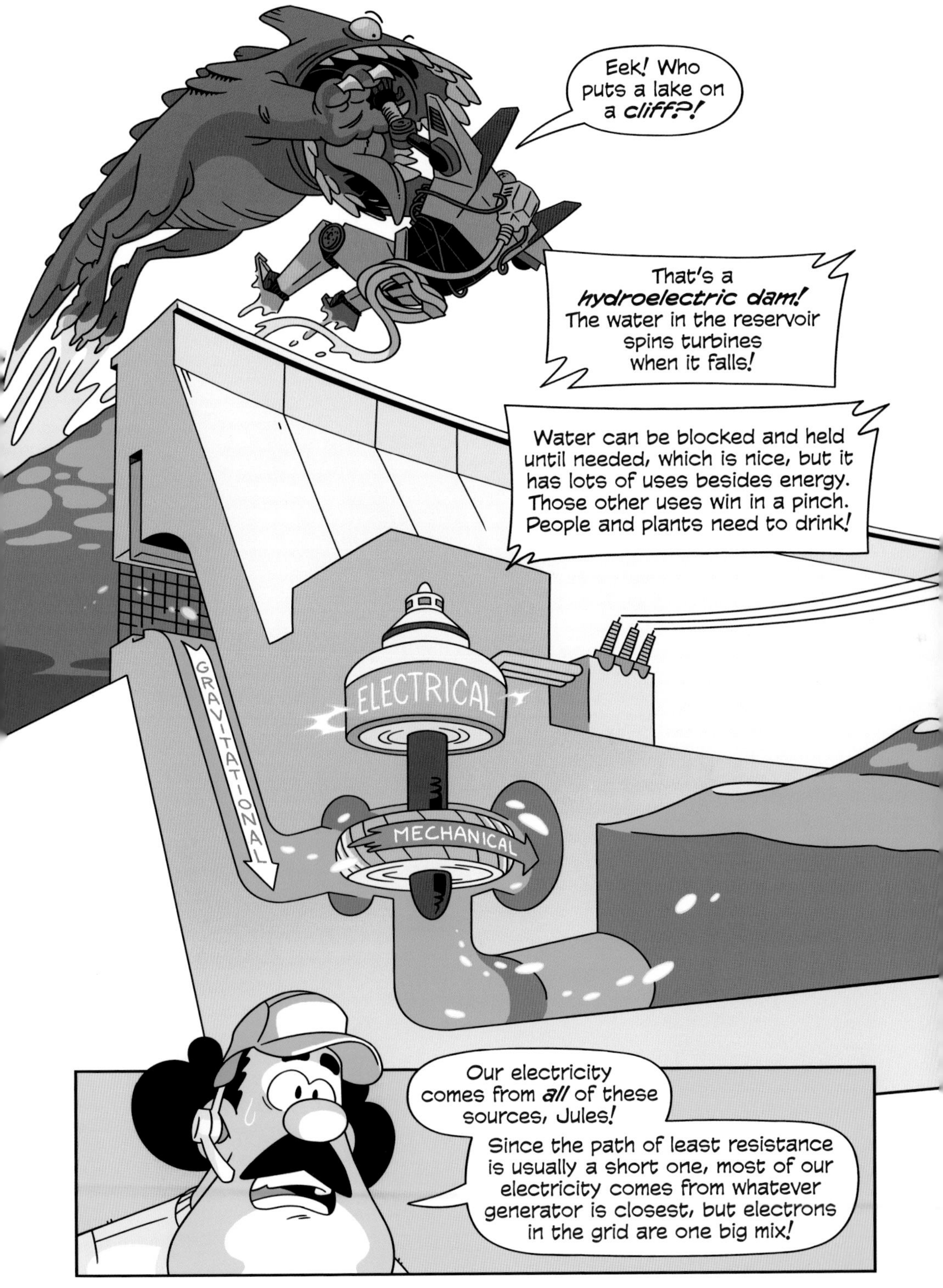
Eek! Who puts a lake on a *cliff?!*
That's a ***hydroelectric dam!*** The water in the reservoir spins turbines when it falls!
Water can be blocked and held until needed, which is nice, but it has lots of uses besides energy. Those other uses win in a pinch. People and plants need to drink!
GRAVITATIONAL
ELECTRICAL
MECHANICAL
Our electricity comes from ***all*** of these sources, Jules!
Since the path of least resistance is usually a short one, most of our electricity comes from whatever generator is closest, but electrons in the grid are one big mix!

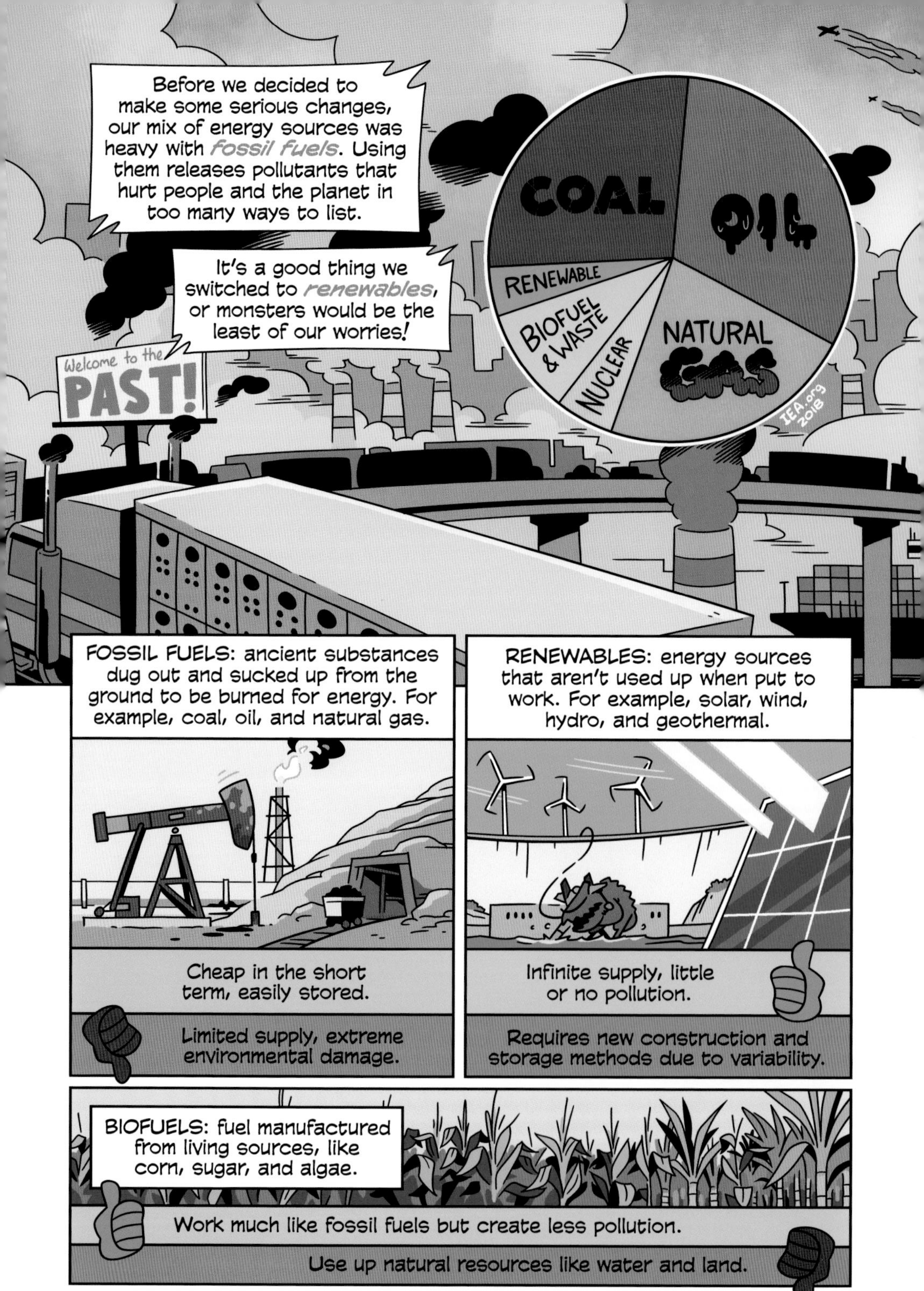
Before we decided to make some serious changes, our mix of energy sources was heavy with fossil fuels. Using them releases pollutants that hurt people and the planet in too many ways to list.
It's a good thing we switched to renewables, or monsters would be the least of our worries!
COAL
OIL
RENEWABLE
BIOFUEL & WASTE
NUCLEAR
NATURAL GAS
IEA.org 2018
Welcome to the PAST!
FOSSIL FUELS: ancient substances dug out and sucked up from the ground to be burned for energy. For example, coal, oil, and natural gas.
Cheap in the short term, easily stored.
Limited supply, extreme environmental damage.
RENEWABLES: energy sources that aren't used up when put to work. For example, solar, wind, hydro, and geothermal.
Infinite supply, little or no pollution.
Requires new construction and storage methods due to variability.
BIOFUELS: fuel manufactured from living sources, like corn, sugar, and algae.
Work much like fossil fuels but create less pollution.
Use up natural resources like water and land.

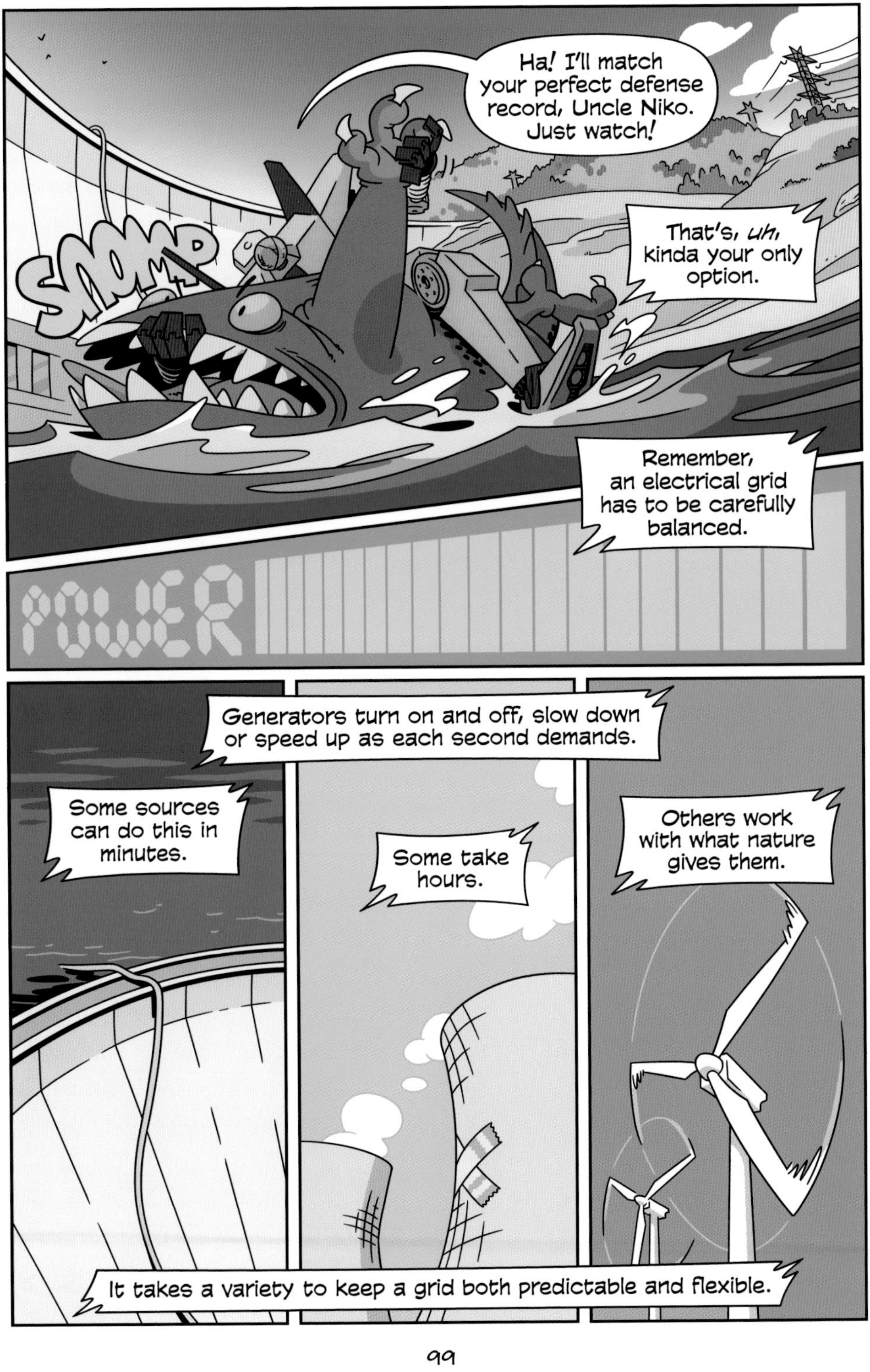
SNOMP
Ha! I'll match your perfect defense record, Uncle Niko. Just watch!
That's, *uh,* kinda your only option.
Remember, an electrical grid has to be carefully balanced.
POWER
Generators turn on and off, slow down or speed up as each second demands.
Some sources can do this in minutes.
Some take hours.
Others work with what nature gives them.
It takes a variety to keep a grid both predictable and flexible.

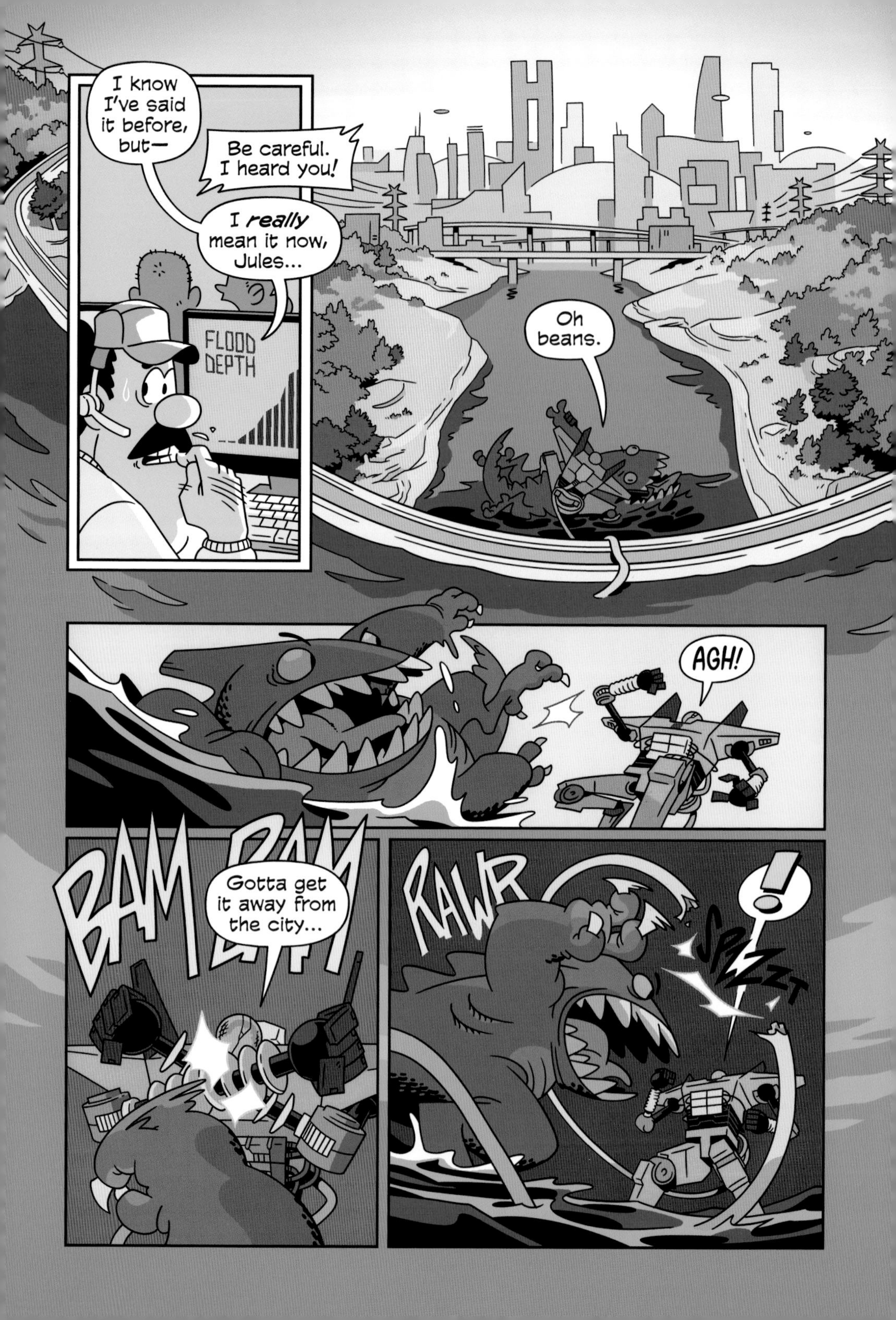

I know I've said it before, but—
Be careful. I heard you!
I *really* mean it now, Jules...
FLOOD DEPTH
Oh beans.
AGH!
BAM BAM
Gotta get it away from the city...
RAWR
!
SPZZZT

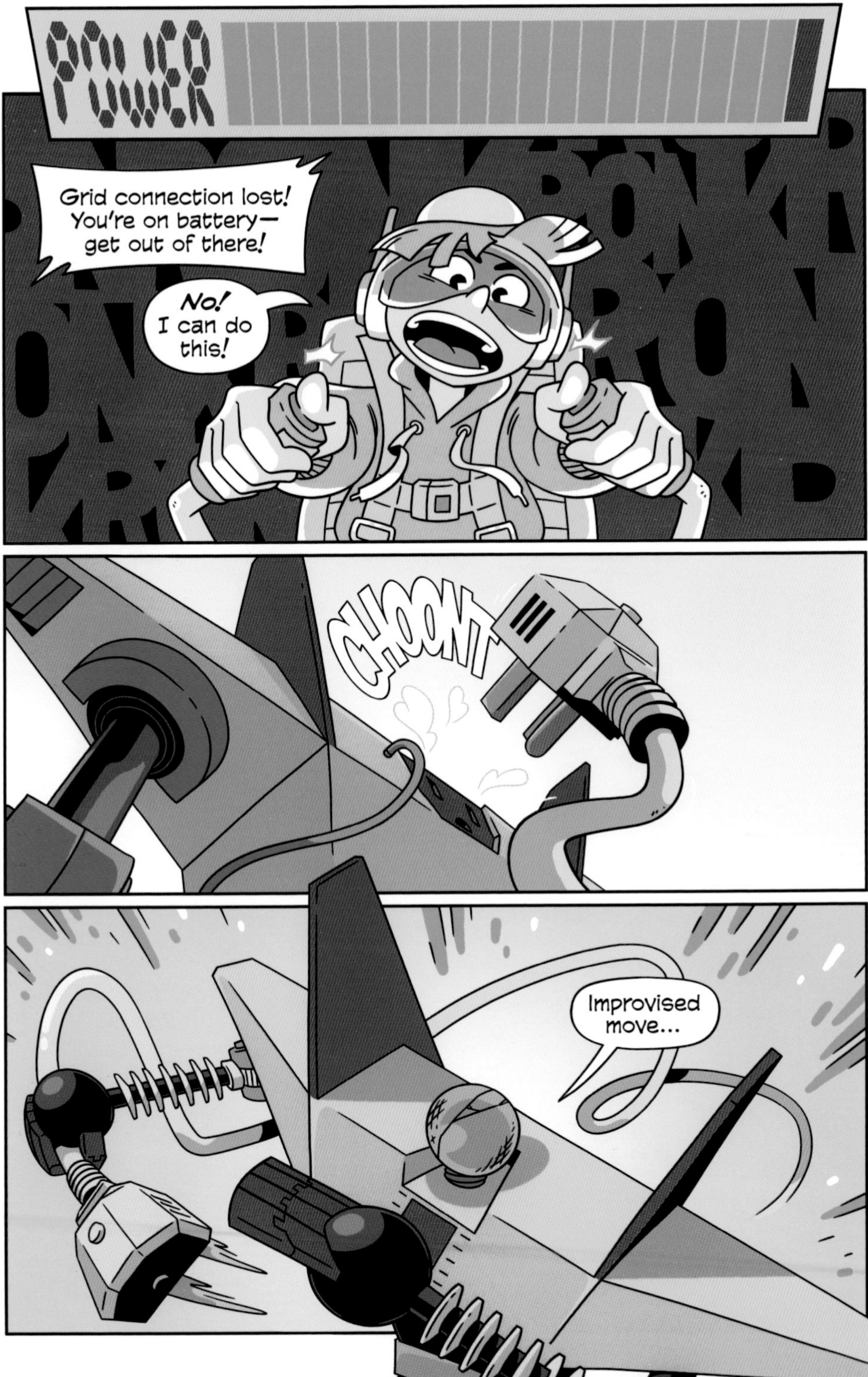
POWER
Grid connection lost! You're on battery—get out of there!
No! I can do this!
CHOONT
Improvised move...

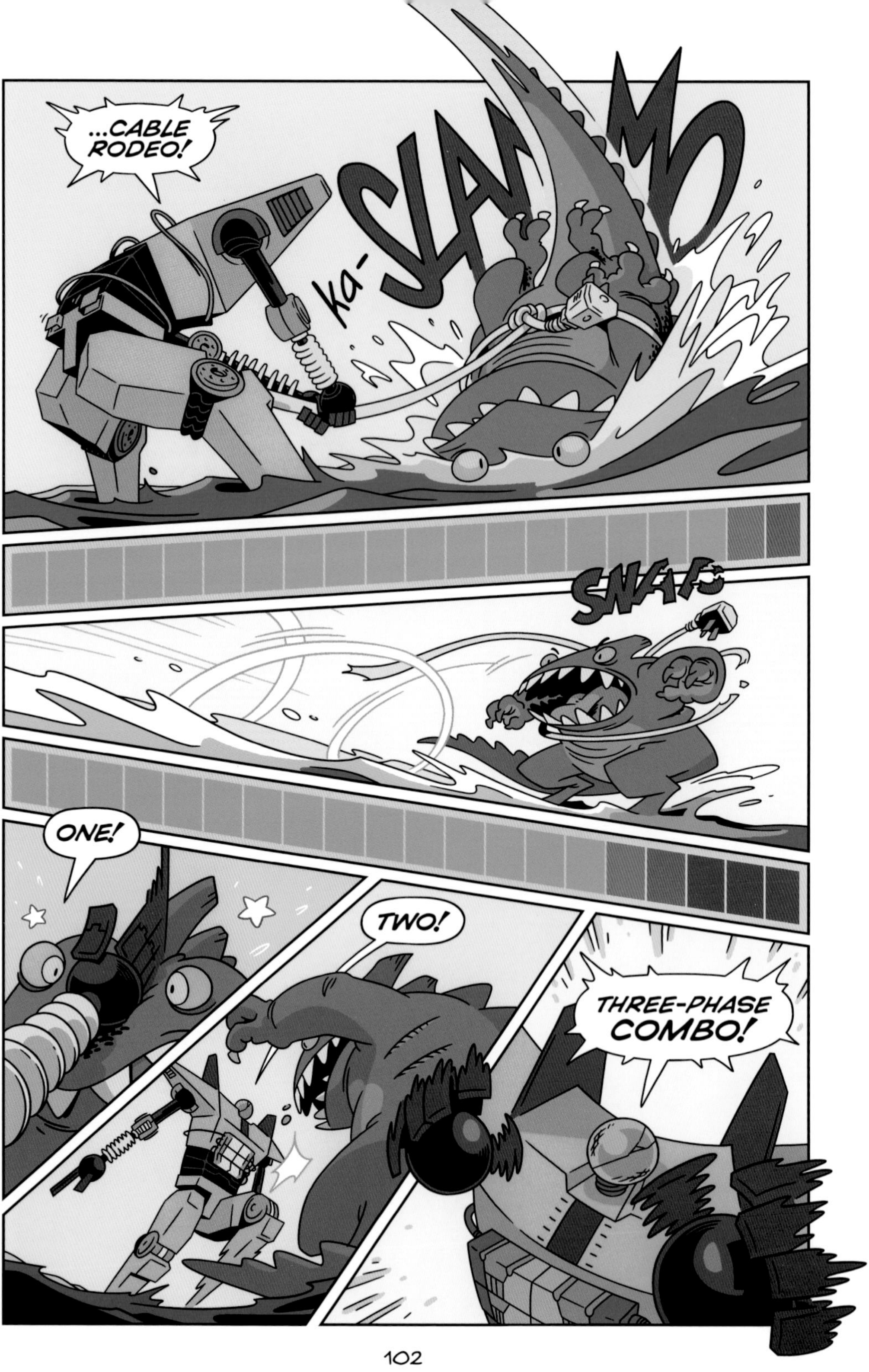
...CABLE RODEO!
ka-SLAMMO
SNAP
ONE!
TWO!
THREE-PHASE COMBO!

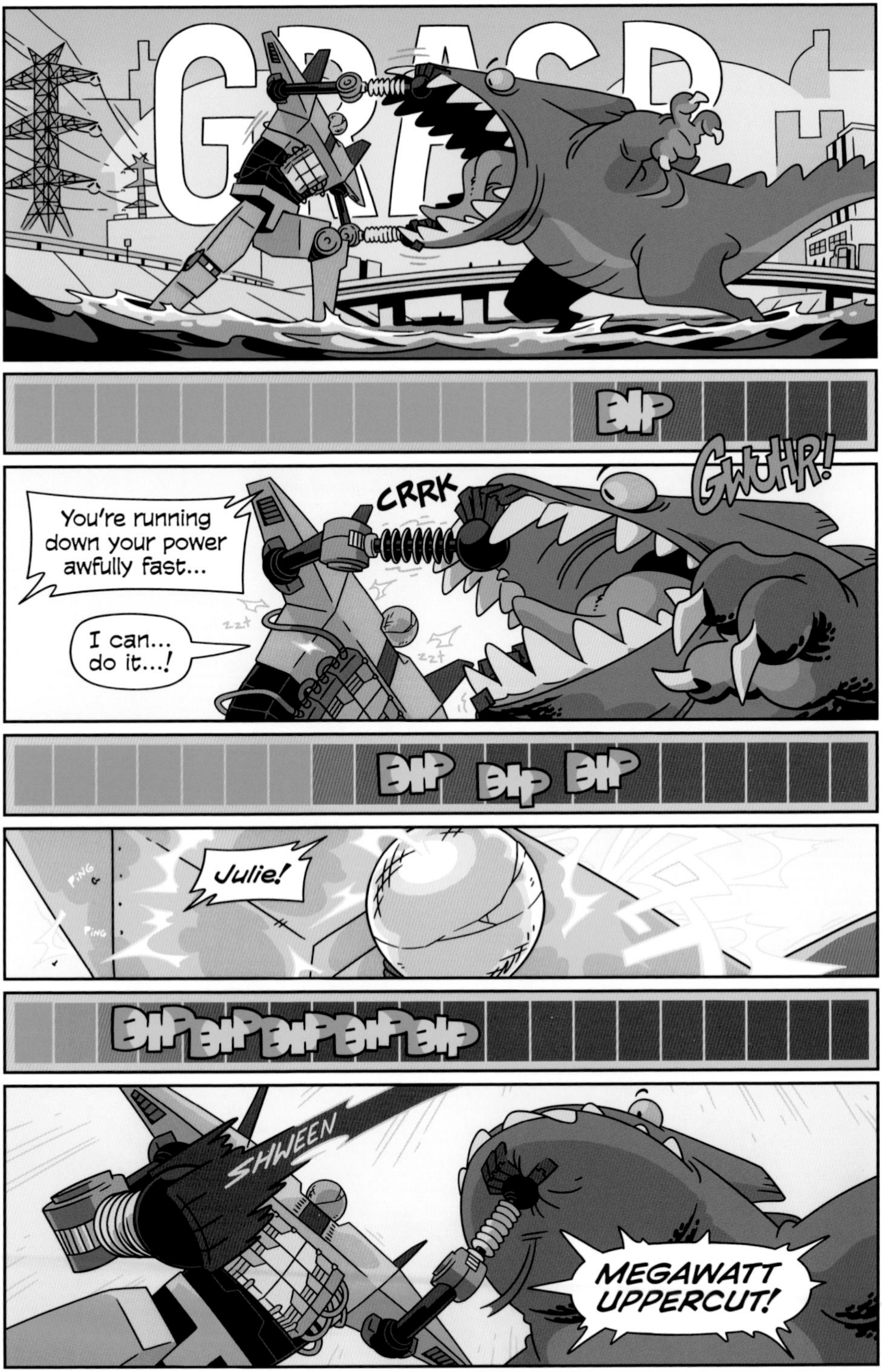
GRASP
BIP
GWUHR!
CRRK
You're running down your power awfully fast...
I can... do it...!
BIP BIP BIP
Julie!
BIPBIPBIPBIPBIP
SHWEEN
MEGAWATT UPPERCUT!

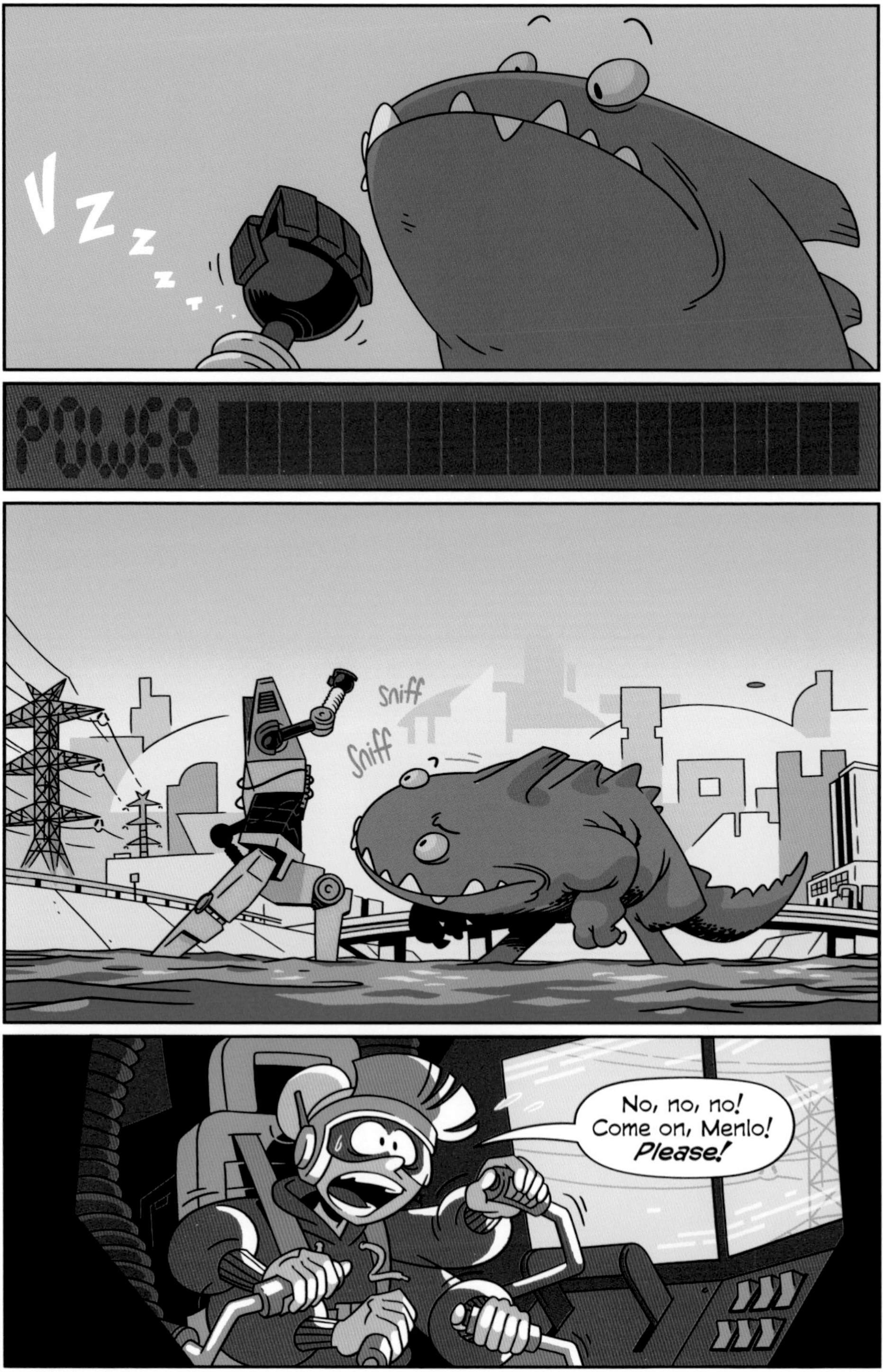
VZZZTTT
POWER
sniff
sniff
No, no, no! Come on, Menlo! *Please!*

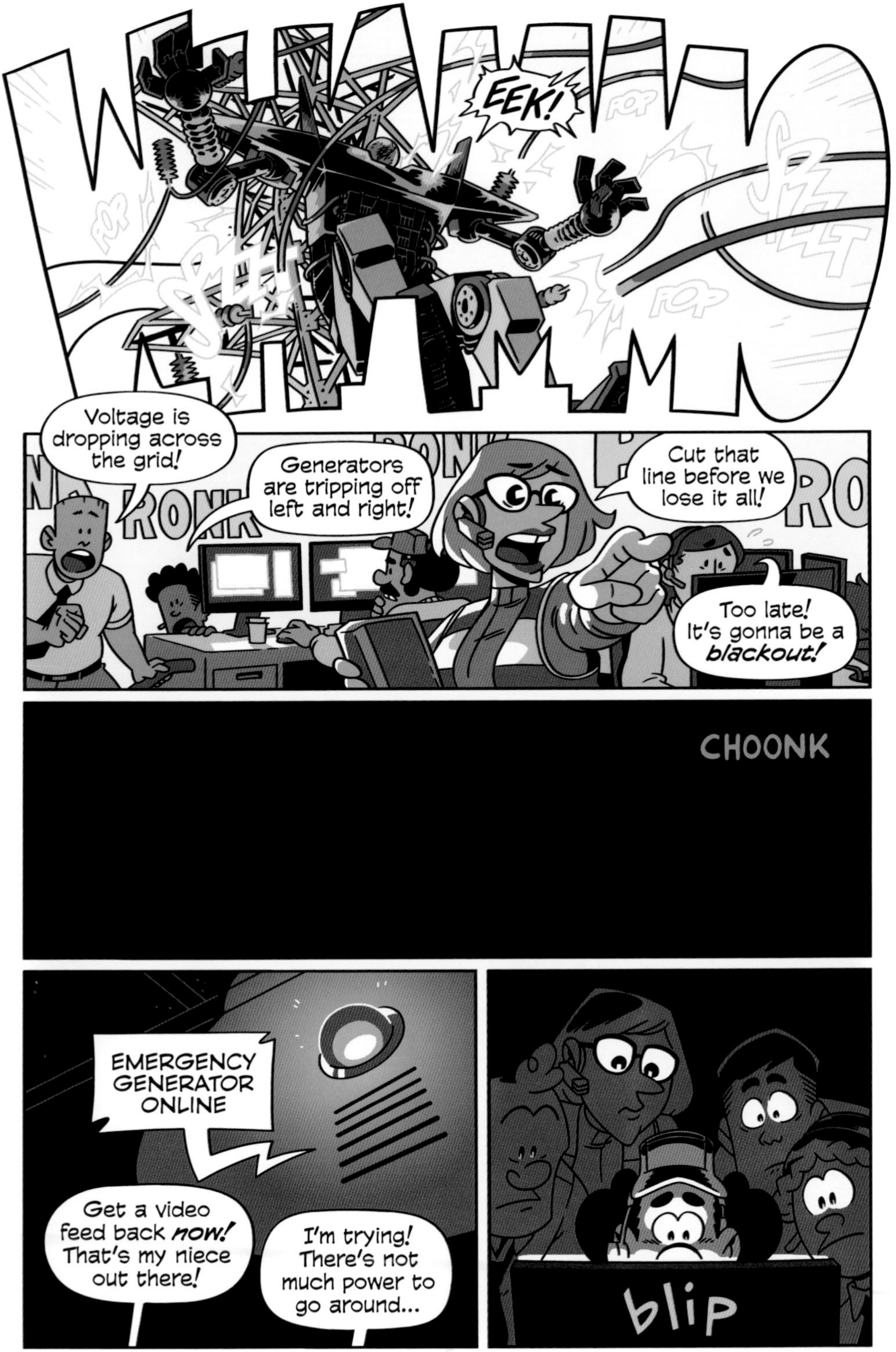
EEK!
FOP
FOP
SPZZT
FOP
Voltage is dropping across the grid!
Generators are tripping off left and right!
Cut that line before we lose it all!
RONK
Too late! It's gonna be a *blackout!*
CHOONK
EMERGENCY GENERATOR ONLINE
Get a video feed back *now!* That's my niece out there!
I'm trying! There's not much power to go around...
blip

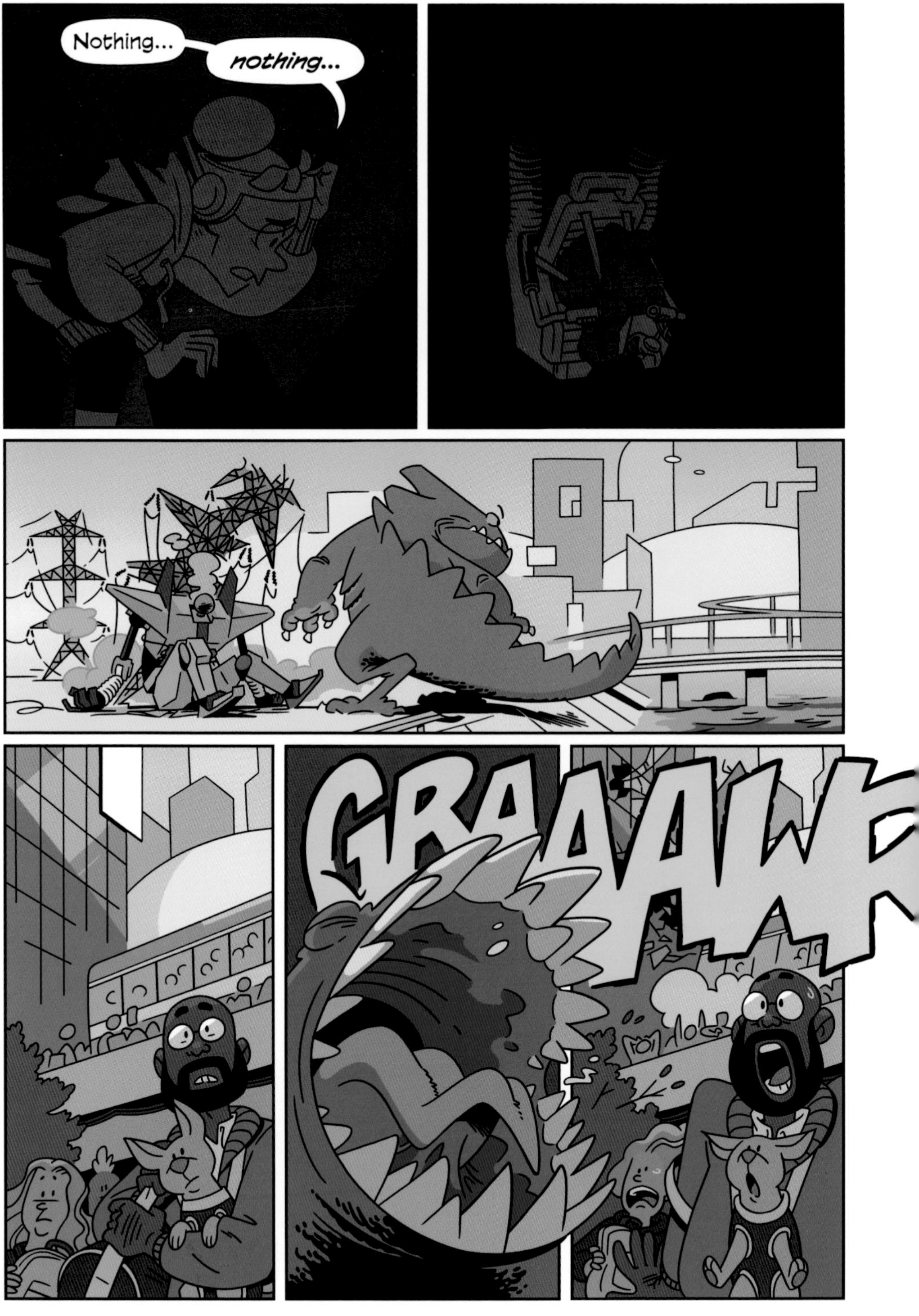
Nothing...
nothing...
GRAAAWR

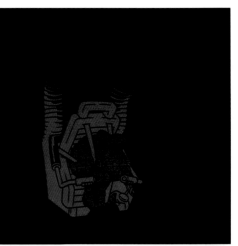

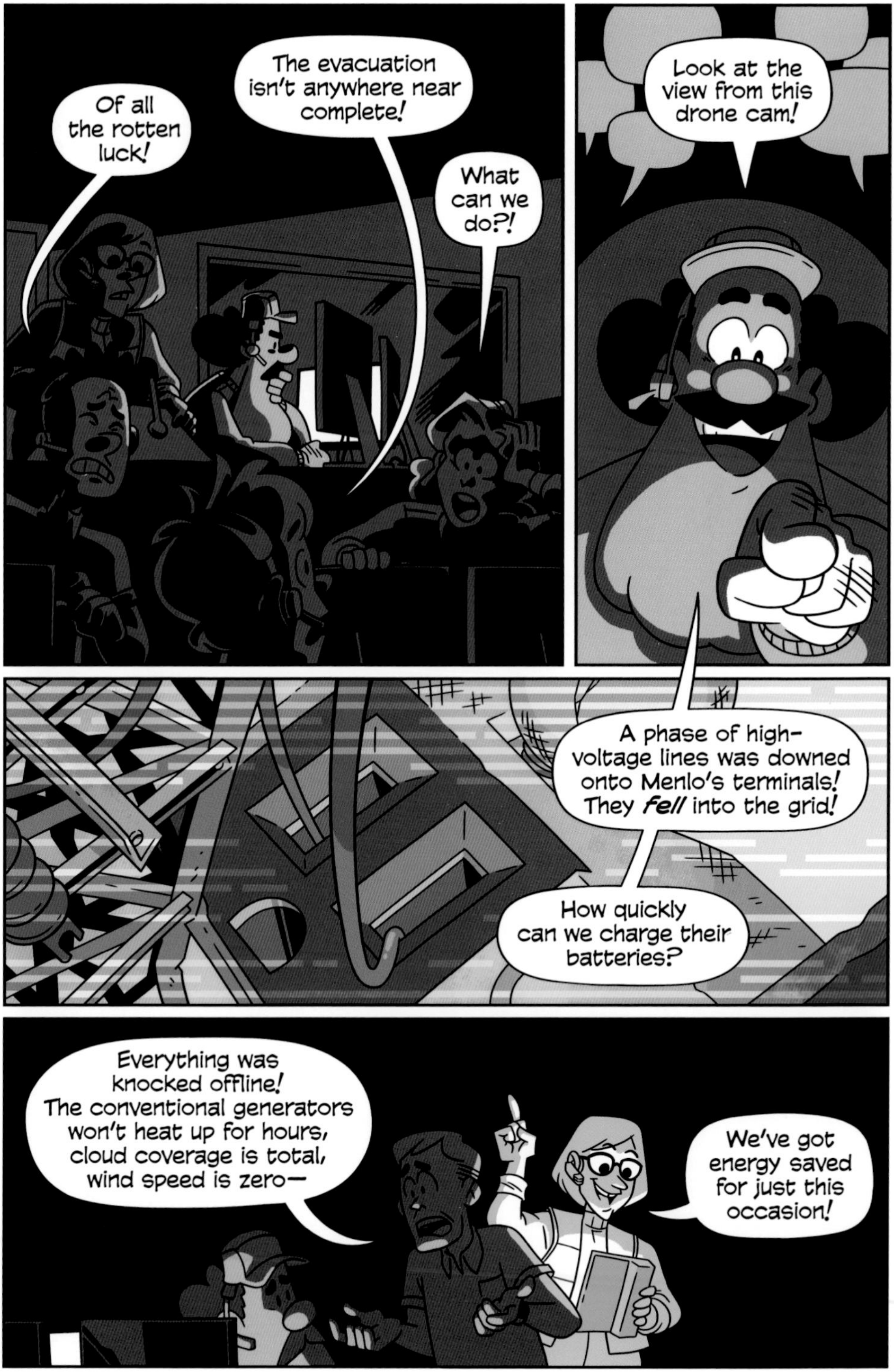
Of all the rotten luck!
The evacuation isn't anywhere near complete!
What can we do?!
Look at the view from this drone cam!
A phase of high-voltage lines was downed onto Menlo's terminals! They *fell* into the grid!
How quickly can we charge their batteries?
Everything was knocked offline! The conventional generators won't heat up for hours, cloud coverage is total, wind speed is zero—
We've got energy saved for just this occasion!

Energy storage is an important part of an electrical grid, especially one based on renewables. We've got to have backup while one source or another isn't producing and to kick-start the grid when *nothing* is producing!

To store energy, we convert it from *kinetic* to *potential*. To use it, we convert it back again!

Gravity makes a great battery. The energy put into raising mass becomes potential energy. The higher the better!

CRRK

That energy then becomes kinetic when the object is lowered.

CRONCH

Electricity fits at either end of the equation!

In a hydroelectric dam, falling water spins a turbine connected to a generator. Extra energy from *another* source can power that same generator, now working in reverse as a motor, connected to that same turbine to send that same water uphill to fall again later.

We can recharge a dam like a giant battery!

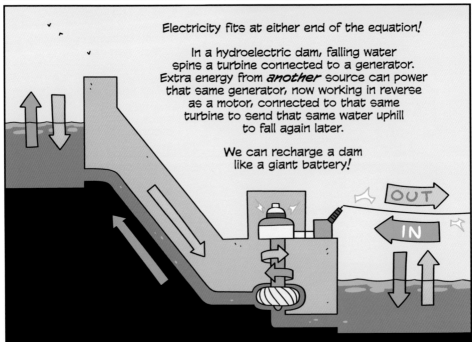

OUT

IN

Just about anything can store *gravitational energy.* If we can put energy into raising it, we can get energy out of lowering it.

We can use other forms of potential energy, too. Air pumped into an underground chamber gets compressed with *elastic energy.* It's like inflating a balloon!

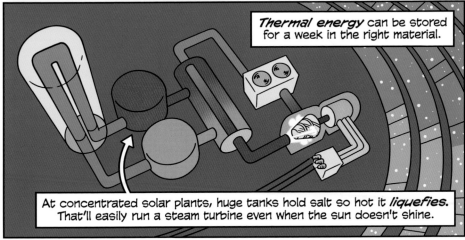

Thermal energy can be stored for a week in the right material.

At concentrated solar plants, huge tanks hold salt so hot it *liquefies.* That'll easily run a steam turbine even when the sun doesn't shine.

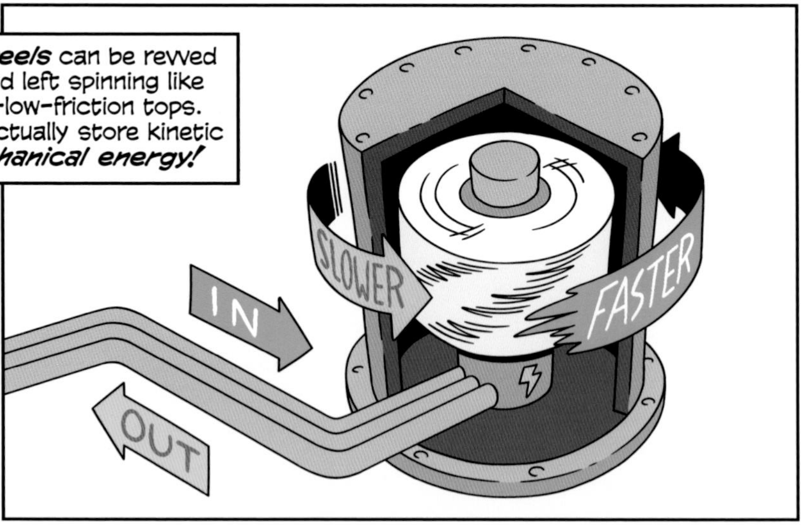
Flywheels can be revved up and left spinning like ultra-low-friction tops. They actually store kinetic mechanical energy!
SLOWER
FASTER
IN
OUT

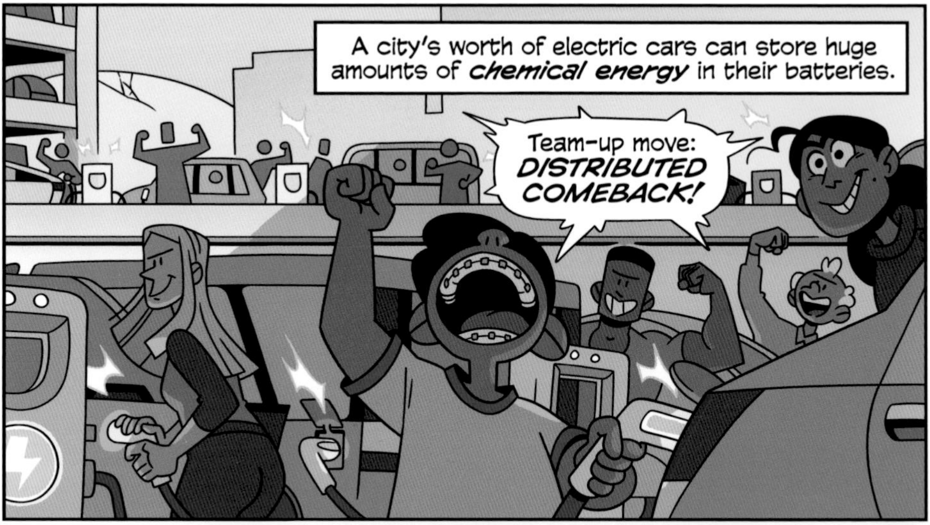
A city's worth of electric cars can store huge amounts of chemical energy in their batteries.
Team-up move: DISTRIBUTED COMEBACK!

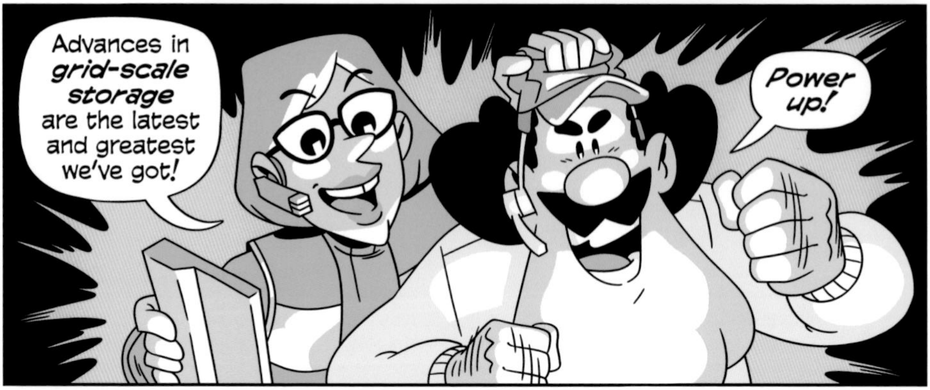
Advances in grid-scale storage are the latest and greatest we've got!
Power up!

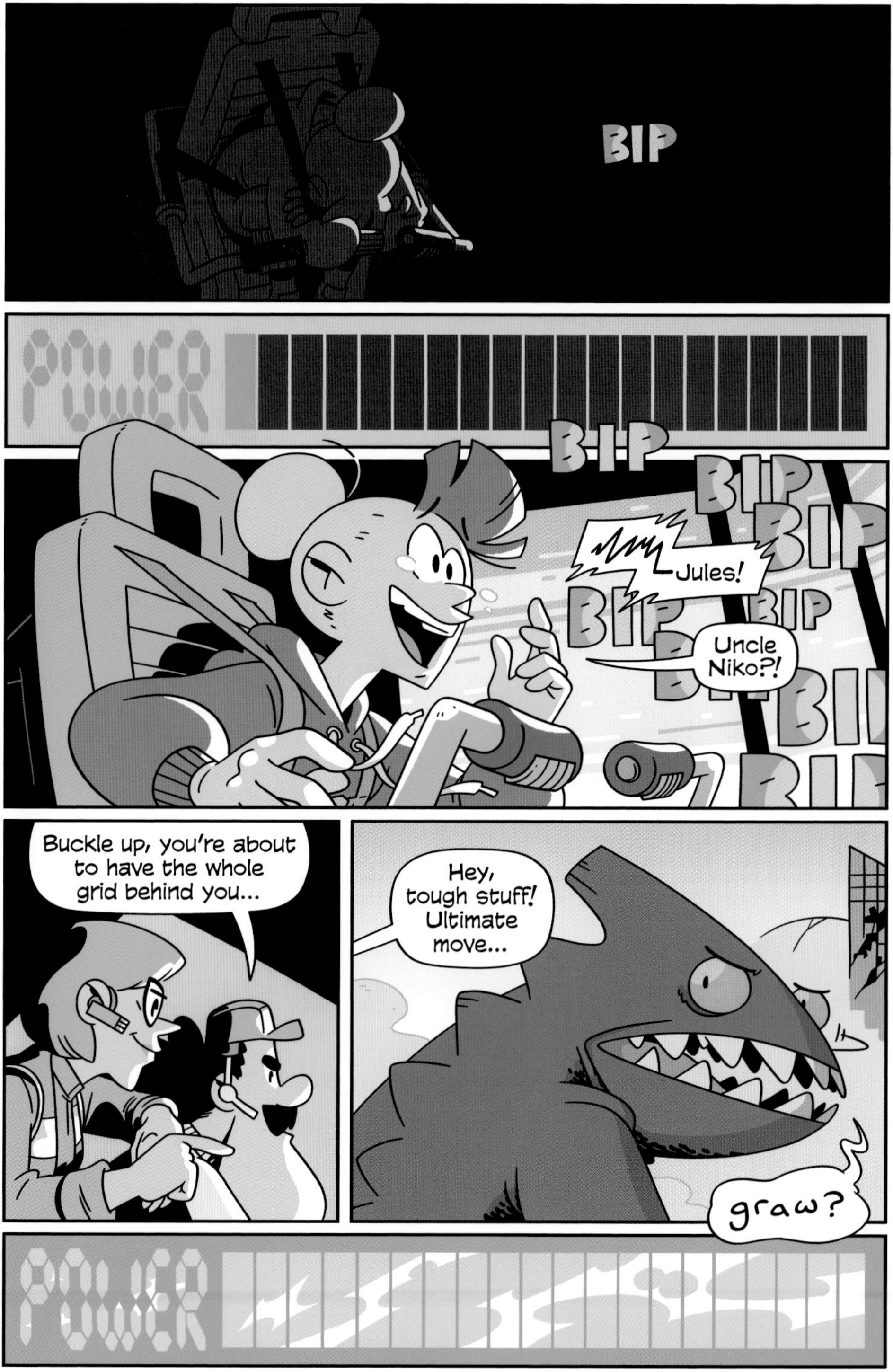
BIP
POWER
BIP
BIP
BIP
Jules!
BIP
BIP
Uncle Niko?!
Buckle up, you're about to have the whole grid behind you...
Hey, tough stuff! Ultimate move...
graw?
POWER

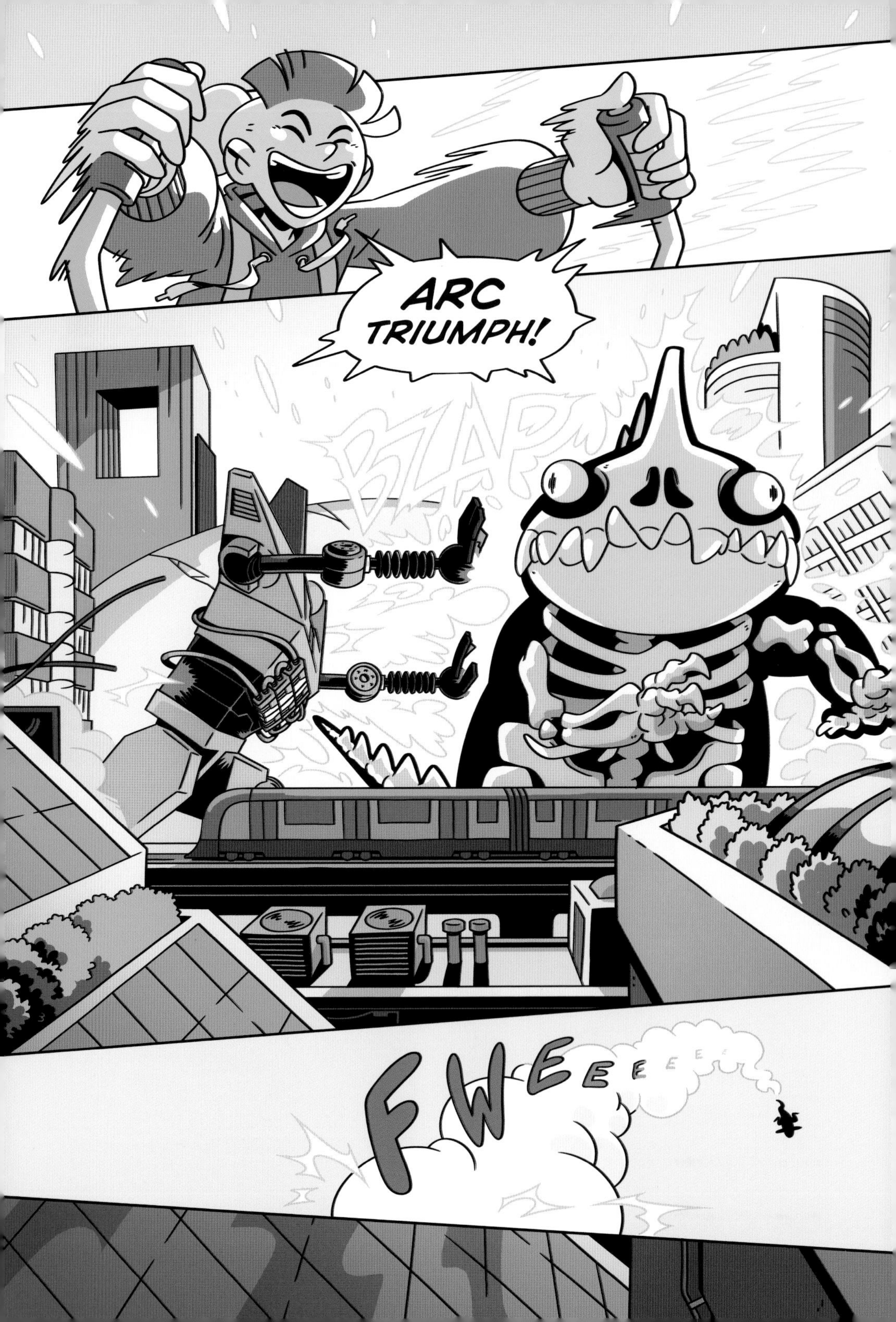
ARC TRIUMPH!
BZZAP
FWEEEEE

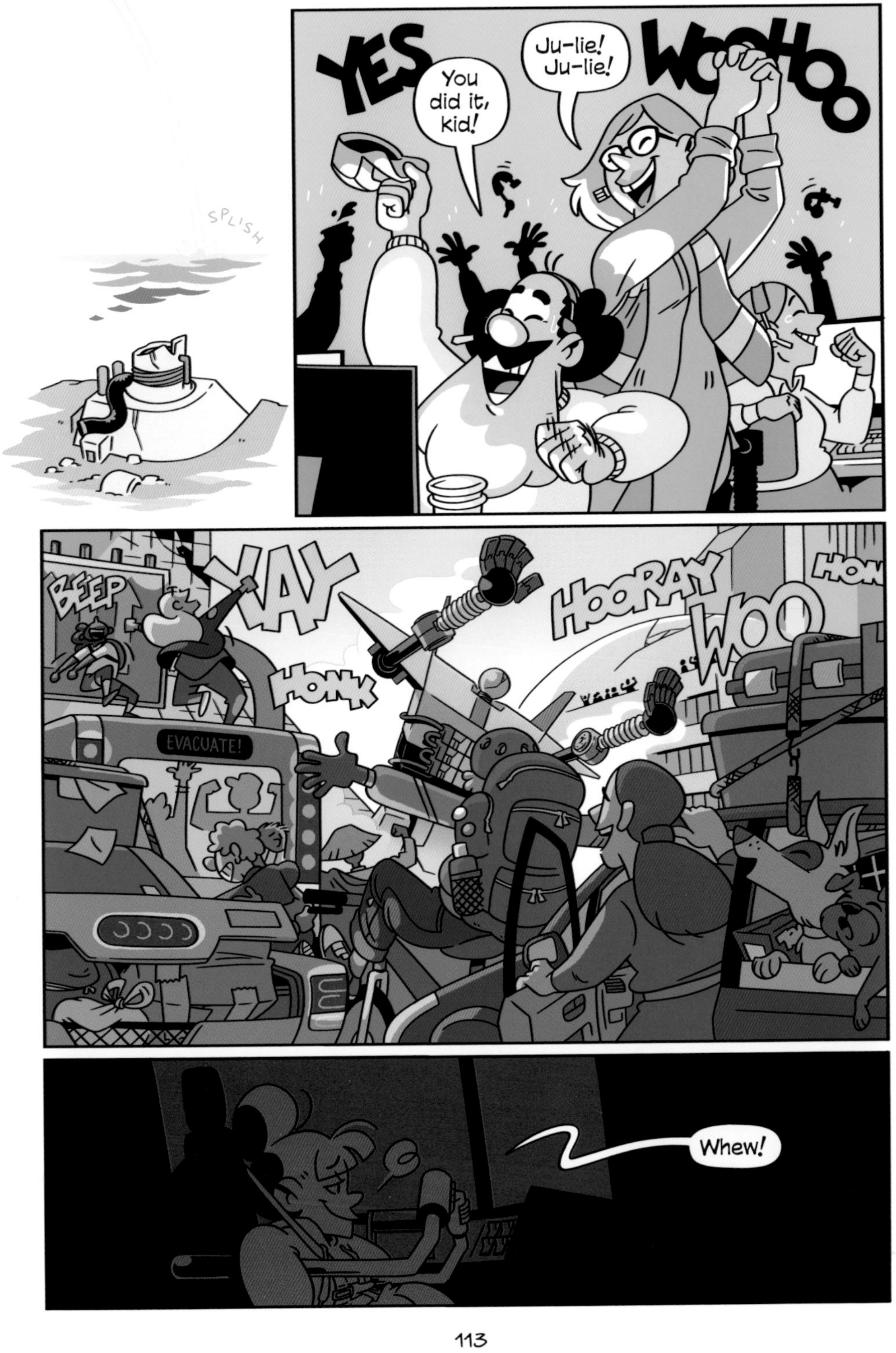
SPLISH
YES
You did it, kid!
Ju-lie! Ju-lie!
WOOHOO
BEEP
YAY
HONK
HOORAY
WOO
EVACUATE!
Whew!

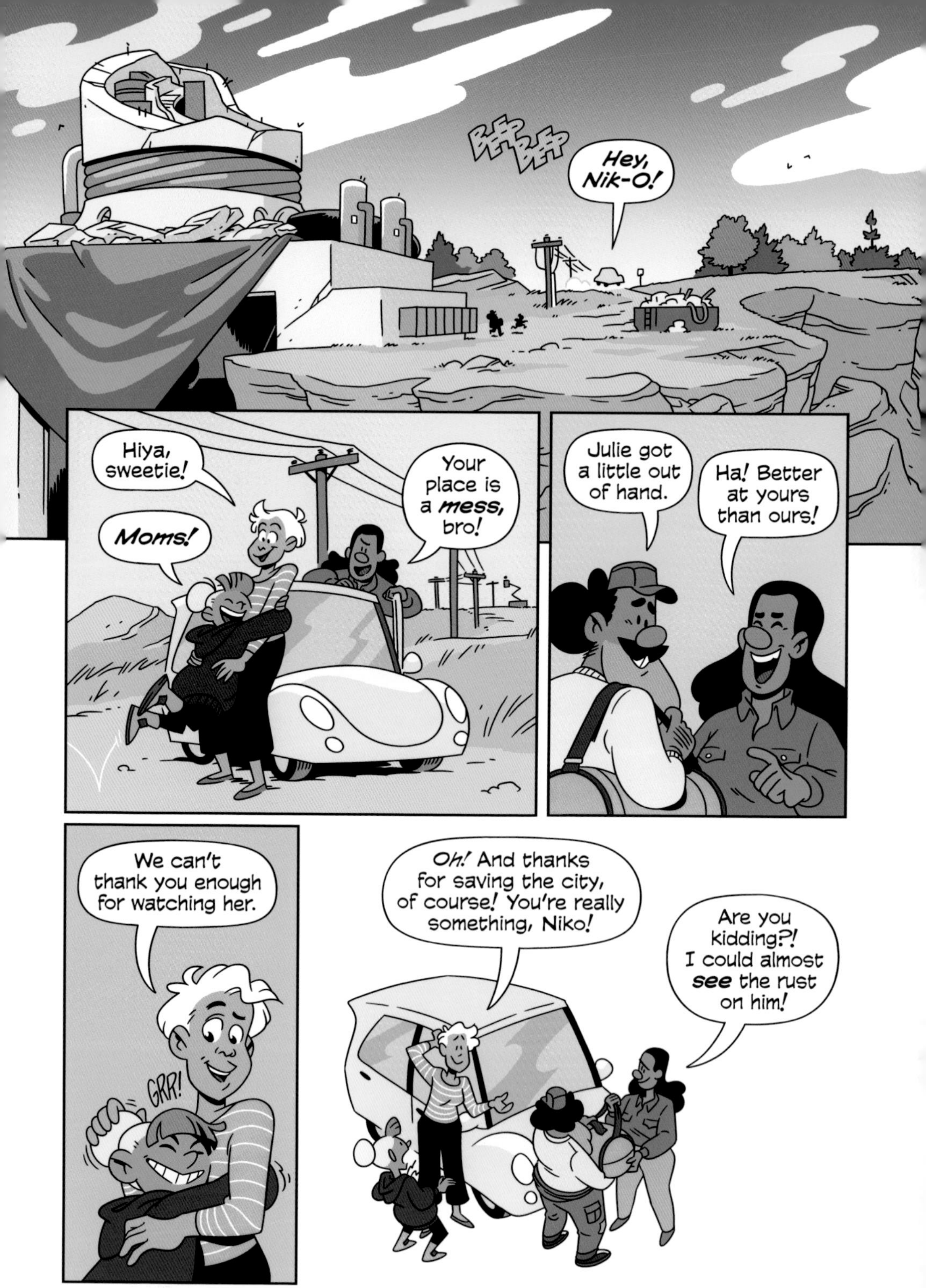

BEEP BEEP
Hey, Nik-O!
Hiya, sweetie!
Moms!
Your place is a *mess,* bro!
Julie got a little out of hand.
Ha! Better at yours than ours!
We can't thank you enough for watching her.
GRR!
Oh! And thanks for saving the city, of course! You're really something, Niko!
Are you kidding?! I could almost ***see*** the rust on him!

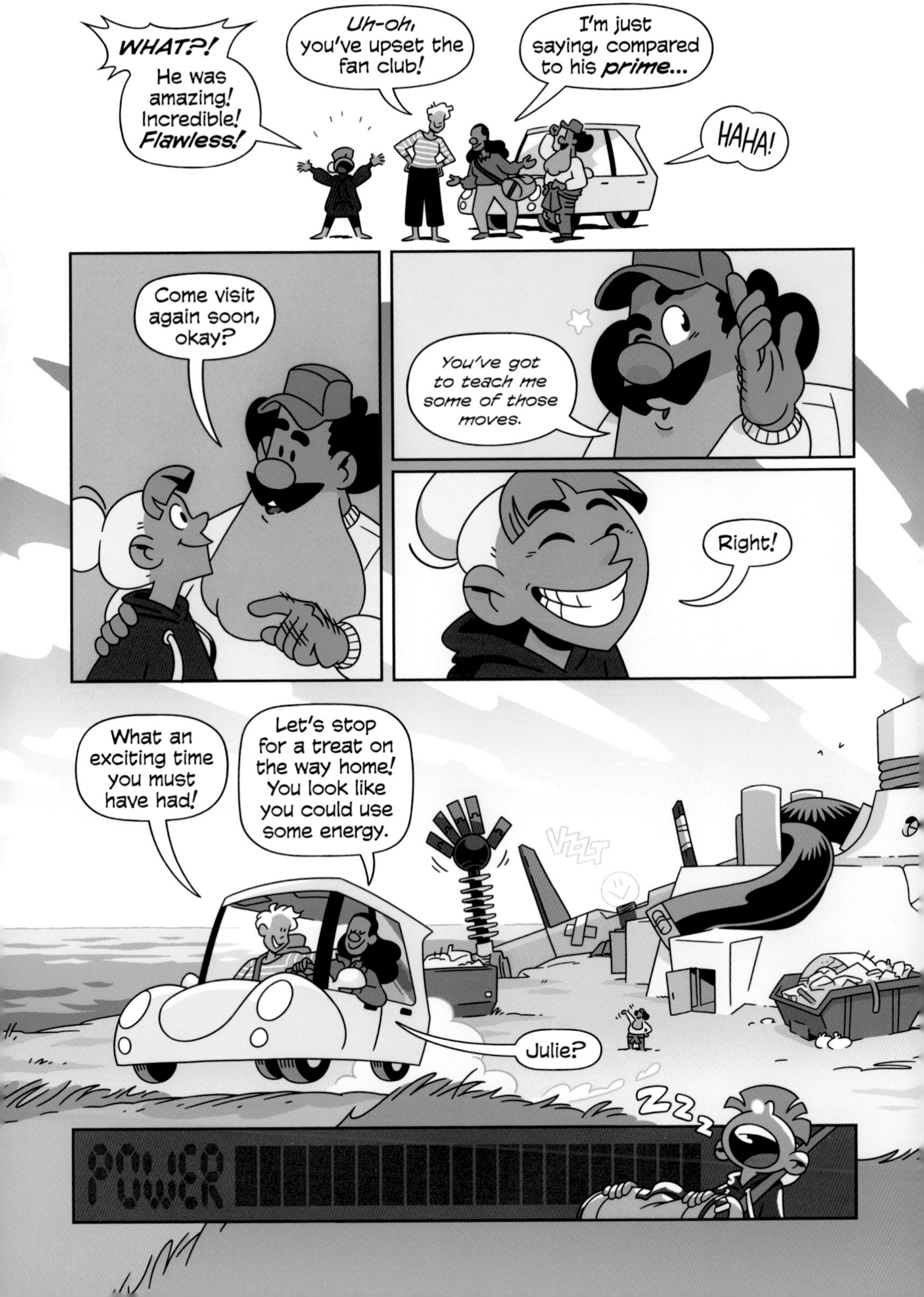
WHAT?! He was amazing! Incredible! Flawless!
Uh-oh, you've upset the fan club!
I'm just saying, compared to his prime...
HAHA!
Come visit again soon, okay?
You've got to teach me some of those moves.
Right!
What an exciting time you must have had!
Let's stop for a treat on the way home! You look like you could use some energy.
Julie?
ZZZ
POWER

—GLOSSARY—

Atom
> A tiny particle that comes in a variety of elemental forms. Atoms are the building blocks of the physical world.

Battery
> A device for storing chemical potential energy that can be converted to electricity. It contains two materials separated by an insulator. The difference in charge between these two creates voltage when connected to a circuit.

Charge
> The property of matter that causes it to react to electromagnetic fields. This is labeled positive, negative, or neutral. *Like charges* repel each other and *opposite charges* attract each other.

Circuit
> A closed, looping path that allows for the movement of electrical energy.

Commutator
> A component of a direct current generator that repeatedly breaks and reverses part of a circuit to keep the overall current flowing in one direction.

Condenser
> A power plant component in which steam cools to become reusable liquid water. It is paired with steam turbines.

Conductor
> The material through which a current moves. This typically refers to a low-resistance material such as metal.

Current
> The flow of electrical energy. *Direct current* moves in a single direction through a circuit. *Alternating current* moves one way and then the other.

Diode
> A circuit component that restricts current flow to one direction. It is high resistance from one end and low resistance from the other.

Electrical grid

A massive circuit incorporating generators, users, and many subcircuits. Electricity generated within a grid must be equal to electricity used within that grid at every moment.

Electric field

The force exerted by one charged particle upon others in the surrounding area. It is strongest near its origin.

Electron

A negatively charged subatomic particle. *Electricity* is the result of their organized movement.

Energy

The ability to do something. It is neither created nor destroyed, but it can change between many forms. *Potential energy*, such as nuclear, chemical, elastic, and gravitational, is still and can do something later. *Kinetic energy*, such as radiant, thermal, sound, mechanical, and electrical, is in motion and can do something now.

Fossil fuels

Ancient substances extracted from the earth to be burned for energy. They are highly energy dense and easily stored, but their supply is limited and environmental effects extreme. Gas, oil, and coal are fossil fuels.

Fuse

A single-use circuit component containing a thin piece of metal that melts, breaking the circuit, when an unsafe amount of current passes through it.

Generator

A device that converts mechanical energy into electrical energy.

Grounding wire

A low-resistance wire that connects a circuit to the earth itself. Used as a safety precaution, it offers electricity a path that avoids damaging people or machines.

—GLOSSARY CONTINUED—

Induction

    The use of magnetic fields to cause a current in a physically disconnected circuit.

Insulator

    A high-resistance material used to restrict or prevent the flow of current. Rubber, wood, and the earth's atmosphere are effective insulators.

Inverter

    A device that converts direct current to alternating current through mechanical or solid-state switches.

Lightning

    A natural phenomenon occurring when opposite electrical charges build up in clouds and the earth beneath. The charges equalize through a brief and intense current. It can also occur from cloud to cloud or within a single cloud.

Magnet

    Any object that produces a magnetic field. Permanent magnets create such fields between their north and south poles even at rest.

Magnetic field

    The force exerted on and produced by both magnets and moving charges. The interactions of these forces and electrons are key to using electricity.

Motor

    A device that converts electrical energy into mechanical energy.

Phase

    The current output from a single pair of coils in an AC generator. Three-phase electricity uses additional coils to maintain consistently high voltage.

Photovoltaic cell

    A device that converts sunlight into electricity by guiding electrons between its layers. Solar panels are made of many photovoltaic cells.

Power
>The rate at which work is done. Electrical power is measured in watts.

Rectifier
>A device that converts alternating current to direct current through diodes.

Renewables
>Energy sources that are not depleted when used. They are in infinite supply and produce little pollution, but they are difficult to store and variable in their availability. Solar, hydro, and geothermal are renewable energy types.

Resistance
>The tendency of a material to allow atoms to trade electrons. Electrical energy moves most easily through low resistance.

Rotor
>The part of a motor or generator that rotates.

Static charge
>An electrical charge in the absence of a current.

Stator
>The part of a motor or generator that stays still.

Transformer
>A device that uses induction to alter voltage and current. They are used at different points in an electrical grid to balance efficiency and safety.

Turbine
>A fanlike machine consisting of blades attached to a rotor. When paired with a generator, the movement of gases, often steam or air, through a turbine results in electricity.

Voltage
>The difference in electrical charge between two points.